Becoming the Story

THE HISTORY OF COMMUNICATION

Robert W. McChesney
and John C. Nerone, editors

*A list of books in the series
appears at the end of this book.*

Becoming the Story

War Correspondents since 9/11

LINDSAY PALMER

**UNIVERSITY OF
ILLINOIS PRESS**
Urbana, Chicago, and Springfield

Library of Congress Cataloging-in-Publication Data
Names: Palmer, Lindsay, author.
Title: Becoming the story: war correspondents since 9/11 /
    Lindsay Palmer.
Description: [Urbana, Illinois] : University of Illinois,
    [2017] | Series: The history of communication | Includes
    bibliographical references and index.
Identifiers: LCCN 2017031827 | ISBN 9780252083211 (pbk. : alk.
    paper)
Subjects: LCSH: War correspondents—History—21st century.
    | September 11 Terrorist Attacks, 2001—Influence. | Pearl,
    Daniel, 1963–2002. | Woodruff, Bob, 1961– | Bahari, Maziar. |
    Fathi, Nazila, 1970– | Colvin, Marie.
Classification: LCC PN4823 .P35 2017 | DDC 070.4/333—dc23
LC record available at https://lccn.loc.gov/2017031827

For Jeff

Contents

Acknowledgments

So many people helped me through the daunting (but rewarding) process of writing this book. I first have to thank my mentor and friend, Lisa Parks. Somewhere on a dusty red road in Macha, Zambia—where we were working on an entirely different project than this one—Lisa told me: "There are many different ways to do research." That really stuck with me, and it helped me to push the boundaries of what was "possible" in writing my first book. So, a special thanks to Lisa, for that vital encouragement! I also want to thank Michael Curtin, Janet Walker, Lisa Hajjar, Constance Penley, Anna Everett, Cristina Venegas, Jennifer Holt, Chuck Wolfe, Greg Siegel, Peter Bloom, and Bhaskar Sarkar. Each of you helped me to think through the ideas in this book, in one way or another! So, too, did Abigail Hinsman, Hannah Goodwin, Rahul Mukherjee, Anastasia Yumeko Hill, Lan Le, Alston D'Silva, John Vanderhoef, Rachel Fabian, Greg Burris, Carlos Jimenez, Teddy Pozo, and Sara Hinojos.

I am very fortunate to have found a new academic family in the School of Journalism and Mass Communication at the University of Wisconsin-Madison. Thank you to my brilliant SJMC colleagues Sue Robinson, Katy Culver, Karyn Riddle, Young Mie Kim, Hernando Rojas, Lucas Graves, Lew Friedland, Dhavan Shah, Doug McLeod, Chris Wells, Hemant Shah, Bob Drechsel, Mike Wagner, Steve Vaughn, Greg Downey, Al Gunther, Jo Ellen Fair, Shawnika Hull, Molly Wright Steenson, and the incomparable Jim Baughman. Alongside my colleagues on the SJMC faculty, I owe a great deal to the impressive graduate students who took my Fall 2015 seminar on ethics in post-9/11 war reporting; their insightful comments in class were a constant inspiration. One of these students, Alicia Wright, served as a project assistant for the research in this book, and so I especially want to thank her and Lanni Solochek, my undergraduate researcher.

A number of other scholars offered me their invaluable assistance or advice in the pursuit of this project, at various points in time: Jad Melki, Daya Kishan Thussu, Stuart Allan, Howard Tumber, Herman Wasserman, Barbie Zelizer, Toby Miller, and Stacy Takacs. Thanks to each of you for taking the time to talk these ideas through with me, and for connecting me with your contacts. A big, big thank you to my editor Daniel Nasset, whose patience and guidance helped me to keep my sanity throughout this process! And perhaps most especially, I'd like to thank my family: my parents, sister, and brother for their interest in my admittedly depressing research, and my amazing husband Jeff—for tolerating the fact that I always seem to be talking about death, and for believing that I could write a book in the first place. Jeff, I don't know where I'd be without you and our beautiful son Cade.

Becoming the Story

Introduction

Shortly after the September 11, 2001, attacks on the Pentagon and the World Trade Center, international correspondent Hashem Ahelbarra found himself covering the aftermath for his then-employer, Abu Dhabi TV:

> Ground Zero to me was—it was really difficult for an Arab journalist to cover that story. Not really a good place to be if you were an Arab. So, I would go for a Latin American name because the tension was really high at that particular moment, at that particular area. (pers. comm., April 2013)

At the same time that Ahelbarra was covering the attacks in the United States from an "outsider's" perspective—and finding it necessary to pass as a different, less "threatening" type of "outsider" in the process—freelance war correspondent Sebastian Junger was woefully far from the action unfolding in his home nation:

> On 9/11 itself, I was overseas on assignment in Moldova. I wasn't in the country. I live in New York, obviously. So, as a war reporter, I had the strange sense that I'd missed the war in my own country. I'm a New Yorker, and I wasn't here when that happened, and it really felt quite remiss. (pers. comm., February 2013)

For war reporters from diverse national backgrounds, 9/11 wasn't just another news event. The September 11, 2001, attacks on the Pentagon and the World Trade Center changed their careers, and in some cases, changed their lives. But 9/11 meant different things to different journalists. For Ahelbarra, it meant new wars in his own region of the world. "I can say that the post-9/11 legacy is particularly characterized by—it's been a hectic, hectic settlement, tense zones, conflicts, wars ever since" (pers. comm., April 2013). For NPR correspondent Lourdes Garcia-Navarro, it meant traveling to Afghanistan and later to Iraq, where she would eventually suffer the harrowing symptoms of posttraumatic stress disorder (pers. comm., July 2014). And for Egyptian-born ABC field producer Hoda Abdel-Hamid, it meant covering Iraq surrounded by U.S.-born colleagues who she felt were "full of hatred" for the "enemy" (pers. comm., April 2013). U.S. war correspondents turned their eyes to their own cities, while correspondents like Ahelbarra wondered what 9/11 would mean for journalists who weren't from the United States (pers. comm., April 2013). In turn, white journalists from Anglophone countries like the United States and Britain began to feel that they were being targeted in the field because of anti-American sentiment abroad.

Meanwhile, foreign-desk editors and bureau chiefs based at mainstream, English-language news organizations scrambled to address a very sudden shift in priorities. Bill Spindle, who was the assistant foreign editor of the *Wall Street Journal* on September 11, watched as his staff of foreign correspondents grew from a grand total of four reporters to fourteen reporters, seemingly overnight (pers. comm., July 2015). Former editor at the *Washington Post* David Hoffman reminisces that the period after 9/11 "fueled this incredible desire to be first and best in the world at what we were doing" (pers. comm., February 2015). And former editor at the *New York Times*, William Schmidt, recalls that the post-9/11 period saw a new attention to foreign correspondents' safety at the *Times* (pers. comm., March 2015). For each of these journalists and editors, the events of September 11 seemed to mark a turning point for the professional practice of war reporting.

This book examines the cultural labor of Anglophone war correspondents after 9/11, drawing upon the theoretical frameworks found in the field of critical-cultural media studies to advance three central arguments:

1. Though 9/11 appeared to be a turning point for conflict correspondents, many of the obstacles that they faced had their roots in nineteenth- and twentieth-century war reporting. 9/11 undoubtedly ushered in an era of intensifying industrial, technological, and political challenges, but these challenges had long histories.

2. The professional practice of twenty-first-century war reporting did see the rise of a new phenomenon that I am calling "safety culture": a highly discursive, performative process through which the entire profession began to think, plan, and *talk* more about safety in the field. Yet, this "safety culture" did not necessarily make correspon-

dents safer at all. In fact, safety training and insurance were distributed according to a hierarchy that was nationalized, racialized, and gendered.

3. Despite the systemic nature of the problems that informed the labor of Anglophone war correspondence after 9/11, the news narratives of this era often focused on individual war correspondents' safety catastrophes. These catastrophes were transformed into melodramas that represented war correspondents as the neoliberal subjects of late capitalism, while simplifying the deep structural problems that engendered correspondents' mishaps—and the geopolitical conflicts they were covering—in the first place.

In making these arguments, I will ultimately show that media scholars need to engage in the ethical practice of "framing the frame" (Butler 2009)—not just in the philosophical sense of which Judith Butler speaks but also in a very literal sense. Though it may be easier to stop at a critical analysis of melodramatic news media texts, the Anglophone war reporting industry isn't nearly as cohesive or simplistic as these news narratives suggest. Far from being a well-oiled "machine," the industry is a diffuse network of moving parts that often work against each other, rather than working cohesively. If we hope to see the improvement of Anglophone war correspondents' reportage, as well as the improvement of the conditions in which they work, it is first necessary to understand Anglophone conflict reporting for the heterogeneous and contradictory profession that it is.

I should clarify from the outset that this book specifically examines the first decade after the September 11 attacks, stopping at 2012. I set these parameters because this was a time when journalists, academics, politicians, and ordinary people were proclaiming that a "new" era had begun. As Vincent Mosco asserts, the "end of history" myth is centuries old; yet it was prevalent in the discourse addressing 9/11 (2005). During this decade, politicians, pundits, and news organizations engaged in the studied obfuscation of history's "baggage" (ibid., 57). For that reason alone, the years directly following 9/11 are important years for media scholars to study.

I have also chosen to examine war reporting during this period because, when the United States and its allies reacted to 9/11 by launching the "war on terror," a vast array of U.S., British, and Canadian journalists descended upon the world's conflict zones. This decade saw a renewed attention to western-based, English-language war coverage and to foreign news reporting more broadly. At the same time, the period also saw a number of safety catastrophes

Figure 1. A damaged television antenna serves as the focal point of the Washington, D.C., Newseum's striking 9/11 memorial, which is a permanent exhibit at the museum.

for war correspondents in the field, incidents that were discussed in the official news coverage and also across the burgeoning, "unofficial" spaces of the web. In order to better understand this phenomenon, the book begins with the incident of Daniel Pearl's kidnapping in 2002 and ends with Marie Colvin's 2012 death in Syria. Each chapter focuses on a particular war correspondent's safety catastrophe, using that case study as a doorway into a larger discussion of conflict correspondents' precarious labor.

While 2002–2012 is an important decade to examine in its own right, I will also place the reporting that occurred during these years in some broader historical context. In doing this, I hope to counteract the popular tendency to think of 9/11 as a temporal rupture with no history of its own, while also illuminating the ways in which the production cultures of conflict correspondence converge with (and diverge from) earlier practices. Scholars have already documented the ahistorical nature of post-9/11 sociopolitical narratives. James Der Derian asserts that the "sheer scale, scope and shock" of 9/11 are partly responsible for the amnesia that numerous sociopolitical actors displayed as they discussed the attacks and the resulting "war on terror": "Before 9/11 and after 9/11: it is as if whole histories, critical questions, and future hopes disappeared into this temporal rift, only to reemerge as official stories and their carnival-mirror opposite, conspiracy theories" (2009, 228). Rather than exposing the public to the messy history of U.S. foreign policy, mainstream Anglophone news organizations—especially those based in the United States—often drew upon simplistic, ahistorical narratives to make sense of September 11 and the wars that followed (Miller 2007; Kumar 2012). As media and cultural studies scholars have suggested, much of this coverage overwhelmingly represented the U.S. military and its allies as heroes, the American people as "victims," and the murky figure of the "Islamic Terrorist" as the villain of the story (Miller 2007; Kumar 2012; Freedman and Thussu 2012; Perigoe and Eid 2014).

According to Elisabeth Anker, this simplistic narrative structure was actually very old, despite its amnesiac quality: it was the narrative structure of melodrama, which situates social conflict within a "moral" framework that propagates the simplistic notion of "good vs. evil" (2014). U.S. news media used this narrative strategy to talk about terrorism at the beginning of Ronald Reagan's presidency (Dobkin 1992). Even earlier, in the nineteenth century, U.S. and British news organizations were deploying hero and villain narratives almost as soon as war reporting became a legitimate civilian profession (Knightley 2004). Despite the long history of melodramatic news reporting, and despite the even messier history of the United States and its allies intervening in the affairs of nations in North Africa and the Middle East (Harms 2010; Jacobs 2011; Baxter and Akbarzadeh 2012; Kumar 2012; Schmidt 2013), the mainstream, English-language news coverage of 9/11 and the resulting "war on terror" was obsessed with an ahistorical "present."

Before I historicize the conflict reporting of the early twenty-first century, I will first take a moment to explain how I am defining the term "conflict correspondence." Conflict correspondence is hardly a monolithic practice, but instead involves a diverse array of participants. For my purposes, the term "correspondent" refers to staff employees and to freelancers, to headlining print journalists and their photographers, to producers and camera people, as well as to on-air television talent. In taking this broad approach, I hope to show the complexity and yet the growing interconnection of war journalists and their labor in the globalized and digital age, where TV networks hire web producers and where newspapers draw upon videographers. It is increasingly rare to encounter a conflict reporter who does not work across multiple forms of media. The thing that these diverse correspondents have in common is their labor for what I refer to as "mainstream" news organizations: news outlets that generally seek a broad audience and that claim to avoid engaging in activism or advocacy, while still generating war coverage that tends to privilege the viewpoints of the political and social establishment (Hallin 1989; Dobkin 1992; Thussu and Freedman 2003; Miller 2007).

For two important reasons, the book primarily critiques "western" war correspondence, drawing specifically upon the accounts of journalists who work for mainstream, Anglophone news outlets headquartered in North America and Britain. On one level, I draw these parameters in order to glimpse the inner workings of the Anglocentrism that surfaces in Anglophone war coverage, most especially in the coverage of the "war on terror" coming out of the U.S. news industry. Post-9/11 U.S. war coverage particularly reveals the news industry's tendentious relationship with ideals of "objectivity" and "balance," as numerous critical media scholars have already shown (Thussu and Freedman 2003; Allan and Zelizer 2004; Miller 2007; Der Derian 2009; Stahl 2009; Freedman and Thussu 2012). And while there are some important differences between U.S. war coverage and the coverage coming out of Canada or Britain—especially depending on which news organizations are being discussed at which precise moments in history—at the level of production, Anglophone war reporting is marked by a great deal of overlap between U.S., British, and Canadian journalists, not to mention the myriad journalists of non-western heritage who work for the news outlets based in the Anglophone west. My goal is to focus on the labor practices that contribute to the impoverished frames through which English-language audiences are encouraged to understand the Middle East, in the age of the "war on terror."

This way of conceptualizing the "Middle East" as a monolithic and "vexed" region has a long history of its own. In the colonial era, British and European powers dominated parts of the region on a material and political level, while also propagating orientalist representations of the diverse peoples who lived there (Kumar 2012). U.S. missionaries built upon these pejorative representations in the nineteenth and early twentieth centuries before a new class of "experts"—mostly businessmen, academics, and journalists—began to contribute to distinctly "American" notions of the Middle East as a place that needed to be "redeemed" and "transformed" through both protestant Christianity and capitalism (Jacobs 2011). The western image of the Middle East had to be cultivated over time, in other words, through cultural as well as political and material practices (McAlister 2005). Anglophone journalists have long participated in these cultural practices of misrepresentation (Spurr 1993; Kumar 2012).

In this sense alone, an analysis of the practices of mainstream, English-language war reporting in the age of the "war on terror" is useful. Yet, I also focus on "western," "Anglophone" war reporting in order to illuminate the contradictions entangled within that label. Though the Anglophone news industry most often tends to narrativize the tragedies faced by white, western conflict reporters, at the level of production there is no strictly "American" or "British" or "Canadian" practice of war reporting. News outlets based in these nations often employ people from various Anglophone countries, complicating any purely "national" perspective. Second, even the more vaguely termed "western" conflict correspondence is an inherently transnational practice, one that relies heavily on the collaboration with stringers, freelancers, translators, drivers, "fixers," and even staff correspondents from various cultural backgrounds. To capture this cultural complexity, I have conducted in-depth, qualitative interviews with 85 very different conflict correspondents and 27 news editors: interviews with people like ABC's Bob Woodruff, NPR's Lourdes Garcia-Navarro, the young Syrian American freelancer Anna Lekas Miller, and the Beirut-based news "fixer" Leena Saidi. Though they each have some things in common, my interviewees offer a wide array of perspectives on the work of war reporting after 9/11.

Not all of my interviewees actually identify as "American" or "British," even when they work for organizations based in those countries. Instead, many of these journalists might be Lebanese, Egyptian, Turkish, or Palestinian. Some of the people I interviewed also work for the English-language version of the Qatar-based Al Jazeera English network, pointing to the important fact that a number of news organizations outside North America and Britain also engage in English-language war reporting—often, to combat the impoverished representations coming out of the Anglophone west. Yet, to complicate things further, some of the Al Jazeera employees I have interviewed actually possess U.S., British, Canadian, or Australian citizenship, and many of them have also worked for western-based Anglophone news outlets at different points in time. Thus, I hope to show that while the ideological approaches of Anglophone news organizations sometimes generate reductive frames through which to see the world, western or Anglophone conflict correspondents comprise a culturally diverse community. Furthermore, mainstream, Anglophone war reporting very simply cannot occur without the help of news employees born and raised outside of the United States, Canada, or Britain. This is something that often goes unnoticed by media scholars who critique western war coverage without always considering the diverse people who participate in war reporting as a professional practice.

Besides defining the term *conflict correspondence,*—which I use interchangeably in this book with the terms *conflict reporter, war correspondent,* and *war reporter*—I also explain what I mean by the terms *conflict*, and *conflict zone*. For the purposes of this book, a *conflict zone* is necessarily produced by the conflict in question, a term that also needs to be defined. I broadly conceptualize *conflict* as something that describes war but also the political and digital dissent that many traditional war reporters cover. When, in the January uprisings of 2011, NBC's celebrity war reporter Richard Engel compared Cairo's Tahrir Square to the war zone in Baghdad, he was certainly glossing over an array of important sociopolitical differences. Still, his rather flippant statement did signal the insidious linkage between certain sites of dissent and the broader rhetoric of the "global war on terror." This rhetoric declares that any and every site, including sites of protest with counterparts on digital media platforms, could possibly be harboring terrorists that endanger the interests of the United States and its allies.

Following this, I use the term *conflict zone* to refer to a space of war or militarized political dissent that is socially produced by a number of different actors. As Henri Lefebvre has asserted, space is not a static thing that society simply inhabits but is instead produced by society (1992). Drawing upon this configuration, I examine how the purportedly "transcendent" journalistic narrativization of the space of war is often at odds with the complexity of space as it is actually experienced and produced by multiple subjectivities, pointing to what Lefebvre calls "spatial violence." Nick Couldry and Anna McCarthy describe this violence as "a gap between representation and material organization that is naturalized out of everyday awareness" (2004). Despite the fact that we tend to forget such a gap exists, this spatial violence is inherent to traditional media practices, which consequently try to transcend the material organization of the site that is so often at odds with the story that is told about it (ibid.). It is this very "spatial violence" that I intend to counteract by "zooming out" on the news narratives that place conflict correspondents within the frame.

The etymology of the word *correspondent* points to the vexed interaction between the war reporter and his or her environment. Apart from the common definition of the word *correspondent* that appears in the *Oxford English Dictionary*—"one who contributes letters to a newspaper or journal"—there appears a second definition that at first seems unrelated. In the "rare use" category, the word is also defined as "an organism *in vital communication* with its environment" (emphasis mine). These definitions have some things in common. Both interestingly draw upon a set of optimistic ideals. The journalistic correspondent is defined by the work that he or she is supposed to successfully complete, while the older and less popular use of the term uncritically assumes the infallibility of this "organism," successfully maintaining "vital communication" with the environment to which it corresponds.

Yet, this older definition also portends the conflict correspondents' embodied labor, the ways in which the correspondent's own vitality is constantly at risk in the process of narrating the injuries and deaths of others. The possibility of failure and transgression acts as a shadow to the word's twin histories. For the more current definition of the word *correspondent*, the possibility of failure is even more difficult to obfuscate, because of the very real tendency of newspaper (and now, television and online) correspondents to refuse certain instructions, to miss an important memo, to flub their assignments, or to get injured on the job. In this sense, I consider the term's explicit and implicit possibilities, conceptualizing instances of industrial failure as productive moments in which to better understand the process of conflict correspondence overall.

I define *correspondence* as the precarious and imperfect labor that ideally—but rarely—involves harmonious communication between the correspondent, the conflict zone, and the larger network of bureaus, headquarters, and audiences in which the correspondent is enmeshed. Though the objective "communication" of an apparently coherent "truth" is still taken at face value by many journalists, who use the phrase "getting the story" to underscore their supposed role as a transmitter of unadulterated information, the journalist's ability to narrativize the conflict zone depends on an array of challenging factors. As many of my interviewees have told me, communication technologies and infrastructures routinely break down in conflict zones, leaving journalists without the means to do their work. What is more, news editors, executives, and accounting officials back home may not understand the situation on the ground, which sometimes results in serious *mis*communication that can decisively impact the tone of a story, or worse: the safety of the correspondent in the field. Alongside these constraints, my interviewees have also noted that they typically run into censorship or competition from the many other human actors whom they encounter at the site of conflict—human actors who may have vastly different perspectives on what is happening.

These obstacles inspire the first argument that I advance in this book: After 9/11, conflict correspondents indeed faced some serious industrial, technological, and political challenges in the field, but some of these challenges also plagued the war reporters of earlier centuries. Rather than being wholly "new," it is more accurate to say that these challenges intensified in the years following the attacks on the Pentagon and the World Trade Center. I want to make it clear, however, that in the process of historicizing the obstacles that conflict correspondents faced, I do not intend to diminish them in any way. Whether or not they were "new," these obstacles had huge ramifications, on individual and collective levels. They constantly threatened the lives of the correspondents themselves, as well as impacting the way that war was narrativized for broader publics.

The first intensifying challenge that conflict correspondents faced from 2002–2012 was industrial in nature. As former CBS correspondent and producer Marquita Pool-Eckert told me, in the early 1980s a sudden trip to Lebanon was a great way to "advance up the ranks" when you were already a staff employee (pers. comm., February 2015). By the first decade of the twenty-first century, however, it was next to impossible to secure a staff position at all, a problem resulting from the slashing of foreign news budgets and the closure of foreign news bureaus over the last decades of the twentieth century (Barkin 2003; Paterson and Sreberny 2004; Williams 2011). This issue led young people with virtually no experience to travel to cities like Beirut in order to try their luck at freelancing. It also led news networks to outsource much more of the labor of war reporting to local stringers and citizen journalists. In the first decade of the twenty-first century, editors began relying more and more heavily on stringers, freelancers, and digital activists to get images and information from places where they could not always afford to send their full-time news teams. This strategy created a staunchly competitive market for staffers and freelancers alike.

While this was certainly a brutal industrial challenge, it must be noted that competitiveness in the profession of conflict correspondence long predates 9/11. All the way back in the nineteenth century, both British and U.S. newspapers fought for lucrative news audiences, racing each other on steamboats, horses, and trains in order to get a scoop that would sell more papers (Knightley 2004; Hamilton 2011). With the advent of the telegraph, correspondents' ability to beat each other to press became all the more important, because with the telegraph came the popular attitude that information was no longer beholden to the vicissitudes of physical space (ibid.). But the telegraph lines often broke down, or were censored by different militaries, leaving the correspondents to find resourceful ways of getting the story to their publishers in a timely manner (ibid.). Editors were less than sympathetic, encouraging their correspondents to put themselves at grave risk in order to bring home the war stories that would almost certainly increase newspaper sales (ibid.). Indeed, nineteenth- and early twentieth-century editors and publishers were more than willing to invest large sums in setting up reporting operations in parts of the world that they deemed "interesting" to their audiences; yet, when those "interesting" areas became more peaceful, news executives would then disinvest in the area, in much the same way they do today (Deacon 2008; Hamilton 2011). News organizations have also long relied on the crucial but devalued labor of freelancers and local stringers (Knightley 2004; Hamilton 2011; Silberstein-Loeb 2014). For example, Archibald Forbes was working on a "pay if used" basis for Britain's *Morning Advertiser* all the way back in the Franco-Prussian War (Knightley 2004). What is more, the period between the two world wars saw a number of young, would-be journalists traveling to foreign locations without specific plans (Hamilton 2011). This also happened during the Vietnam conflict, where inexperienced "proto-journalists" traveled to Saigon and started reporting, hoping to eventually sell a story (Knightley 2004). History shows that there is nothing new in the tendency for freelancers to travel somewhere risky on the gamble that they might make it big in the war reporting industry.

What *is* new is the unstable news market on which these freelancers now depend. The end of the twentieth century was marked by financial crisis for news organizations, as well as by a significant drop in the coverage of foreign news (Hamilton 2011). By 2002, "freelance rates ha[d] declined by more than 50 percent since the 1960s," while the cost of living had gone up in various places around the world (ibid.). According to my interviewees, the ability to get a staff job became more and more difficult over the first years of the twenty-first century, as news organizations overwhelmingly outsourced labor to the employees who would work without benefits. Though the Anglophone news industry had seen a number of financial crises (and recoveries) in previous decades (ibid.), twenty-first-century war reporting was decisively impacted by a particularly punishing round of bureau closures and budget cuts.

On top of this issue, news organizations also began to regularly draw upon the completely free labor of digital citizen journalists. Although activists have long attempted to tell their own "alternative" stories of sociopolitical conflict (Kind-Kovács and Labov 2013; Harcup 2013), when citizen journalism "went digital," it arguably became far more visible to mainstream news organizations (Allan 2009). Major news outlets like CNN began to use this citizen journalism without paying for it (Palmer 2012), causing professional freelancers and staff reporters to compete all the more passionately to get the story and to be paid for their work. This became more difficult in the wake of bureau closures and the pendulumlike swing of news organizations first investing, then disinvesting in specific conflicts. When bureaus closed, freelancers or individual staff correspondents were then expected to do the work that once would have been assigned to entire bureau staffs, helping to maintain the illusion of a news organization's "presence" in the field.

Alongside the intensifying industrial challenges that conflict correspondents faced in the first decade of the twenty-first century, war reporters also dealt with technological conditions that seemed profoundly new. As the *Washington Post's* Liz Sly told me, in the early 1980s she filed some of her very first stories on a Telex machine that was based at Beirut's famous Commodore Hotel—a hub for foreign journalists who wanted to stay in the center of the action during Lebanon's civil war (pers. comm., June 2015). Sly struggled to build contacts in a preinternet era, spending much of her time at the long bank of pay phones in the Commodore lobby. Slow, arduous technology was Sly's only link between Beirut and news desks around the world. Looking at stories like Sly's, it would be easy to assume that the rise of digital technology in the late '90s and in the first years of the twenty-first century changed conflict reporting for the better.

But the celebration of speedier communication and better interconnection long predates the internet. This utopic rhetoric also accompanied the advent of the telegraph and, later, the wireless radio (Mosco 2005; Perlmutter and Hamilton 2007). As it does today, the utopic technological discourse of the nineteenth and early twentieth centuries often obscured the tendency for technology to break down in the war zone (McLaughlin 2002), as well as belying the increased pressures that nineteenth- and twentieth-century war correspondents faced as their deadlines became shorter and shorter (Knightley 2004; Hamilton 2011). When people addressed the dangers of these "new" technologies, they did so through the lens of the "sublime," praising the technologies for their "epochal and transcendent characteristics" while also "demoniz[ing them] for the depth of the evil [they] can conjure" (Mosco 2005, 24).

According to Mosco, this notion of the sublime informed earlier discussions of technology, and this same notion continued to inform the cultural discourse on the digital in the early twenty-first century (2005). For at least the past two centuries, popular discourse has attributed a remarkable amount of power to individual technologies, engaging in the technological determinism critiqued by the cultural studies scholar Raymond Williams ([1974] 2003). That same attitude informed the discourse of the technologies associated with the early twenty-first century, and the technologies used by war reporters were no exception. Despite the tendency for commentators in the Anglophone war reporting industry to blame new technology for the industry's problems (and successes), it was not the technology itself that contributed to this challenging environment for conflict correspondents. Instead, the challenges were posed more by the social practices that animated these technologies and made them meaningful.

For instance, the explosion of the internet and the rise of 24-hour news networks throughout the '90s and 2000s certainly inspired the feeling in correspondents and news editors that all news was now 24-hour news (Ullmann, pers. comm., February 2015). Yet, that idea itself had a long history (Knightley 2004; Hamilton 2011), and the competitive nature of the news industry played a huge role in the expansion of 24-hour news television and online news platforms. After CNN caught the world's attention with its coverage of the Persian Gulf War, a number of 24-hour news networks sprang up around the world (Cushion and Lewis 2010). The combination of technological advancement and professional competition led most major Anglophone news organizations to place more and more pressure on their correspondents in the field, demanding that they do multiple live "standups," and that they constantly update their stories even when the traditional news day had ended.

The competitive nature of the industry also contributed to correspondents' drive to familiarize themselves with the murky, unpredictable spaces of the web. The internet especially caught the eye of the war reporting industry during the conflict in Kosovo in the late '90s. As Donald Matheson and Stuart Allan argue, "rudimentary forms of web reporting attracted considerable attention," in Kosovo (2009, 29–30). Some journalists celebrated the immediacy and potential for more personal forms of reporting while others thought that "rigorous" and "responsible" war journalism was in danger (ibid.). These competing attitudes would continue as web reporting matured during the first decade of the twenty-first century. By 2012, correspondents and their editors would be no less suspicious of the internet's reliability as a reporting tool, but they would feel far more pressure to use this tool anyway, maintaining visible online personas that could compete with the myriad "amateur" perspectives that flooded social media.

War correspondents of the early twenty-first century often invoked the lighter and more mobile digital technology that citizen journalists and militants used to "broadcast themselves to the world." Industry commentators claimed that the invention of this new technology was to blame for the increasing expectation that war reporters get closer and closer to the perilous site of conflict (Matheson and Allan 2009). But news artists of the nineteenth century were also expected to get near the action, and this mandate

Figure 2. A 1990s-era satellite uplink, used by Associated Press journalists in the field. Bulky equipment like this was once heralded for its contribution to speedier and more flexible war reporting. On display at the Newseum, in Washington, D.C.

continued for the photographers of the twentieth century (Knightley 2004; Hamilton 2011; Carruthers 2011). The expectation preexisted the technology that ostensibly engendered it. Rather than directly causing conflict reporters to venture too close to the fighting, the rise of equipment such as the satellite BGAN and the videophone over the course of the late '90s and the early 2000s contributed to the intensification of the already existing expectations that war reporters put themselves in danger.

Besides facing these technological challenges, twenty-first-century conflict correspondents also grappled with an array of intensifying political challenges. In the years between 2002–2012, war journalists had to deal with a notable amount of censorship. On the one hand, they navigated censorship at the hands of the "foreign" governments who monitored their use of social media or blocked cell phone and internet access. On the other hand, they dealt with censorship from their own governments, who controlled where correspondents could travel and what they could say in their news coverage. The embedded reporting model deployed in Iraq 2003 serves as one of the most widely discussed examples. In this configuration, journalists would don a military uniform, travel with a particular military unit for the duration of the war, and sign an agreement limiting what they could and could not reveal in their stories.

Critical-cultural media scholars have argued that this reporting model generated stilted news coverage often fixated upon military prowess, technological innovation, and the "bravery" of the U.S. military and its allies (Kellner 2003; Miller 2007; Der Derian 2009; Stahl 2009; Carruthers 2011).

Yet, it is important to note that no Anglophone journalist has ever covered a war entirely without censorship or, at least, without some kind of military influence on the correspondent's access to information (Hallin 1989; Knightley 2004; Mander 2010; Hamilton 2011; Bourrie 2012). In both of the World Wars, correspondents wore military uniforms and signed agreements to omit certain information from their reports (Knightley 2004; Hamilton 2011). Though Vietnam is often seen as the "uncensored war" (Hallin 1989), military officials censored themselves heavily during that conflict, resulting in deep frustration from conflict correspondents who could move through the battlefield with relative ease, but who could get no real information from the military officials they interviewed (Knightley 2004; Hamilton 2011). Part of the problem was the fact that war correspondents overwhelmingly privileged official military sources in the early coverage of Vietnam (Hallin 1989), and news editors based in the United States did as well (Knightley 2004; Hamilton 2011). Thus, Vietnam was not the journalistic free-for-all that so many people claim it to be. The first war in the Persian Gulf, the conflict in the Falklands, and the conflicts in Granada and Panama all saw what Thomas Rid refers to as more "restrictive," "top-down" censorship policies on the part of the U.S. and British militaries (2007), but these policies had their roots in the policies of the early twentieth century. Thus, English-language war reporters have long grappled with the censorship inherent in the practice of embedding during the 2003 invasion of Iraq.

What many correspondents and editors themselves claim to be *new* about the political landscape of the early twenty-first century is the overt hostility that journalists faced in the process of doing their jobs: hostility toward their messages as well as toward their physical well being. The conflict correspondent's need to compete with social media during this decade had a darker side, where political issues were concerned. Former ABC correspondent Ray Homer told me that when he was covering the Lebanese Civil War in the 1970s and '80s, people in Beirut could not see the final product of his work, because there was no internet: "So they didn't know what we were reporting or really anything that we were doing. If they did an interview with us, they couldn't necessarily see what had gone on the air. Now, they know everything." (pers. comm., June 2015).

Homer's assertion highlighted a belief that many of my interviewees shared: the transnational, multichanneled flow of information has made war reporters more expendable in the twenty-first century and, thus, more of a political target. As ABC producer Matt McGarry put it:

> I think that the world has become much more dangerous for journalists because of the development of the Internet and the technology which allows people to broadcast themselves to the world. Several decades ago, I think most people in the world understood that journalists were impartial observers. . . . Now, the people with an iPhone and an Internet connection can broadcast their own story. So they don't need international journalists knocking on their doors. (pers. comm., January 2013)

McGarry's statement points to the popular notion that the first decade of the new millennium was a time when professional journalists were losing their monopoly on meaning itself. No longer the only ones narrativizing the space of war, conflict correspondents felt that they were competing for the story on a political as well as industrial level. In these cases, they had much more to fear than being "scooped." A number of my interviewees told me that conflict correspondents were increasingly being targeted by nondemocratic governments, as well as by militant groups who associated western, English-language journalists with western foreign policy (or with the western money that could result in a hefty ransom for a kidnapped journalist). Judging from the melodramatic political narratives so often found in mainstream, Anglophone news coverage, this claim unfortunately makes sense: if more and more people around the world can see what western journalists are saying in their news coverage, and if this coverage tends to bolster the rhetoric of the United States and allies, then the likelihood of journalists being targeted for political reasons could conceivably increase.

But there is also another side to this issue, and it gets far less discussion in the mainstream, English-language war reporting industry. Not only were journalists targeted by militant groups and authoritarian governments at the turn of the twenty-first century. They were also targeted by the U.S. military. Starting in 1999, and exploding in the first decade of the new millennium, the U.S. military engaged in a "pattern of violence" against journalists working in war zones (Paterson 2014, 58). This violence overwhelmingly impacted journalists who were born and raised in places such as Iraq and Afghanistan, even when these journalists were working for "western" news organizations like Reuters or the BBC (Paterson 2014). While industry commentators might have denounced this issue behind the scenes, they rarely addressed it in their news coverage (ibid.). For instance, CNN senior executive Eason Jordan had to leave the network when he "publicly expressed concern" for this problem (ibid., 11). Most news organizations didn't even venture so far as Jordan, remaining silent in the news coverage that could have brought this issue into the public eye.

The conflict correspondents of the nineteenth and twentieth centuries were certainly injured, targeted, and killed (Knightley 2004; Tumber and Webster 2006; Hamilton 2011; Armoudian 2017). Anglophone war reporters died in the Turko-Serbian war of the nineteenth century (Knightley 2004), for example, and numerous correspondents were arrested, deported, and kidnapped in the process of doing their work (Knightley 2004; Hamilton 2011). Journalistic death tolls were particularly high during the Vietnam War and the conflicts in the Balkans in the 1990s, with 66 correspondents killed in Vietnam and 61 killed in the Balkan wars (Hamilton 2011). But it is striking that since 2003, 177 journalists have died covering the ongoing conflict in Iraq, more than doubling the number of journalists killed in Vietnam (Committee to Protect Journalists 2016). Partly because of numbers like these, and partly because of the various other tragedies that have befallen correspondents in the field, a number of journalists and media scholars argue that the twenty-first century has seen an increase in the dangers that war reporters face (Paterson 2014; Cottle, Sambrook, and Mosdell 2016; Armoudian 2017). Whatever the case may be, one thing is certain: conflict correspondents faced a number of political and physical dangers in the years following 9/11, and their news editors often very publicly attributed their incidents to journalistic targeting—when the people doing the targeting could be represented as sociopolitical "Others."

I offer a glimpse into these harrowing conditions so that critical media scholars can gain a clearer understanding of the factors that impact the production of journalistic media texts. These challenges make it difficult for conflict correspondents to *survive* the story, let alone *tell* the story in a more politically nuanced fashion. And yet, it is easy to forget that many of these same challenges also inform the work of news editors back at headquarters, albeit in different ways. As Owen Ullmann, managing editor of world news at *USA Today* told me, editors carry the "huge burden" of waiting to hear from their people in the field, "and until they are out of that conflict zone, it stays with you constantly" (pers. comm., February 2015). Such an assertion speaks to the oppressive weight that foreign-desk editors and producers must also bear, when dealing with the question of journalistic safety.

This leads me to the second argument that I advance in this book: The new millennium saw the rise of a highly discursive and performative "safety culture," where the entire profession began to think, plan, and *talk* more about safety in the field. As veteran correspondent Judith Matloff put it:

Editors used to send you forth with a bottle of Scotch and the words "good luck." I never heard the word "trauma" uttered until 9/11, and now it's part of the pre-and post-assignment briefing. Editors today tend to ask correspondents how they are, and advise them of confidential hotlines, and send them on hostile environment courses. (pers. comm., June 2013)

Matloff's assertion was echoed by many of my interviewees. Though hazardous environment courses first came onto the scene with the Balkan conflicts of the early '90s (Brayne, pers. comm., February 2013; "About Us" 2016; "Who We Are" 2016), many editors and war reporters argue that the popularity of these classes "exploded" after 9/11, with more and more news organizations sending their staff employees to get this expensive training. Yet, the training was highly performative. Some of my interviewees traveled to the English countryside for these courses, where they interacted with trained actors playing the role of militants. The performance of risk was helpful to a few of my interviewees, who felt that the classes taught participants how to conduct individual risk assessments; others found them to be a waste of time, citing experience in the field as a far better training ground. These competing attitudes toward safety informed the Anglophone news industry's discourse on security more generally (Cottle 2016).

If anything, the proliferation of these safety training classes in the early twenty-first century was indicative of a post-9/11 shift in editorial attitudes toward safety. In 1894, when correspondent James Creelman was injured covering the Spanish-American War, his boss William Randolph Hearst told him, "I'm sorry you're hurt, but wasn't it a splendid fight! We must beat every paper in the world" (cited in Knightley 2004, 61). This logic continued into the twentieth century. For instance, when BBC correspondents covering the Second World War complained that they should be given more compensation for injury or death than the "average army equivalent," because they faced greater danger than the average soldier, their superiors retorted "that front line reporting traded extra risk for extra excitement" (Nicholas 2005, 150). And though, by the Vietnam War, some publications were paying their injured reporters' hospital bills (Knightley 2004), it was the turn of the twenty-first century that saw a more collective, organizational push toward proactively preparing for safety risks in the field (Brayne, pers. comm., February 2013; Ullmann, pers. comm., February 2015; McLaughlin 2002). As Pool-Eckert ruefully said of her years covering the Lebanese Civil War in Beirut, there were no hazardous environment courses for journalists in those days; instead, Beirut "*was* my hazardous environment training!" (pers. comm., February 2015).

John Maxwell Hamilton attributes the rise of this safety culture to the more general corporatization of news that solidified over the second half of the twentieth century (2011). Perhaps this is why some of my interviewees scoffed when I asked them about the usefulness of hazardous environment training. A few of them suggested that these courses were more important to insurance companies than they were to anyone else in the news business, and others repeated the familiar adage that "you only learn by experience." Paul Ingrassia, the managing editor of Reuters told me that when his news agency was acquired by Thomson in 2007, the new editorial leadership team was asked to "be especially systematic and stringent" when it came to safety (pers. comm., February 2015). This led them to be criticized by some of their own correspondents for being too restrictive and allowing competitors to scoop them in the field (ibid.).

While some of my interviewees asserted that the growing safety culture was too invasive, other correspondents I interviewed said that it did not go far enough—especially because some reporters were better protected than others. This points to a crucial paradox in the news industry's safety culture. Though the Anglophone news industry paid more and more money for security advisors, hazardous environment training, and safety equipment as the first decade of the twenty-first century unfolded, in practice, these expensive safety measures were distributed unevenly, without much formalization (Cottle, Sambrook, and Mosdell 2016). The pressure to compete in a dangerous environment continued to haunt conflict correspondents—especially the freelancers. Additionally, safety training and medical insurance was allotted to only certain war reporters—mostly the white, western staff correspondents (Cottle 2016; Palmer 2016). Freelancers, stringers, "fixers," and employees born and working outside the United States, Canada, or Britain did not receive these perks nearly as often. If they were lucky enough to acquire a flak jacket or hazardous environment training, members of this economic and racialized "underclass" of war reporters usually had to pay their own bills (Palmer 2016).

For instance, a Turkish reporter for a major U.S. newspaper (who wished to remain anonymous) told me that she had to beg her news organization to send her to hazardous environment training (pers. comm., July 2015). The newspaper did so only after this reporter had been promoted to the position of "staff employee." Even then, she was given a watered-down version of the course. My interviewee felt that this was directly due to her status as a non-western reporter (ibid.). Suzan Haidamous, a full-time news assistant for the *Washington Post* in Beirut told me that she has also never received hazardous environment training (pers. comm., June 2015). And news assistant for the

New York Times in Beirut, Hwaida Saad, asserted that certain employees at the bureau are paid more in general, "because they're Americans" (pers. comm., June 2015). My interviewees provided myriad examples of this kind of industrial discrimination.

This issue points to the fact that some English-language war reporters are valued more than others, a problem that is difficult to tackle when considering the fact that the mainstream, Anglophone news industry is a contradictory, heterogeneous system that exceeds any one individual. The hierarchical valuation of war correspondents is generated and sustained in the disjointed practices of the myriad desk assistants, editors, news executives, bureau secretaries, bureau chiefs, producers, correspondents, freelancers, news departments, and accounting officers who all play a role in producing the news. These various entities often never meet each other, nor do they always understand the roles that the others play. This is why the inequalities that some war reporters face need to be addressed at the institutional level, rather than at the level of the individual.

Such reform is tough to achieve when the English-language war reporting industry remains so fascinated by the figure of the individual. This leads me to the third and final argument I advance in this book. Despite the systemic nature of the problems that inform the labor of war correspondence, post-9/11 news narratives that featured war correspondents' safety catastrophes represented conflict reporters as the neoliberal subjects of late capitalism. War reporters appeared in these news narratives as self-sufficient individuals who were responsible for their own well being. This insidious "individualization" of the war reporter obfuscated the need for industrial reform and justified the rhetoric of the "war on terror"—rhetoric which melodramatically celebrated the neoliberal individual over any collective notion of the world.

Anker argues that the philosophy of neoliberalism is inherent to the United States' own special brand of melodrama, because this narrative has for decades focused on "freedom" (2014). In Anker's formulation, the notion of freedom is really a mask for the dangerous sense of entitlement to unrestrained power that has long surfaced in the discourse of the U.S. government and its allies (ibid.). As Anker declares:

> The norm of freedom that circulates in melodramatic political discourse is rooted in particularly liberal and Americanized interpretations of freedom as self-reliance, as unconstrained agency, and as unbound subjectivity. It combines these interpretations together as normative expressions of a sovereign subject, one who obeys no other authority but one's own, who can determine

the future and control the vagaries of contingency through sheer strength of will." (ibid., 9)

Anker locates this "norm of freedom" in the larger political narratives that circulated throughout the Cold War and then intensified after 9/11 (2014). Following Anker, I argue that this same neoliberal bent informs the 2002–2012 war coverage that focused on the figure of the war correspondent, where the war reporter was represented as the sovereign subject and the virtuous hero. Through this mechanism, Anglophone news outlets capitalized upon the injury or death of their correspondents while still obscuring the ways in which such incidents could have been prevented. The precariousness of the correspondents' labor was sometimes foregrounded, either by the correspondents' news editors or by the correspondents themselves, in a way that distracted from the larger systemic causes for the mishap.

In addition, instead of interrogating the politics and policies that made it easier for such tragedies to happen, mainstream, English-language news organizations and western governments blamed the sociopolitical "Others" that were "hunting" these journalists. Perhaps this is why so many of the war reporters featured in these news narratives were white. In the rarer instances when these melodramatic narratives featured correspondents who were *not* white, the western affiliations of these reporters were heavily foregrounded. This uncritical and politically biased way of representing professional catastrophe deserves interrogation, because it ignores the negative experiences of nonwhite, or non-western war reporters—experiences that were sometimes the result of the U.S. military's very direct attack on journalists in the field (Paterson 2014)—while also contributing to the larger political discourse that sanctions the "war on terror."

Judith Butler argues that the philosophical "frame" that shapes this political discourse is biopolitical in nature, since it suggests that some populations are worth cultivating and salvaging, while other populations are not (2009). Butler offers two interrelated terms: *precariousness*—the existential danger we all face and thus experience on a collective level—and *precarity*: the mechanism that engenders the "politically induced condition in which certain populations suffer from failing social and economic networks of support and become differentially exposed to injury, violence, and death" (ibid., 25). Melodramatic news narratives deploy the mechanism of precarity, representing some groups of people as being so villainous as to be inhuman, while representing other groups as the heroes (or victims) that are most recognizable to power.

For Butler, "recognizability" is at the heart of precarity, and this recognizability is a staunchly ethical issue. Butler adapts the ethical philosophy of Emmanuel Levinas to the questions posed in the field of cultural studies, echoing Levinas's assertion that the face-to-face encounter with the Other can lead us to help, rather than hurt, each other (cited in Butler 2004). Yet, Butler argues that precarity renders some people "faceless": "Those who remain faceless, or whose faces are presented to us as so many symbols of evil, authorize us to become senseless before those lives we have eradicated, and whose grievability is indefinitely postponed" (ibid., xviii). Thus, Butler says, we need to "frame" the frame in order to see that this philosophical outlook is always exceeded by something uncontainable (2009). For her, "framing the frame" is a radically ethical solution to the problem of precarity.

Applying Butler's framework to the Anglophone news industry's representation of conflict correspondents, it becomes clear that the "framers" of whom Butler speaks are not the war correspondents themselves, but the larger melodramatic narratives—and sociopolitical perspectives—that preexist and outlast individual reporters' presence in the war zone. While conflict correspondents undoubtedly sometimes write stories that contribute to the logic of melodrama, they are simultaneously *written by* the very narratives they appear to bolster. Indeed, war correspondents are valued or devalued according to the same unethical logic that Butler critiques: some of them are represented as the recognizable heroes, while others are rendered "faceless," hidden from what falls within the frame. The melodramatic news narratives that feature war correspondents as heroes do the work of demarcating which journalists are recognizable to which audiences, while also contributing to the larger social narratives that mark the "Other" as an unrecognizable enemy. In turn, these narratives present the white westerner as the most recognizable Self.

It is important to remember that these narratives are larger than any one individual. They draw upon diffuse cultural traditions that are deeply entrenched in the news industry, as well as in western, Anglophone society. This is why it is essential for critical media scholars to zoom out from the news narratives themselves and examine them in the broader context of production culture—a culture that cannot exist outside the larger sociopolitical culture in which it operates. The cohesiveness of the melodramatic news narrative makes it easy to overlook this important fact. Each of the case studies explored in this book shows that journalistic catastrophe vastly exceeds the representations that fall within the frame. Behind each of these narratives of certain correspondents' tragedies, there were larger, messier challenges that diverse war reporters had to face in diverse contexts. The practice of war reporting will always exceed the news story itself. Because of this, I trace the important interconnections and divergences between journalistic media texts and the cultural act of producing them, following humanist media production scholars in "consider[ing] the interrelationships between industry, text, audience, and society" (Holt and Perren 2010, 5).

This critical approach informs each of the chapters in this book. Chapter One investigates the 2002 kidnapping of *Wall Street Journal* correspondent Daniel Pearl in Pakistan. Pearl's case reveals the relative laxness of security protocol for foreign journalists working in the region at that time. Though the 1980s and '90s saw the high-profile kidnapping of correspondents like the Associated Press's Terry Anderson in Beirut and Tina Susman in Somalia, Pearl's kidnapping was quickly represented as a "new" danger, a turning point for journalists working after 9/11. One of the Anglophone news industries' primary talking points was the "digital" nature of Pearl's kidnapping: he had been lured into a trap via email, and his captors were making their demands online instead of by phone. Perhaps not surprisingly, mainstream war reporters' own lack of digital savvy loomed large within the public discussion of Pearl's plight, as did their lack of security protocol for covering the "war on terror." Meanwhile, the *WSJ* editors decided to make Pearl's kidnapping a highly visible news story in and of itself, while barely mentioning the demands that Pearl's kidnappers had made—demands that included the release of Pakistani prisoners who were illegally being held in Guantánamo Bay.

Chapter Two looks at the issue of physical injury in conflict correspondence. I examine the 2006 brain injury of ABC's Bob Woodruff in Iraq, an injury that was not supposed to happen to a reporter engaged in what the Pentagon claimed was the "safest" reporting option: embedding with the U.S. troops. Woodruff was supposed to be reporting in the safest possible way, despite the fact that his mobility as a reporter was limited by the troops with whom he traveled. Since Woodruff was embedded when he suffered his infamous injuries to the neck and head, his injury exposed the inadequacy of embedding as a safety precaution. With the transnationally circulated image of Woodruff's wounded body, the safety promised by the Pentagon was profoundly called into question. Yet, the U.S. news industry wove Woodruff's experience into a larger narrative of U.S. patriotism, distracting from the holes in the Pentagon's rhetoric.

Chapter Three addresses the 2009 exile of Iranian-Canadian journalists Maziar Bahari and Nazila Fathi, after their coverage of the postelection uprising in Tehran. Both Bahari and Fathi were working for U.S.-based publications when they reported on the Green Movement, an uprising that was militarized once the Iranian Revolutionary Guard and the Basij started cracking down on protesters. Though Bahari and Fathi were Iranian citizens and had family in Tehran, their association with *Newsweek* magazine and the *New York Times* led to their persecution at the hands of Iranian officials. Bahari was imprisoned for months before fleeing the country, and Fathi grabbed her family and fled to Canada after receiving threats that she would also soon face imprisonment. At the time of this writing, neither Bahari nor Fathi have been able to return to Iran. Thus, Chapter Three examines the racialized and nationalized challenges for reporters who work with mainstream, Anglophone publications, but whose cultural identities are spread out across multiple continents. For these correspondents, exile looms large as a devastating threat.

Chapter Four analyzes the sexual assault of CBS war correspondent Lara Logan, who had been covering the 2011 uprisings in Egypt. On January 25, 2011, Logan was attacked and sexually assaulted in Tahrir Square, an event that quickly became the subject of much internet chatter. Obsessed with Logan's "difference" as a female reporter inhabiting the "masculine" space of conflict, this digital discourse prompted Logan to give an interview about her experience on CBS's *60 Minutes* program. In the interview, Logan claimed to be "breaking the silence" for other female correspondents reporting from conflict zones, asserting that sexual harassment and assault is a risk that many female journalists specifically face in the field. Yet, the *60 Minutes* interview in no way interrogated the news industry's studied avoidance of gender-specific safety precautions at that time, nor did it address the sad truth that male war reporters also face the risk of sexual assault. Instead, this interview placed the blame onto Logan herself, as well as onto the racialized figure of the "Egyptian male," subtly conflating Logan's attackers with the entire group of protesters and citizen journalists who had pushed for Egyptian President Hosni Mubarak's resignation.

Lastly, Chapter Five considers the 2012 death of a well-known newspaper correspondent in Syria: the *Sunday Times of London*'s Marie Colvin. The veteran reporter died in February of 2012, shortly after smuggling herself into the embattled city of Homs. CNN, the BBC, and Channel 4 News each captured Colvin's final hours in Homs by conducting live interviews with her—interviews thought to have contributed to her being targeted by the Assad regime (Conroy 2013). CNN obsessively replayed the interview with Colvin in the days following her death, capitalizing on the "live" testimony of a dead correspondent who was still being made to labor for the news outlets even when her physical body was gone. But as Colvin's freelance photographer Paul Conroy later said, Colvin's decision to do this interview might have caused Syrian forces to locate the media house where she was hiding. Because of the digital technologies used to connect Colvin to CNN's newscast, Syrian forces were reportedly able to figure out where the western journalists—and the many opposition activists doing their own digital reporting—were located (ibid.). Following this, Chapter Five raises questions about the centrality of death to the practice of conflict correspondence, especially interrogating the extreme competitiveness of the industry that sells stories of death to its audience.

On a deeper level, this book interrogates the popular tendency to romanticize the labor of conflict reporting, despite the fact that such romanticization seems difficult for both scholars and industry practitioners to avoid. Conflict correspondents have fascinated their publics since the nineteenth century, surfacing as characters in novels and later in film (Korte 2009), as well as becoming celebrities in their own right (Knightley 2004; Hamilton 2011). Perhaps there is something reassuring in the fantasy of the rugged figure, scurrying over the sand dunes and dodging bullets in order to act as "the world's eyes and ears in troubled times and places" ("In the Line of Duty" 2013). Perhaps people simply want to know that someone is out there, documenting the sights often rendered unpalatable for most eyes. Yet, the conflict correspondents' legendary status has potentially been most dangerous to these reporters themselves, and to the media producers who take grave risks in order to live up to the lofty stories that are told about them. With this book, I hope to introduce some different stories.

1

The "Blood Messenger"

Daniel Pearl's 2002 Kidnapping in Pakistan

> Those who would threaten Americans, those who would
> engage in barbaric, criminal acts, need to know that
> these crimes only hurt their cause, only deepen the
> resolve of the United States of America to rid the world
> of these agents of terror. May God bless Daniel Pearl.
>
> —President George W. Bush, on Pearl's 2002 kidnapping

On January 23, 2002, *Wall Street Journal* reporter Daniel Pearl was abducted in Karachi, Pakistan. Pearl was driving to the Village Restaurant in Karachi, under the impression that he was meeting with a potential interviewee for a story on the connection between Al-Qaeda and Richard Reid, the infamous "shoe bomber." Instead of completing that interview, Pearl was kidnapped by a group that called itself the National Movement for the Restoration of Pakistani Sovereignty (NMRPS). Members of this group had been posing as Pearl's potential news sources for several weeks, communicating with him through a phony email account. Shortly after the NMRPS kidnapped Pearl, they sent another email, this time to an array of western news organizations. This email listed a series of demands in exchange for Pearl's safe return: better treatment for prisoners in Guantánamo Bay, the release of Pakistani detainees from that prison so they could be tried in a legitimate Pakistani court, and the completion of what Pearl's captors said was a previously halted shipment of F-16 fighter jets to the Pakistani government. Attached to the email were a series of digital pictures of Pearl in captivity.

Though they treated these demands with varying degrees of skepticism, the Anglophone news media rushed to report on the kidnapping itself. Industry commentators lamented that, despite the fact that Pearl was "far from the fighting" in Afghanistan, he was still a casualty in the U.S.-led "war on terror"

(Rieder 2002). Years after Pearl's eventual murder, the *Columbia Journalism Review* recalled that "Pearl's plight inspired an enormous international media campaign," one that did not at all help to save his life (Bach 2014). In fact, Pearl's highly visible case haunted the 2008 cases in which *New York Times* reporter David Rohde and Canadian Broadcasting Corporation correspondent Mellissa Fung were kidnapped in Afghanistan, leading their organizations to call for a media blackout until they escaped. Even in mid-2002, when Pearl was only a few months dead, industry pundits conceded that Pearl's captors had "cast themselves as lead actors on a global stage, focusing a powerful spotlight on their demands" (Ricchiardi 2002b). By drawing upon the expansive capabilities of the media in the digital era, Pearl's captors used him as a medium through which to send what some journalists viewed as a "blood message" to the United States.[1]

David Allen Grindstaff and Kevin Michael DeLuca argue that Pearl's body itself was the medium, meant to send a message of violence and fear to the U.S. government, its allies, and its journalists (2007). Certainly, western news commentators saw a message emanating from a widely distributed video of Pearl's decapitated body, and "the message was stark: Pearl's execution signaled an era of greater danger and vulnerability outside of combat zones" (Ricchiardi 2002b). Though conflict correspondence had always been a dangerous job, and though kidnapping a journalist was certainly not a novel trick, news outlets saw Pearl's kidnapping and subsequent murder as a turning point in post-9/11 war reporting. Because of the kidnapping's "digital" quality, and because of its positioning within the Bush administration's new "war on terror," the mainstream, Anglophone news industry flagged Pearl's kidnapping as a grim sign that western journalists faced a far more dangerous world.

In order to better understand the world in which journalists were operating in 2002, Chapter One first looks at the industrial tensions and technological practices that underwrote correspondents' experiences in the months following the 2001 attacks on the World Trade Center. This was a time of industrial instability, especially for the newspapers that were struggling for relevance and revenue in the still rather new digital era. Accordingly, this chapter will also examine the discourse surrounding Pearl's abduction, investigating the anxiety that his hi-tech kidnapping inspired. Pearl's case made industry commentators feel that the danger was not simply tethered to the war zone itself but could follow correspondents into locations far from the front lines. On top of that, war reporters could now be monitored and lured through the anonymous use of digital technologies.

Correspondents and their editors perceived these ostensibly new dangers at precisely the same time that many in the Anglophone news industry began to make a more concerted attempt at discussing the safety of conflict correspondents. The *Wall Street Journal* was no exception: in fact, Pearl participated in the paper's early conversations on how to properly evaluate and prepare for the risks that correspondents faced in the "war on terror" (Spindle, pers. comm., July 2015). Yet, Pearl's kidnapping showed that much more needed to be done. In one sense, the incident raised concrete questions about whether news organizations should publicize their reporters' kidnappings, or whether they should call for a media blackout—especially in the internet age, when information could fall in the "wrong" hands.

In another sense, Pearl's kidnapping operated as a marker for what some in the English-language news industry saw as a temporal rupture—the entryway into an era when war reporters were becoming more visible targets for militant groups. For journalism industry commentators, the precarious visibility of correspondents in the context of digitization was shadowed by the even more unsettling invisibility of the "enemies" using the internet. Pearl's abduction drove this point home for the western news organizations who flooded the mediascape with coverage of Pearl's abduction, while ignoring the political demands that his captors made. Following this, Chapter One ultimately explores the melodramatic narrativization of Pearl's case, particularly in the context of U.S. journalism. Though Pearl's situation certainly struck a chord with British and Canadian journalists, U.S. news organizations especially suggested that Pearl's case served as a justification for the Bush administration's "war on terror," tightly linking Pearl's visibly absent body to the "barbarism" and "inscrutability" of the extremists that U.S. officials were determined to destroy.

Covering the "War on Terror": Industrial, Technological, and Political Challenges

By the time the World Trade Center fell in 2001, the figure of the war correspondent was familiar to people in North America and Britain. The twentieth century saw the rise of a variety of wars in which the United States and its allies had been involved, and thus, it also saw the rise of the modern, English-language war correspondent (Knightley 2004). An older guard of journalists had built their careers on patriotic coverage of the World Wars (Knightley 2004; Hamilton 2011). The Vietnam era saw another generation of war correspondents gain notoriety, this time because they were seen (perhaps incorrectly) as being "rebels"—questioning the war and revealing its horrors (Hallin 1989; Knightley 2004; Korte 2009; Hamilton 2011). Some of the correspondents who covered Vietnam went on to cover the Persian Gulf War, providing older news audiences with a sense of continuity (Knightley 2004; Hamilton 2011).

For news audiences in North America and Britain, the first war in the Persian Gulf was the most visible war since Vietnam. Though the British military had fought in the Falklands in 1982, British officials blocked most reporters from the action and kept them from covering what happened (Rid 2007; Carruthers 2011). Journalists were also blocked from covering the U.S. military's 1980s excursions in Grenada and Panama (ibid.). By the time U.S. forces descended upon the Persian Gulf in the early '90s, both U.S. and British officials had devised a new censorship plan that would allow journalists to "cover" the war, albeit under strict military supervision (ibid.). Television news coverage of this conflict especially focused on new military technology and military might (Carruthers 2011). The young, 24-hour news network CNN played a starring role in the coverage of the Persian Gulf, giving rise to a new style of reporting that was focused more on "liveness"—on the televisual simulation of temporal and spatial instantaneity—than on providing adequate historical and political context (Paterson 2010).

Despite the U.S. media's brief focus on covering the Persian Gulf War, news organizations in the United States, and to some extent Britain and Canada, closed a substantial number of news bureaus throughout the 1990s. They also struggled to retain their news audiences throughout that decade (Manthorpe 1999; Starr 2002; Greenslade 2002; Knox, pers. comm., March 2015). Public news organizations like the CBC had been the subject of federal budget cuts (Nayman pers. comm., March 2015), while private news organizations had increasingly dealt with the corporatization of their news practices and products (Barkin 2003; Paterson and Sreberny 2004; Williams 2011). Perhaps unsurprisingly, foreign news coverage dropped sharply over the course of the 1990s, as the Cold War came to an end (Hamilton 2011). The industry's haphazard coverage of the conflicts in the Balkans and on the African continent throughout the 1990s occurred within this precarious industrial context.

Because of these challenges, educating the public about the intricacies of foreign policies in politically complex regions like the Middle East had not been a top priority for the mainstream, English-language news outlets in North America and Britain (Tomlin 2001b; Macdonald cited in Tomlin 2001a; Nayman, pers. comm., March 2015; Knox, pers. comm., March 2015). This was despite the fact that after the end of the Cold War, U.S. officials and their international allies viewed the region with more and more suspicion (Dobkin 1992; Kumar 2012). Instead of investigating and interrogating this suspicion, television networks represented "Islamic terrorism" in a simplistic, melodramatic fashion (Dobkin 1992). And TV networks weren't the only offenders; other news outlets also failed to provide an appropriate amount of historical background information on the sociopolitical tensions between the United States and the Middle East (Carey 2002; McChesney 2002; Zelizer and Allan 2002).

When the 9/11 attacks occurred, news organizations celebrated the opportunity to tell their public a riveting story of war, drawing upon the salacious melodramatic narratives that had informed the news coverage of earlier eras (Dobkin 1992; Knightley 2004; Anker 2014). But this was no simple task, as television networks and newspapers in North America and Britain lacked the resources they needed to cover the story. Since they had dismantled their international infrastructure of international reporters (or had never built such an infrastructure in the first place), these news organizations often had to start from scratch. An article in the *American Journalism Review* put it bluntly, saying: "The biggest news story in a generation or more occurred just as the pain of newsroom downsizings, buyouts, and layoffs was beginning to fade. The gut-punch that the attacks laid on the economy seems certain to trigger that pain anew even as the story mushrooms" (Farhi 2001).

Notwithstanding these obstacles, news executives saw 9/11 and the resulting war in Afghanistan as a story with a life of its own, one that would help news organizations "cement" relationships with newly interested audiences (McClellan 2001). For instance, CBS's vice president of news coverage, Marcy McGinnis said: "This is the biggest thing that's ever hit. There have been no discussions of money. There will never be enough money to cover something like this. . . . You just do it, and nobody is going to tell you not to" (cited in McClellan 2001). News executives in Canada and Britain also felt this drive to cover the fallout from 9/11, despite the lack of resources (McNamara 2001; Petrick 2002; Tomlin 2001a; Nayman pers. comm., March 2015). For example, former executive producer for the Canadian Broadcasting Corporation David Nayman told me that though the CBC had experienced budget cuts, there were reserve funds that had to be used to cover "epochal" stories like this one (pers. comm., March 2015). And numerous news outlets in Britain also rushed to get their correspondents into Afghanistan, inspiring correspondents like the BBC's John Simpson and the *Sunday Express*'s Yvonne Ridley to go so far as to disguise themselves in Afghan clothing in order to gain access to the story (Tomlin 2001c; Morgan 2001a).

In the early days of the Afghanistan conflict, news analysts noted that some U.S. news networks were spending around one and two million dollars a day to cover the "war on terror" (Farhi 2001; McClellan 2001). At the same time, advertisers were increasingly pulling their funds because of the unstable political climate. The downturn in advertising especially hit newspapers, the still very traditional news outlets that had already been struggling to maintain their relevance in the burgeoning digital media sphere. As news outlets focused more heavily on foreign reporting than they had in years, they indeed saw some initial payout in terms of newspaper circulation and network ratings (Mostafa 2001; Shields 2001; McNamara 2001). Yet, this success was accompanied by a huge "advertising drought" that quickly inspired a number of English-language news organizations to reassess their budgets (Shields 2001; Petrick 2002; McNamara 2001) and implement layoffs ("American Pie" 2001; Morgan 2001b; Petrick 2002).

Within this economically unstable context, western news outlets also had to compete with global news organizations such as Al Jazeera, the young Arabic-language network whose views were continually excoriated by U.S. government officials (Samuel-Azran 2010). The increased use of the internet had exposed U.S. news audiences to a variety of perspectives from international news organizations, and industry pundits were taking notice (Rieder 2002; Vane 2002). On top of international competition—which, on a smaller scale had troubled U.S. and British newspapers since the nineteenth century (Knightley 2004; Hamilton 2011)—news outlets feared the growing presence of amateur internet sites that could potentially distract, lure, and influence audiences through the still relatively "new" technology. The danger of being scooped by "amateurs" undeniably informed the industry's ambivalent discourse on digital technologies more generally.

News coverage of the Persian Gulf War and the Balkan Wars in the 1990s had inspired particular interest in the nascent digital technologies that would become so important to covering the "war on terror," engendering a wealth of journalistic ambivalence toward the internet even in the early years of its mainstream accessibility (Matheson and Allan 2009). Some conflict reporters embraced online journalism at this early stage, celebrating its potential to make news reporting more personal and immediate (ibid.). Others feared the unreliability of the internet, asserting that digital reporting and the industry's interaction with bloggers would hurt the credibility of professional journalism (ibid.). This ambivalence continued into the new millennium, impacting the Anglophone news industries' notions of the digital at the beginning of the "war on terror."

For instance, one U.S. trade article referred to "weblogs" as "so much blather," while in the same breath referring to them as "maverick sites . . . well worth exploring" (Seipp 2002). Other industry commentators characterized the internet more generally as "a medium plagued by horrible navigation, utterly hopeless search tools and general clutter" (Palser 2002). Canadian journalism pundits celebrated "computer assisted reporting" (McKie 2002) while also raising questions about the credibility of digital citizen journalists (Hayhoe 2002). And in the United States, Britain, and Canada, news commentators celebrated both the pitfalls and the promises of media convergence (Robins 2001b; Healy 2002; Vranckx 2002) while they simultaneously tracked the risks and payoffs of newspapers' forays into the online world (Bunder 2001; Robins 2001a; Shields 2001; "New Media Hits Profits" 2001). This ambivalence toward "new" technology repeatedly surfaced in the industrial discourse after 9/11, with news organizations celebrating the internet as a hands-on tool through which to secure viewer loyalty (Palser 2002) while also worrying that the "facts" that news audiences could now retrieve and share with others may have come straight from the Taliban (Rieder 2002). Such discourse invoked the notion of the "digital sublime," both celebrating and denigrating the power of new technology (Mosco 2005).

Pearl's abduction added a new layer to this industrial anxiety. Throughout the early days of the war in Afghanistan, journalists and news editors worried over the rash of journalists' deaths that had already occurred. At one point in 2002, the *American Journalism Review* announced that "eight journalists had been killed in Afghanistan—all within a 17-day period, the profession's heaviest death toll in such a short amount of time in recent memory" (Ricchiardi 2002a). The *Columbia Journalism Review* featured an article by correspondent Jim Wooten, who had narrowly escaped death alongside some of these less lucky reporters (Wooten 2002). In turn, *Broadcasting and Cable* noted that the Taliban had threatened CNN's Nic Robertson, saying they would "dismember" Robertson if he did not leave the country (McClellan 2001). And a later *AJR* article lamented that the September 11 attacks had "upped the ante on American journalists," leading to numerous assaults, deaths, and the kidnapping of Pearl (Ricchiardi 2002b). These accounts suggested that war reporters were operating within a new political environment, where they would now be more directly associated with the interests of the U.S. government. This discourse overlooked the fact that journalists had been associated with their nation's governments long before 9/11 (Knightley 2004), reproducing the sociohistorical amnesia that informed the broader understanding of 9/11 as a political event. It also overlooked the U.S. military's own growing tendency to target journalists who looked too much like "terrorists" (Paterson 2014).

Though Pearl was not, strictly speaking, a "war reporter," he was a foreign correspondent for the *Wall Street Journal*, covering issues related to terrorism in Karachi. He had also been to the Balkans in the '90s, writing long-form and feature-driven pieces on the conflicts there (Spindle, pers. comm., July 2015). Once Pearl was kidnapped in Karachi, the English-language war reporting community repeatedly invoked Pearl as one of its own, while also continually remarking that Pearl's kidnapping—executed through a series of duplicitous email exchanges that lured Pearl into captivity—was proof of the murkiness of the "front lines" in the "war on terror." This discourse suggested a linkage between Pearl's incident, the "war on terror," and the precariousness of conflict reporting in the digital age. I now turn to a more detailed discussion of that discourse, focusing on the paradoxical connections and disconnections between the industry's burgeoning "safety culture" and the melodramatic strategies used to narrativize Pearl's kidnapping.

Kidnapping and the New "Safety Culture"

The capture of foreign journalists historically predates Pearl's own abduction. For example, U.S. correspondent Richard Harding Davis was briefly captured and held by German troops during World War I (Knightley 2004). The Germans were especially suspicious of Davis because he was carrying a photograph of himself wearing a British military uniform, pointing to the strong identification of war correspondents with particular governments decades before the conflict in Afghanistan (ibid.). War correspondents were also kidnapped by militant groups long before Pearl's kidnapping. Terry Anderson, a reporter for the Associated Press, was kidnapped in Beirut in 1985 at the height of the Lebanese Civil War. Affiliated with Lebanon's Hezbollah group, Anderson's captors circulated images of Anderson in their custody, in an effort at galvanizing the public to meet their demands. Thus, kidnapping journalists was certainly not a new practice in 2002.

Perhaps this is why the risk of kidnapping was built into the hazardous environment training courses that were first launched in the 1990s. Many of the correspondents I interviewed told me that they were trained to deal specifically with kidnapping when they took their hazardous environment courses. For instance, freelancer Don Duncan and an anonymous NBC reporter both mentioned the frightening realism of having a hood placed over their heads during the training (pers. comm., June 2012; Duncan, pers.

comm., January 2013). The BBC's Alastair Leithead told me that his safety training course emphasized that the exact moment of the kidnapping is also the exact moment when you should try to escape (pers. comm., May 2013). In turn, Al Jazeera English reporter Yasmine Ryan noted that her hazardous environment course taught her about the necessity of humanizing yourself to your captors, making them realize that you are a person just like they are (pers. comm., April 2013).

In each of these examples, my interviewees recited a list of facts about kidnapping that they had learned in the performative, simulated environments of their safety training courses. They were encouraged to "feel" the fear associated with being captured. They were also taught how to relate to their kidnappers on an ostensibly more "human" level. These skills were offered to my interviewees as part of the growing "safety culture" of the Anglophone war reporting industry. Yet, this safety training subtly placed the responsibility for safety onto the correspondents' own shoulders, revealing the tension between the news industry's celebration of the neoliberal notion of individualism and the industry's need to address the issue of safety on a more institutional level.

At the time of Pearl's kidnapping, hazardous environment courses were still relatively new. As former BBC correspondent Mark Brayne told me, these classes were first conceptualized during the Balkan conflicts of the 1990s, but they became the norm only in the years after 9/11 (pers. comm., February 2013). In 2002, safety training in general was far from systematic. Though Pearl himself had helped *WSJ* editor Bill Spindle draft the *WSJ*'s new, post-9/11 safety protocols, these measures were untested at the time of Pearl's kidnapping (pers. comm., July 2015). In fact, Spindle told me that before 9/11, *WSJ* reporters were not allowed to go to active front lines, and so editors left the more detailed security issues up to the correspondents themselves (ibid.). Just after 9/11, the *WSJ* began to reassess its security measures, encouraging reporters to "check in" with their editors more often. Pearl had been part of this discussion, according to Spindle: "I had been out to Pakistan just a few weeks, probably a month, before [Pearl] was abducted. . . . So we had gone over a lot of that kind of stuff."

Despite his participation in these new safety discussions, Pearl was kidnapped only weeks after Spindle left Pakistan. Reflecting on this incident, Spindle said:

> [Pearl's kidnapping] was a pretty extraordinary situation. And one that was hard to figure out. How do you really respond to this [kidnapping], because it

had its own peculiarities and uniqueness. . . . The groups that were operating in Beirut [during the Civil War] were targeting journalists along with others. But they seemed to have a purpose. A political purpose. And they seemed to have some set of demands that you could deal with. I think the difference [in Pearl's case] was that they were targeting journalists, and they didn't seem to really have any political objective in mind other than just to create publicity. And it was new in that sense. (Spindle, pers. comm., July 2015)

In this statement, Spindle is sharing his undoubtedly painful memories of an event that happened several years ago. Yet, it is important to note that Pearl's captors did indeed have a set of identifiable demands, which the U.S. government categorically refused to consider. As many news organizations reported in the early days of Pearl's kidnapping, these demands included better treatment for prisoners in Guantánamo Bay, the release of Pakistani detainees from that prison so they could be tried in a legitimate court in Pakistan, and the completion of a previously halted shipment of F-16 fighter jets to the Pakistani government. Later communications by Pearl's kidnappers also referenced the extensive civilian casualties caused by the U.S. military—an issue that mainstream, English-language news coverage did not adequately address (Paterson 2014).

Spindle's statement is likely the product of a more collective level of socio-historical amnesia that continues to inform journalistic discussions of post-9/11 war reporting. His statement also suggests that it was the kidnappers, and not the western press, who sought publicity in the wake of Pearl's kidnapping. This suggestion overlooks the role that U.S. media played in publicizing Pearl's tragic incident, as well as overlooking the insidious ways in which the discussion of Pearl's safety was woven into a melodramatic narrative that distracted from the messier political issues. While U.S. officials, including Secretary of State Colin Powell, Secretary of Defense Donald Rumsfeld, and President George W. Bush, all emphasized the U.S. government's effort at finding and saving Pearl from his captors, none of them actually addressed his captors' demands. Instead, Rumsfeld fretted that such negotiation would "create an incentive for people to take hostages," making kidnapping "a major business" (*NBC Nightly News*, February 3, 2002).

Rather than taking these demands seriously, journalists and U.S. government officials engaged in a highly public discussion about the quality of Pearl's work and the caution with which he approached his stories. For instance, an ABC broadcast on January 28, 2002, featured State Department official Richard Boucher declaring that Pearl was "a respected journalist," and for that reason alone, he should be released immediately (*ABC World News Tonight*, January 28, 2002). On the same day, CNN showed an interview with the *Wall Street Journal*'s managing editor Paul Steiger, who said: "Danny is not what some folks call a cowboy. He's a very experienced, careful journalist" who has "been with us for a dozen years. . . . He knows his way around. He's known as a cautious, careful reporter, but a terrific reporter" (CNN, 28 January 2002).

This initial discourse on Pearl functioned in two important ways. First, it suggested that Pearl did not fit the pejorative journalistic stereotype of "adrenaline junkie." Instead, the discourse presented Pearl as an exemplary individual who knew how to take care of himself. The rhetoric of "caution" and "preparedness" would haunt the profession of war reporting for the rest of the decade, especially as news organizations worked to improve their safety protocols in an industrial climate that made it difficult to spend the extra money on such measures. But at the time of Pearl's kidnapping, safety protocols were still a new idea. Thus, when Steiger invoked the notion of "caution," he was mostly talking about Pearl's individual strategies for staying safe, a maneuver that subtly offloaded the brunt of the safety responsibility onto Pearl himself. Steiger represented Pearl as the "free" subject of a neoliberal society, accentuating his individualism and directing the conversation away from the need for a more institutionalized and politically aware response to the risk of kidnapping.

Steiger's remarks also functioned in another way. These remarks flagged the fact that Pearl was a civilian—an "independent" journalist—and not a soldier, thus shaming his captors for kidnapping a "neutral" observer. This discourse drew upon the Geneva Conventions on the treatment of journalists in wartime, suggesting that civilian journalists should not be attacked by militants or governments for any reason. Yet, these statements did not then turn to an analysis of the U.S. military's 2001 bombing of the Al Jazeera headquarters in Kabul, nor did they discuss the escapades of the "civilian" CIA in the Middle East (Wilford 2011). Only Pearl himself fell within the frame, obscuring the messier issues entangled within the broader "war on terror."

The *Wall Street Journal* repeatedly mentioned that Pearl was not affiliated with the CIA (despite his captor's accusations), but was "solely a journalist" who had "no connection whatever with the government of the United States" ("Pakistani Group Says" 2002). This declaration was important because Pearl's captors had accused him and other western journalists of being spies. In light of these accusations, some industry commentators in the

United States blamed the accusation of espionage on the very real tendency for CIA agents to pose as journalists in the field (Fitzgerald 2002). Yet, British journalism commentators had a different perspective. The *Press Gazette* blamed the accusations that Pearl was a spy on the *WSJ*'s earlier decision to give the U.S. government a laptop that the newspaper had secured—a laptop that was thought to have been used by Al-Qaeda (Blythe 2002). None of the U.S. trades or U.S. news coverage of Pearl's kidnapping mentioned this. But the *Press Gazette* reported that "just two days later, Pearl was lured to his death" (ibid.).

Rather than considering this potential connection between Pearl and the U.S. government, U.S. news commentators lamented the attack on a "neutral" observer, while either ignoring or ridiculing the political demands made by Pearl's captors. For example, Pearl's own newspaper did list the demands, but followed up with quotes from U.S. officials who suggested the demands were ludicrous. For example, one early report from the *Journal* first quoted Pearl's captors:

> "Unfortunately," the email said of Mr. Pearl, "he is at present being kept in very inhuman circumstances quite similar in fact to the way that Pakistanis and nationals of other sovereign countries are being kept in Cuba by the American Army." It said that "if the Americans keep our countrymen in better conditions we will better the conditions of Mr. Pearl and all the other Americans that we capture." (cited in "Pakistani Group" 2002)

The story directly followed this quote with another statement:

> A senior Bush administration official said, "We want to see Daniel Pearl reunited with his family as soon as possible. Mr. Pearl is a journalist trying to do his job. We dismiss any attempt to link Mr. Pearl's abduction with the disposition of detainees in Guantánamo Bay in Cuba, where the United States is holding al Qaeda and Taliban captives." (ibid.)

In this way, the *Journal* subtly destabilized the argument that Pearl's captors were making, dismissing their complaints about the prisoners in Guantánamo and distracting readers from the civilian casualties incurred in the new "war on terror."

On top of this, the *WSJ* often drew upon trivializing language when describing the captors. One article listed the demands as follows:

> The [kidnappers'] statement expressed annoyance that Pakistanis are being held by U.S. forces in Guantánamo Bay, Cuba, at a facility set up to hold and interrogate al Qaeda and Taliban fighters captured in the war in Afghanistan.

The note also expressed unhappiness that Abdul Salam Zaeef, the Taliban's former ambassador to Pakistan and its most recognized spokesman, is being held by the U.S., and anger that the U.S., citing Pakistan's nuclear program, refused several years to deliver F-16 fighter jets that Pakistan had ordered and paid for. The disagreement was settled during the Clinton administration. ("Journal Staffer's Abductors Deliver" 2002)

Attributing feelings such as "annoyance" and "unhappiness" to Pearl's kidnappers served to infantilize them, casting doubt on their motives. The terse assertion that the matter of the F-16 jets had been "settled during the Clinton administration" in turn suggested that the captors were either unaware of their own history or that they were clinging to "old" grudges. The *WSJ* repeatedly gave more credence to the dismissive statements of U.S. government officials than to the people whose complaints had led them to kidnap one of the *Journal*'s own reporters. Thus, Pearl's captors were simplistically cast as childish and ineffective villains, and the political gray area that their demands illuminated was all but erased from the story.

This melodramatic framing strategy resonates with Justin Lewis's argument that western coverage of terrorism typically shies away from discussions of political motivation, "especially when these involve an examination of the ugly side of Western foreign policy" (2012). As Bethami Dobkin also asserts, U.S. television news networks have long relied on the melodramatic narrative in order to resolve any "moral ambiguity" (1992, 56), reductively casting certain actors as villains and, thus, justifying military intervention in a particular region (1992). In Pearl's case, the journalist himself was represented as both a hero and a victim, even in the early stages of Pearl's kidnapping. The issue of journalistic safety in the field was written into the melodrama, in a way that subtly justified the "war on terror." Thus, the U.S. news industry's coverage of Pearl's kidnapping relied on the larger political and philosophical frame of precarity; this frame situated certain subjects as "terrorists" and "others"— unrecognizable, in Judith Butler's formulation, to the power that organizes and cultivates the survival of sanctioned populations (2009). The melodrama continued after Pearl's murder, with industry commentators declaring that "Pearl's executioners would have cause to celebrate if their vicious deeds forced a media pullout" from Pakistan and Afghanistan (Ricchiardi 2002b). Others characterized Pearl as a martyr who had "paid the ultimate price" to tell the story of the "dispossessed" (cited in Ricchiardi 2002b). Through this discourse, the Anglophone journalism industry emphasized Pearl's own voluntary choice to travel to Pakistan and take such personal risks, suggesting an individual valor that sat in tension with the equally simplistic "evil" assigned to Pearl's kidnappers.

This juxtaposition of Pearl as a brave and innocent victim with the portrayal of his captors—and, by extension, the "Islamic World"—as harbingers of unfathomable evil served to distract from the United States' own complicated historical role in the political affairs of the Middle East. The fact that President Bush himself drew upon Pearl's death as a way of condemning terrorism and justifying the "war on terror" demonstrates the insidious ways in which certain conflict correspondents can be turned into symbols of a particular sociopolitical system. Pearl's death—brutal though it was—could have engendered an intelligent discussion about the demands made by his captors. Instead, Pearl's capture led to a rash of discourse on the ostensible interconnection between the use of digital technologies and terrorism. The next section of this chapter examines that discourse, showing how the specter of digital technology was written into the melodramatic narrative of Pearl's death.

Melodrama and the Digital

Before Pearl's death, news organizations relied heavily on the digital still shots of Pearl in captivity, in order to help news audiences visualize the reporter who had gone missing. The specter of Pearl's potential death loomed large in the early coverage of his kidnapping, though at this point, no one could determine whether Pearl was dead or alive. Indeed, the still shots filled a visual hole in the coverage, serving as examples of what Barbie Zelizer has called the "about to die" image—an image that suggests, but does not show, the potential or impending death of an individual (2010). The image that showed Pearl with a gun to his head especially functioned in this way. Before the official announcement of Pearl's murder, this image suggested that Pearl could potentially be killed in captivity.

Yet, the digital photographs also inspired a number of industry comments on the duplicity of the internet and of digital technologies more generally. Since these images had been emailed to news organizations, and since Pearl had been lured to his kidnapping through the anonymous use of the web, news organizations focused obsessively on the role that digital technology played in Pearl's abduction. U.S. television networks especially drew upon the digital images of Pearl in captivity, as well as highlighting the way in which Pearl had been tricked by internet users who were purportedly more technologically "sophisticated" than average journalists like Pearl. NBC even played a sound bite of President Bush assuring the public that "we're following the trail of emails" in order to save Pearl (*NBC Nightly News*, February 1, 2002) while CBS said that the trail being followed "in cyberspace" kept "going cold" (*CBS Evening News*, January 31, 2002). ABC, NBC, CBS, and CNN all showed footage of old computer rooms and internet cafés, suggesting that the activity in these spaces was directly linked to the elaborate scheme that resulted in Pearl's capture. And repeatedly, U.S. television networks aired the photos of Pearl in captivity, remarking upon the digital nature of the medium as often as they remarked upon the kidnappers' message.

Through this type of coverage, U.S. television news networks anxiously wrote the specter of digital technology into their melodramatic narratives on Pearl's kidnapping and eventual murder. While Pearl was represented as both the "hero" and the "victim" of the story, digital technology became a character in its own right, associated with the "terrorists" who had captured Pearl. On top of that, the rather literal visualization of the equipment associated with the internet—of desktop computers, printed emails, and internet cafés—illuminated the television networks' efforts at capturing and narrativ-

Figure 3. The laptop that Daniel Pearl was using in the field, before he was kidnapped. On display in the Washington, D.C., Newseum.

izing something that, for many journalists in 2002, seemed woefully intangible. No matter how many pictures of computer monitors and keyboards appeared in these newscasts, digital technology could still be "anywhere" and "everywhere." It could be used by even the most "evil" of "villains," and it could compete with official narratives in its effort to make sense of the "war on terror."

Pearl's own news organization wrote the role of digital technology into the story as well, though the *Wall Street Journal* approached this issue differently than the U.S. television networks. Rather than flooding its coverage with the vivid captivity images, the *WSJ* described the images textually. Almost every description mentioned the fact that one of the photos showed Pearl with a gun to his head; yet, the *Journal* did not actually display the image itself. Instead, the paper drew upon the medium with which it was most familiar: the written word. At certain points, the *WSJ*'s print stories also raised suspicions about the digital photos, asserting that the they "purport[ed] to show" Pearl in the clutches of his kidnappers. In one article, the *WSJ* even stated: "Pakistani police raised the possibility that the email was a hoax. With digital technology available, the possibility of altering pictures always exists" ("Pakistani Group Says" 2002).

Through this statement, the *WSJ* article subtly drew upon the same ambivalent discourse that journalists had directed at digital media for the past few years, highlighting the photos' potential lack of credibility and calling the emails themselves into question. It is especially relevant to consider this representation of digital technology within the larger context of mainstream newspapers' downward spiral in the first decade of the twenty-first century. Newspapers in Canada, Britain, and the United States had all suffered financially in the years leading up to Pearl's capture. They had plodded reluctantly toward carving out a space on the internet. It had already become commonplace for twenty-first-century commentators to simultaneously celebrate and bemoan the rise of media convergence (Robins 2001b; Healy 2002; Vranckx 2002). It was also common during this time period for industry pundits to anxiously track the risks and the payoffs of newspapers' online efforts (Bunder 2001; Robins 2001a; Shields 2001; "New Media Hits Profits" 2001). When viewed against this backdrop, it could be argued that these newspapers' suspicion of digital technology was just as related to their own financial and technological failures as to the political suspicion of "terrorists" using the internet.

Significantly, the *Journal* refrained from publishing the pictures that Pearl's kidnappers had circulated. In every print story discussing Pearl's death, the newspaper either included Pearl's professional headshot or opted out of using photos at all. There are a few likely reasons for this, and one is simply pragmatic: at that time, the print version of the *WSJ* was not running many photos at all. The stories that accompanied the newspaper's print coverage of Pearl's kidnapping were text-based, perhaps because the *Journal* had not traditionally focused on images up to that point. Words had long been the medium of print news reporting, and the digital images did not fit within that framework. It is also possible that the *Journal* did not wish to run such sensitive images of its own employee—partly because this employee was an American citizen, and represented as a hero in the "war on terror." Rather than engaging in the logic of the "about to die" photo (Zelizer 2010), the *WSJ* avoided it altogether.

Consequently, none of the archived web stories on WSJ.com displayed the digital pictures at the time of this writing. The reason for this could be due to the fact that most major newspapers were still experimenting with their websites in 2002, often treating them as separate entities that may or may not prove successful. The *Journal's* website had enjoyed some notoriety, for its ability to "st[and] tall in the shards of September 11" (Mostafa 2001). Since the *WSJ* headquarters had been damaged in the 9/11 attacks, *WSJ Online* kept the paper's news coverage going in the following days, working out of a building in New Jersey. The website gained somewhere between 20,000 and 30,000 subscribers in the wake of 9/11 (ibid.) suggesting that it was another important venue through which the *WSJ* could report on the kidnapping of its employee. But even on its website, the *Journal* apparently relied more heavily on text than images, describing the salacious photos in detail, but not showing them.

It would have been difficult for the *Journal* to avoid addressing Pearl's kidnapping at all. From the beginning, Pearl's captors had distributed their message in a multichanneled fashion, sending the photos of Pearl to an array of western news organizations. Since many of these outlets also covered the kidnapping—and ran the digital images of Pearl with a gun to his head—the *WSJ* had to make a choice between remaining silent or joining the larger discussion. This conundrum points to the precarious industrial balancing act in which news editors also must engage, negotiating the pressure to compete with other organizations while still carrying the burden of care for their employees. Spindle himself remarked on this issue: "It's just that you're on 24 hours. You have 20 reporters out there, all of them potentially [at risk] . . . it just got to be really, really difficult to deal with" (pers. comm., July 2015).

The burden grew heavier after news outlets announced his death on February 21, 2002. An anonymous person was reported to have given a video to U.S. intelligence agents posing as journalists in Pakistan. That video allegedly recorded Pearl's execution. As soon as this news got out, U.S. television networks rushed to cover the murder, typically refraining from showing the video but providing detailed descriptions of its content. U.S. television networks suddenly joined publications like the *WSJ* in avoiding the visualization of Pearl's experience, likely because of the longer tradition of censoring the more graphic images of American deaths from the view of the public (Griffin 2004; Kennedy 2008; Zelizer 2010). For its own part, the *Wall Street Journal* stuck to its earlier strategy of describing rather than showing, though without the previous qualifications that the entire thing might be a hoax. Now that U.S. officials had confirmed Pearl's death, the *Journal* took the images of Pearl at face value, lamenting the permanent loss of one of its reporters.

The U.S. news reporting community took the video very seriously—so seriously that when the video began to circulate online, two news organizations decided to make its contents available to their own audiences. On May 14, 2002, CBS showed parts of the video on its evening newscast. Only days later, the *Boston Phoenix* posted a link to the video on its home page ("Freedom to Choose" 2002). In both cases, the organizations' news executives decided to issue a statement explaining the logic behind their decisions to show certain segments of the video to their readers and viewers. For example, the CBS newscast opened with a lengthy justification from anchor Dan Rather:

> A gruesome piece of propaganda. It is videotape of the execution of *Wall Street Journal* reporter Daniel Pearl, who was kidnapped and murdered earlier this year in Pakistan. And this video, slickly produced, is being used by terrorists to recruit new soldiers for their cause. CBS News has obtained this video, and we're about to show you edited portions of it, so that you can see and judge for yourself the kind of propaganda terrorists are using in their war against the United States. Be assured we will not show you any graphic scenes, although many are on the full videotape.

This opening to the CBS News report operated in a few important ways. First, it immediately labeled the video of Pearl's death as "gruesome propaganda," in an attempt at casting suspicion on the captors' assertions about civilian casualties and the mistreatment of Pakistani prisoners. Second, this opening mentioned the video's "slick" production, simultaneously invoking and excoriating the digital sophistication of these "terrorists" who were not professional media producers. Lastly, Rather's opening included a defense of CBS's decision to air even a small piece of the video—"so that you can see and judge for yourself the kind of propaganda terrorists are using in their war against the United States." Rather then quickly tempered his assertion of the video's "terrorist" message with the promise that CBS would not show anything "graphic," and thus, anger its audience.

From the very beginning of this newscast, then, CBS attempted to strike a balance between the marketability of Pearl's narrative and the outrage that could be inspired by the network's decision to air the tape. Television news networks have long enjoyed the marketability of melodramatic narratives, since melodrama is "a format that reassures and satisfied audiences" (Dobkin 1992, 56). Yet, this particular report also showed the graphic death of an American citizen, risking the ire of audiences and, by extension, advertisers. Crucially, CBS attempted to resolve this contradiction by obfuscating the kidnappers' original message, one that situated the United States as the perpetrator of violence in the Middle East. Instead, CBS framed the video according to the logic of precarity, where some people are presented as recognizably human, while the humanity of the "Other" is obscured from view (Butler 2004, 2009). From the outset of CBS's report, Pearl's captors were framed as simplistic villains, and their political demands were ignored.

CBS also framed the video's anonymous online "viewers" as potential "villains." In an effort at regaining control of a narrative that was no longer solely in the hands of professional journalists, CBS called upon reporter Dave Martin to analyze the video. Martin's analysis was imbued with a sense of dread for the fact that thousands of anonymous "Arab" internet users were viewing and discussing Pearl's death. Framed by CBS, the video showed Pearl on the right side of the screen, speaking from what appeared to be a prerehearsed script. On the left side of the screen hovered a window with other moving images: of women, children, and men either dead, suffering, or under military attack. As Pearl spoke in English, Arabic subtitles lined the screen's bottom half. Yet, CBS viewers could not hear very much of what Pearl was saying, because Martin's voiceover pointedly spoke for him: "Interspersed with news clips, the video of Pearl's final hours is a coldblooded recruiting poster for America's enemies, complete with Arabic subtitles." The report then suddenly cut to a sound bite from Saudi Arabian journalist Ali Al-Ahmed: "The translation is Arabic, because the audience is Arabic."

This assertion swiftly situated the video within the context of its online circulation, invoking the purportedly duplicitous internet users capable of interacting with the video of Pearl's death. Martin then explained that Al-Ahmed found the video on an Arabic-language website that mostly targeted college-aged Saudi youths. His report showed Al-Ahmed sitting at a computer, Arabic characters flooding its screen, before cutting to what at first appeared to be more of the Pearl video. Yet, it soon became evident that CBS viewers were in fact watching a screen shot of an unknown "internet user" navigating the Pearl video online. Through this strategy, the CBS report drew upon the discourse that had been surfacing in professional news commentary since the 1990s: The internet was potentially dangerous. The danger stemmed from the fact that the web could harbor anonymous "bad guys" who could manipulate the very thing that professional journalists had always claimed as their own—information itself. Without gatekeepers like CBS, the Pearl video could fall into enemy hands and be interpreted in the "wrong" way, inspiring more and more people to join the "terrorist" cause.

This perception drew heavily on the logic of the "digital sublime," "demoniz[ing]" digital technology "for the depth of the evil it can conjure" (Mosco 24). According to Mosco, the *digital sublime* is a descendant of the *electrical sublime*, which surfaced in popular discourse on the technologies that came of age in the nineteenth and twentieth centuries. Despite the long history of viewing "new" technologies with such existential suspicion, journalists like those at CBS felt that they were in truly uncharted territory. Because of this, the specter of digital technology was written into the melodramatic narrative, potentially inspiring fear in the hearts of news audiences but also potentially securing their undivided attention. CBS's portrayal of purportedly duplicitous "Arab" internet users was meant to justify the network's decision to show salacious excerpts of the video on its newscast, while also raising the concern that a nameless and faceless enemy could manipulate Pearl's image in cyberspace.

Like the editors at CBS, the editors of the *Boston Phoenix* also invoked the video's online presence in their own defense, claiming that the video had been posted to a site called Ogrish.com ("Freedom to Choose" 2002). Unlike the CBS editors, the *Phoenix* editors were ostensibly more concerned about the U.S. government's own manipulation of Pearl's image—"censor[ing] politically sensitive, yet legal content" (ibid.). Because of this effort at government intervention, the editors said they had chosen to make the video available to their readers:

> Deciding whether to link to the video from our home page was clear-cut. "This is the single most gruesome, horrible, despicable, and horrifying thing I've ever seen," *Phoenix* publisher Stephen Mindich wrote in an online note below the link. "If there is anything that should galvanize every non-Jew hater in the world—of whatever faith, or of no faith—against the perpetrators and supporters of those who committed this unspeakable murder, it should be viewing this video. (ibid.)

As this statement shows, the *Phoenix* also reframed the kidnappers' original message in order to justify its decision to expose its readers to the video of Pearl's murder. Yet, this publication was not interrogating the U.S. military's own attacks on civilians—including journalists (Paterson 2014). Deploying a simplistic binary between "Jew haters" and "non-Jew haters," the paper's editors argued that Americans needed to see the graphic images, since these images signaled the anti-Semitism and anti-Americanism of the "terrorists" in Pakistan. As in the CBS report, no one paid attention to the video's discussion of civilian casualties in the "war on terror." Instead, the *Phoenix* attempted to harness the unruly potential of the web, giving readers access to this "important" political document through the supposedly more respectable gateway of its own website. At the same time, the *Phoenix* capitalized upon the visual and digital elements of Pearl's story.

This did not go unnoticed by the *WSJ*, whose editors published an opinion piece asking: "Is a snuff film news?" (Varadarajan 2002). In this column, the author slammed both the *Phoenix* and CBS for their "heartless" decisions to make the videos available to news audiences. Rather than "add[ing] a new layer of understanding" to the Pearl story, the author claimed that the *Phoenix* was merely adding a "new texture of horror" by appealing to viewers' voyeuristic tendencies (ibid.). In other words, the author's critique subtly aligned the *Phoenix* with what many journalists at that time were still viewing as the sensationalism and tastelessness of the internet, especially when compared with the alleged authority and professionalism of traditional news reporting. The author also suggested that the *WSJ* was above such antics, citing common decency as something that was more important than spectacle.

This editorial fails to note that traditional news outlets had been making a spectacle of Pearl's plight for months before the video became available. Even the *WSJ* had, to some extent, participated in the construction of this spectacle. By saturating the media sphere with patriotic stories about Pearl's kidnapping—either through the use of digital images or the more traditional medium of the written word—mainstream, English-language news outlets had unwittingly collaborated with the very "villains" they were critiquing. This was despite their efforts at reframing the kidnappers' message and weaving Pearl tightly into the larger melodramatic narrative of the U.S.-led "war on terror."

Conclusion

The kidnapping and murder of Daniel Pearl frightened the English-language war reporting industry. Former security strategist for the *New York Times*, William Schmidt, told me of the shift that Pearl's death signaled for people like himself: "I never thought that I would be kidnapped or taken, and this was as recently as the early '90s. And then after Daniel Pearl, we began to change that dynamic too. We had to think of the safety of our people abroad in different ways. We had to think about the way we prepared people to go abroad" (pers. comm., March 2015). Though correspondents kept working in Pakistan after Pearl's kidnapping, they also wrestled with the very real possibility of getting hurt or captured in the process. For instance, *San Francisco Chronicle* freelancer Juliette Terzieff told the *American Journalism Review* that her safety precautions could be divided into the categories of "pre- and post-Pearl": "Pre-Pearl, I would have jumped in the car and hit the road. Post-Pearl, I notified other colleagues of my plans, my approximate schedule and destination. I spent three days scoping out the situation before I felt it was safe enough to try" (cited in Ricchiardi 2002b).

This post-Pearl attitude only partially impacted the policies of news organizations where reporters were concerned. A February 3, 2002, article in *Broadcasting and Cable* reported that U.S. television networks would allow their staff members to decide for themselves whether or not they wanted to leave Pakistan after Pearl's captors issued the warning to western reporters (Trigoboff 2002a). Yet, many executives asserted that their correspondents had chosen not to leave, emphasizing the voluntary nature of their presence in Pakistan (ibid.). CNN reportedly began mandating that its correspondents take the hazardous environment training courses that include kidnapping simulations after Pearl's kidnapping and eventual death (Trigoboff 2002b). But in a way, this was just another effort at putting the onus on the correspondents, as these courses taught journalists to take individual responsibility for their own safety. News outlets' larger narratives of political risk were subtly underwritten by a different narrative in which journalists were subject to a hierarchy of protection—indeed, a hierarchy of "recognizability." While Pearl's death was highly publicized, the deaths of Afghan and Iraqi journalists at the hands of the U.S. military were not (Paterson 2014). And even journalists as privileged as Pearl were encouraged to take individual responsibility for their own safety.

In the years following Pearl's abduction, this individualization of the war correspondents' safety would sit in tension with the industry's growing "safety culture." And when more journalistic kidnappings occurred in 2008, western media outlets deployed a very different strategy. Instead of flooding newspapers and broadcasts with details on war reporters' kidnappings, news organizations later called for an industrywide media blackout, refusing to allow the kidnappers' messages to gain the desired international exposure. For example, news organizations enacted media blackouts in Chinese-Canadian reporter Mellissa Fung's 2008 kidnapping, as well as in the 2008 kidnapping of *New*

York Times reporter David Rohde. In both of these cases, the majority of the mainstream news outlets in the Anglophone world played along, refraining from mentioning the kidnappings in their reportage. Consequently, in both of these cases the abducted correspondents were eventually able to return home, and the expansive media coverage of their traumatic experience was postponed until after they were physically safe. What impact the dramatic, postcaptivity coverage had on these individuals is a question for another day.

In Pearl's 2002 case, the precariousness of his situation served as the story itself. U.S. news outlets appropriated the event of Pearl's kidnapping and eventual murder, in many ways depending upon the digital photos, the emails, and the video that they also deeply feared. This appropriation—enacted through the use of "new" media technologies—revealed a great deal about the unease with which these corporate news outlets viewed their increasingly globalized and digitized world. The fact that an American journalist could be "lured" through the technology of the internet, and then killed on a video that global viewers could access again and again, shook the core of the U.S. news industry. Rather paradoxically, news outlets also saw a lucrative news narrative in Pearl's story, one in which a journalist could represent an "average" American man, victimized by "terrorists."

Pearl's status as a *Wall Street Journal* reporter bolstered the news outlets' "war on terror" narrative, partly because of the much-discussed evacuation of the *Wall Street Journal* offices during the September 11 attacks on the World Trade Center. These offices were located almost precisely at the site of the 9/11 attacks. By the time of Pearl's kidnapping, *WSJ* managing editor Paul Steiger had become something of an industry hero. This was because he went missing for several hours on 9/11, and then later turned up unharmed. The November/December 2001 issue of the *Columbia Journalism Review* even used a photograph of Ground Zero from the perspective of the *WSJ* offices for its November/December 2001 cover photo, framing the entire event through the eyes of the news organization that survived and became the story.

Oddly enough, that same photograph of Ground Zero from the perspective of the *WSJ* office appeared once again in the *CJR*, five years later. In the September/October 2006 issue, the editors of *CJR* included the image in their "Opening Shot" piece, where they also listed a number of journalistic failures they had noticed since 9/11: failures which could have been avoided with "more foreign bureaus, more reporters and editors who know the rest of the world inside and out." By this point in 2006, the industry trade publications both in and outside the United States were rife with critiques of the U.S. military's invasions in the Middle East, especially of the occupation of

Iraq that had stretched long past the heady days of the 2003 invasion. Even in 2003, the trade articles perpetually invoked the impending Second Gulf War as one that could be more dangerous for journalists than past wars. In February of 2003, Dan Trigoboff of *Broadcasting and Cable* wrote: "Network executives aren't just talking platitudes when they say they worry about their human capital. They remember the Afghan war and the murder of journalists, especially *Wall Street Journal* reporter Daniel Pearl" (Trigoboff 2003). Yet, in 2003, U.S. journalists seemed to celebrate the new embedding system that would purportedly allow journalists a new kind of mobility in the war zone.

When the *CJR* reran the *WSJ*'s photo of Ground Zero in 2006, the publication displayed a definitive shift in tone. The war that should have ended in only weeks had stretched on for years, and the journalists who had been ecstatic to tell the story of the Iraq conflict were dying or suffering injuries in unprecedented numbers. One of the journalists to suffer an injury was ABC's longtime correspondent and newly appointed anchor Bob Woodruff, hit by an improvised explosive device (IED) while traveling with the U.S. 4th Infantry Division in Taji, Iraq. Chapter Two explores this incident in greater detail. Woodruff's 2006 injury drew a huge amount of attention, because of his status as the new face of *ABC World News Tonight*. When Woodruff took shrapnel to the brain on 29 January 2006, industry commentators obsessed over why an anchor had been covering Iraq and whether or not Woodruff would ever be able to return to the coveted anchor's chair

2

The "Walking Wounded"

Bob Woodruff's 2006 Injury in Iraq

> They called these men the "walking wounded." Most
> often the scars were invisible, but the damage inside
> the brain was permanent. It had become the signature
> wound of this war.
>
> —Lee Woodruff, after her husband Bob Woodruff's 2006
> head injury in Iraq (Woodruff and Woodruff 2007).

In the months preceding and directly following the 2003 U.S. invasion of Iraq, the Pentagon repeatedly drew upon the discourse of safety in order to discourage journalists from moving independently through Baghdad and elsewhere in the country. Pentagon officials said they could not guarantee the protection of those journalists who operated outside the "new" embedding system—a reporting model where journalists would don military gear and travel with one specific unit "for life," or for the duration of the war. Though this reporting model seemed new at the time, it actually had a long history. U.S., British, and Canadian soldiers traveled with their nation's militaries in both of the World Wars, often wearing military uniforms, signing agreements that censored what they could say in their stories, or dealing with stubborn silence from military officials in the field (Knightley 2004; Mander 2010; Hamilton 2011; Bourrie 2012). Even in the Vietnam War, which is still often remembered as an "uncensored" conflict, war correspondents sometimes accompanied military troops into battle (ibid.). Yet, by the time of the First War in the Persian Gulf, U.S. officials were still invoking Vietnam as a war that the media lost for them (Rid 2007; Carruthers 2011). In response to this, officials developed the military pooling system for the Persian Gulf War, where war correspondents would travel in large groups with military babysitters and share carefully censored information (ibid.).

The memory of this pooling system loomed large as English-language news outlets prepared to cover the 2003 invasion of Iraq, despite the fact that since the first conflict in the Gulf, war correspondents had also covered the conflicts in the Balkans—where military officials engaged in the strategy of "information saturation" rather than direct censorship (Rid 2007; Matheson and Allan 2009). War reporters had also recently covered the 2001 invasion of Afghanistan, where the Taliban as well as the U.S. and British militaries had tried to limit the very presence of journalists in the field (Matheson and Allan 2009). Perhaps because of the censorship strategies deployed from 1991–2001, the mainstream, Anglophone journalists—especially those hailing from the United States—largely embraced the embedded reporting model as their best option. Not only did many industry commentators believe that embedding would give them unprecedented access to the war zone, but they also thought that this was the safest way to report on a dangerous conflict. The Pentagon asserted that war reporters would be safe only if they embedded with the U.S. or coalition military troops, and this rhetoric bled into the news industry's own discourse on "safety culture" in the new century. Both Pentagon officials and news industry commentators declared that embedded reporting was the safest way for journalists to cover the 2003 invasion of Iraq.

Soon after the 2003 invasion, the U.S. military and its coalition forces were faced with a sophisticated and persistent insurgency that prolonged the conflict and gradually lost public support for the U.S. presence in Iraq (DiMaggio 2009). The number of embedded journalists plummeted, as did the overall number of journalists reporting from that nation. By 2006, *embedding* referred to a slightly different practice: now, embedding could more quickly be arranged and could involve a trip with the military that lasted for only a few days. Then, the journalist could return to Baghdad to continue reporting independently, albeit in an environment that had become so perilous that most western correspondents remained inside their compounds, sending underpaid and underprotected Iraqi stringers to gather information instead (McLeary 2006; Ricchiardi 2006). Journalism industry commentators in turn became more ambivalent about the embedding model, voicing concern over the potential for reporters to be used in the U.S. propaganda machine, while still often asserting that it was safer for journalists to embed than to work independently.

When ABC's correspondent and coanchor Bob Woodruff was seriously wounded on a 2006 embed in Iraq, journalists and editors struggled to make sense of the dissonance between Woodruff's nearly fatal injury and the conflicting safety rhetoric that had long encouraged war correspondents to avoid working unilaterally in or outside of Baghdad. Some commentators emphasized the unpredictability of postinvasion Iraq, declaring that no one could truly prepare for the insurgents who relied upon Improvised Explosive Devices (IED's) to kill anyone who opposed them. Others split hairs over the fact that Woodruff had been riding in an Iraqi military vehicle that had joined the U.S. convoy, implying that Woodruff had been embedded with purportedly inferior Iraqi soldiers, rather than with U.S. troops. Many industry pundits said that Woodruff had chosen to travel to Iraq and that he knew the risks involved, subtly offloading the responsibility for his safety onto Woodruff himself. Almost all of the people who commented on Woodruff's injury aligned him with the U.S. troops, narrativizing his incident in patriotic terms.

Chapter Two "zooms out" on the narrativization of Woodruff's injury in Iraq, looking first at the broader adaptation of the embedding model. I show that embedding was a favorite talking point in the news industry's discourse from 2003–2006, not the least of which because of the technological and economic potential entangled within a practice that promised an "intimate, immediate, absorbing, almost addictive coverage" (Smith 2003). Yet, I also hope to show that the Anglophone news industry's use of the embedding model was not as monolithic and uncritical as some cultural studies scholars have previously suggested (Kellner 2003; Miller 2007; Butler 2009; Stahl 2009). Though the celebratory and, indeed, "brainwashed" journalistic embrace of embedding is often taken for granted by critical media scholars, a more cautious historical approach shows that the embedding model was adapted unevenly, with a fair degree of ambivalence.

In addition, the embedding model changed significantly over the years following the 2003 invasion of Iraq, something that complicates existing representations of embedding as a homogenous practice that resulted in an equally homogenous news coverage (ibid.). By 2006, embedding was not nearly as immersive or immediate as it ostensibly was in 2003. Instead, this later form of embedding usually referred only to journalists' decisions to accompany troops for a few hours or days before returning to Baghdad to report on their own. Alongside the practice of embedding, there were also other reporting strategies in play, during 2003 as well as in 2006. For example, some journalists engaged in unilateral reporting despite the Pentagon's warnings, and this at times resulted in these journalists being targeted by U.S. forces (Paterson 2014). These unilateral reporters contributed to the news coverage of Iraq at great personal risk. On top of this, western news outlets also relied upon Iraqi journalists to do their field reporting, especially once white, western journalists pronounced that it was too dangerous to venture outside their compounds in Baghdad. Thus, though the embedding model certainly deserves critique, I also hope to emphasize the fact that at the level of production, the Anglophone war coverage of the conflict in Iraq was not as homogenous as media scholars have previously argued. Many other unilateral or "surrogate" journalists contributed to this war coverage as well, and their labor tends to be erased from the scholarly discussion.

Unfortunately, big-name, western reporters like Woodruff tend to dominate Anglophone news texts, at the expense of the myriad other journalists who inhabit the war zone (Paterson 2014). Following this, Chapter Two interrogates the industrial discourse on Woodruff's injury, revealing what should, but does not, appear within the frame. The early television coverage of Woodruff's incident in Iraq attempted to resolve the contradiction that his injury symbolized: an embedded reporter had been hurt on the job, despite the Pentagon's assertion that embedding was the safest option. News coverage grappled with this contradiction by focusing on Woodruff's individual responsibility as a "free," neoliberal subject, while simultaneously aligning him with the U.S. troops he was covering. The discourse did not focus on the dangers faced by numerous other journalists in the field, nor did it discuss the larger sociopolitical ramifications of the U.S. occupation of Iraq. Instead, it situated Woodruff as both the hero and victim of the melodramatic narrative, simplifying the messier questions that his injury could have inspired.

The industrial discussion of Woodruff's long recovery also functioned in this fashion. Chapter Two closes with an analysis of this later coverage, illuminating the industrial imperatives—both economic and technological— that underscored the melodramatic narrativization of Woodruff's healing process. Woodruff's wounded body appeared in various states of disarray, until he finally returned to ABC to report (but not to anchor) the flagship evening news program. His return to ABC was highly publicized, and it was celebrated as a patriotic victory for America in the same way that injured soldiers are often represented in U.S. discourse (Kinder 2015). Driven by the need to secure more viewers and better ratings in the new "digital future," the coverage of Woodruff's injury and recovery represented Woodruff, and by extension, the U.S. troops, as melodramatic heroes. Woodruff and the soldiers were portrayed as being recognizable to power, while the experiences of other journalists and Iraqi civilians were obscured from the frame.

The Embedding Model and "Safety Culture"

Despite the fact that many in the English-language news industry thought of the embedding model as "new," the industry's initial attitudes toward that model had a great deal to do with history. The U.S. and British militaries had long been censoring the press in war zones, and after the perceived "freedom" of the press in Vietnam, these militaries felt the need to take more control of press operations during wartime (Rid 2007). This philosophy surfaced in the British military's staunch censorship of reporters during its 1982 campaign in the Falklands, as well as informing the U.S. military's decision to virtually exclude journalists from covering its 1983 campaign in Grenada and its 1989 campaign in Panama (McLaughlin 2002; Rid 2007; Carruthers 2011). In response to complaints about this censorship, the MOD and the Pentagon devised the military pooling system for journalists who wanted to cover the Persian Gulf War in 1990. Though this reporting model did give journalists more access to the soldiers than they had enjoyed in past campaigns, the pooling system was later excoriated by reporters and news editors as being too restrictive (Carruthers 2011).

After their very brief and limited excursions in the Persian Gulf, English-language war reporters turned their eyes to the conflicts in the Balkans. As Thomas Rid asserts, "The peacekeeping operation in Bosnia . . . was the first time the U.S. army used an open access press policy and called it 'embedding'" (2007, 95–96). Reporters traveled with troops, slept on cots, ate rations, and were discouraged from reporting anything too critical (2007). During the later conflict in Kosovo, journalists were not typically embedded, but they were treated to a newer form of censorship: "information saturation" (Rid 2007; Matheson and Allan 2009). Deploying this strategy, NATO officials took advantage of satellite television and the burgeoning internet to bombard journalists and news audiences with so much information—slanted in a predictably pro-NATO fashion—that critical voices could get lost in the background (ibid.). This same strategy informed the Pentagon's later approach to embedding in 2003 (Lewis et al. 2006).

During the 2001 invasion of Afghanistan, the United States and its allies returned to a "closed-mouth" policy, shutting journalists out of their operations in the field (Matheson and Allan 2009). Thus, when mainstream, English-language journalists appeared to very suddenly embrace the "new" embedding strategy, they were working within this larger historical context, viewing the embedding model as a better option than what they had faced in previous conflicts. The 2003 embedding model at first glance appeared to offer much more insight into the conflict than past reporting models had done. As David Hoffman, former foreign news editor at the *Washington Post* told me, "There was a great sort of rushing into this [embedding model]. . . . I understand why. I mean, I lived through that period where we had been shut out and kept at a distance, and so this time, in some ways, it was a triumph of reason that the military brought the media along, but it also led to a lot of one-sided coverage" (pers. comm., February 2015). Likewise, Bob Arnot asserted that embedding was "10 times better" than what happened in the First Gulf War," (Arnot 2003), while Rem Rieder proclaimed in 2003 that "the great embedding experiment was a home run as far as the news media—and the American people—[were] concerned" (Rieder 2003). Rieder's gleeful declaration partly depended on his belief that

> this is a regime that has hardly been known for its openness as far as journalists are concerned. That had been particularly true in wartime. In Afghanistan, the Pentagon warmly embraced the little-to-no access policy that characterized Grenada, Panama and Gulf War I. There was to be no hanging out with the GIs, World War II- or Vietnam-style. (ibid.)

In the process of making a comparison between other post-Vietnam models of war reporting and the embedding system, Rieder and many others certainly celebrated embedding as an improvement over disparate historical models of reporting. Yet, this is not to say that the English-language news industry commentators voiced absolutely no concerns about embedding on the whole. Though a number of British journalists participated in the embedding system, some British news commentators were highly ambivalent about this reporting style, with Jon Swain writing in the *British Journalism Review* that "all too often, the military has used bogus security concerns, particularly in the Gulf War and in Afghanistan, as a device to control the information flow" (2003). Swain saw the embedding model as another potential extension of this history of military control. Phillip Knightley also wrote in the *BJR* that "those journalists prepared to get on side—and that means one 100 per cent on side,—will become 'embeds' and receive every assistance. Those who try to follow an objective, independent path, the so-called 'unilaterals,' will be shunned" (2003). In turn, the Canadian trade press vociferously criticized the embedding system, with the *MEDIA Magazine*'s Leslie Hughes proudly noting that the CBC had opted out of embedding in Iraq 2003, while Stephen Ward wrote in the same publication that both the U.S. and British press were producing reports that served as mere reflections of military strategy (2003).

Even in the United States, a number of industry commentators invoked the potential dangers of embedding with the U.S. or British militaries. First, journalists and editors revealed an initial skepticism on whether the U.S. military would keep its promises. Rieder, in the same article quoted earlier, also remarked that "when the Bush administration revealed its plan to 'embed' journalists with military units, everyone wondered where the catch was" (2003). Ken Kerschbaumer of *Broadcasting and Cable* echoed this skepticism, writing that "although the Pentagon promises to let the press 'tell the factual story, good or bad' and let reporters report from the frontlines with soldiers, how it will play out is still a good question" (2003a). Going a step further, *AJR's* Sherry Ricchiardi gave voice to news outlets' fears that correspondents might "be relegated to reserve battalions far from the action," or subjected to media blackouts that would not allow them to file their material until the war was over (2003a). And prominent CBS news anchor Dan Rather voiced his own fears:

> As journalists, we have to realize there's a very fine line between being embedded and being entombed. And what I mean by that is, there is a way to cocoon the journalists and place them in a position so they report only what the top tier of the military wants reported and so they don't have an opportunity to be truly independent. (cited in Kerschbaumer 2003c)

Rather echoed what many other members of the mainstream news industry also asserted, revealing that not everyone was categorically embracing the new embedding model, nor were they being brainwashed into believing the Pentagon's rhetoric. Instead, the embedding model was met with at least some suspicion on the part of news organizations.

Of course, this suspicion did not keep approximately 600 reporters from embedding with military troops in 2003 (Samuel-Azran 2010), a fact that can be better understood within the larger industrial context during that time. In 2003, western news outlets continued to suffer financially, and they had already spent a large chunk of money covering the war in Afghanistan. Against this backdrop, the war in Iraq seemed like an excellent way to regain the attention of news audiences. Journalism commentators repeatedly invoked the cutting-edge reporting technologies that embedded reporters would be using, technologies that they felt had become more sophisticated since the 2001 invasion of Afghanistan. CNN's Walter Rodgers went on his assigned embed in a Humvee that was loaded with satellite equipment, for example (Rodgers 2005). Indeed, the 2003 invasion of Iraq marked a time in which the mainstream Anglophone news industry was widely celebrating the professional use of new digital technologies in international reporting.

For better or for worse, many Anglophone commentators associated these technological practices with the embedding model. For instance, in the same *BJR* essay in which Swain criticized embedding, he also said: "It is in [the military's] blood to want to corral us into their cause, but military censorship is not possible in the way it once was, now that reporters can carry their personal communications gear—sat phones and laptops—everywhere with them" (2003). This assertion represented technology as the utopic force that might save reporters from the military's censorship. In an even more celebratory voice, Ken Kerschbaumer proclaimed: "Lipstick cameras and small handheld cameras will be a major part of the broadcast journalist's arsenal, giving any coverage the potential of real-life drama that could make *Fear Factor* look like *Romper Room*" (2003b).

With statements like these, some journalists and editors appeared to invoke the more utopic version of the digital sublime (Mosco 2005), drawing upon the much older rhetoric of the electrical sublime to celebrate the wonders that these new digital technologies could ostensibly engender. Yet, news discourse during 2003 also drew upon the underbelly of the digital sublime, sometimes representing the new technologies in a negative fashion. For instance, while some journalists appeared to celebrate embedded reporting as a technological extravaganza promising a "first-person experience" for news audiences (Stahl 2009), others lamented that "the networks [that] have put ENG crews in harm's way, go to great expense and trouble to bring the video home, and then as often as not use it as wallpaper, as an ever-changing background collage of war images for anchors, reporters and talking heads" (Jessell 2003). Critics remarked that despite all the hype, the pictures from the embeds were "not very special," suggesting that the expensive investments in all the latest technology were ill advised (Friedman 2003). As the 2003 invasion wore on, the promise of totalizing, high-tech reporting gave way to the reality of routinely broken equipment and competition with other global news networks and media producers—both professional and amateur—working within Iraq itself (Friedman 2003; Matheson and Allan 2009). One trade article even told of a U.S. journalist's visit to a suspected poison plant in northern Iraq that turned out to be a makeshift media center:

> These back-to-the-land zealots planning their Islamic revolution—high in the mountains, without electricity, running water, or telephones—had set up a generator-powered film production studio. There were video cameras and

editing decks and miles of wiring. They had even put some of their films on a multimedia website, www.ansarislam.com. (Bourzou 2003)

In a xenophobic and also rather hypocritical maneuver, this article suggested that in the discovered media center, "a different sort of wartime weaponry" (ibid.) was in effect: propaganda. The article went on to recount how U.S. missiles later took the whole place out: "The Ansar's 'image war' wasn't effective enough to save it from the real thing" (ibid.).

This statement ignored the Pentagon's own "image war," being fought in part through the implementation of the embedded reporting model. As one embedding architect, Admiral Terry McCreary said, the Pentagon's embedding model was meant to help reporters understand even the unfortunate decisions that the U.S. military makes in wartime (cited in Lewis et al. 2006). The idea was that embedded reporters would then help the American—and, increasingly, the global—public "understand" the Pentagon's broader political choices. The figure of the unilateral reporter operating outside of the embedding system posed a very real threat to the Pentagon's narrative of the war in Iraq, as did the myriad international news organizations that were covering this war from their own perspectives. The Pentagon combated this threat by repeatedly invoking the notion of correspondents' safety—most especially the safety of the unilateral reporters (ibid.).

While about 600 correspondents embedded with coalition troops in 2003, there were reportedly a minimum of about 2,000 unilaterals reporting on the 2003 invasion (Samuel-Azran 2010). This was despite the fact that from the very beginning, Pentagon officials had proclaimed that they could in no way guarantee the safety of any reporters—even correspondents from the United States—who were not embedded with U.S. or coalition troops. One rhetorical maneuver on the part of the Pentagon emphasized the military's "inevitable" difficulty in distinguishing between unilateral journalists and Iraqi enemies, a distinction that the military was, in fact, required to make according to the Geneva Conventions protecting journalists in wartime. Though in 1949 the Geneva Conventions largely focused on the premise that war reporters should be protected as prisoners of war if captured—because in World War II they had traveled with military units and worn military gear—in 1977, the Conventions further emphasized journalists' status as civilians, stating that they must receive the same protections that civilians are promised in war. These protections include the prohibition of journalists' "murder" in the conflict zone, something that occurred several times during the Iraq conflict (Trombly 2003).

A fairly visible example of this targeting was the March 22, 2003, death of the British ITN correspondent Terry Lloyd, who had been reporting from Iraq as a unilateral. When two Iraqi cars pulled up alongside Lloyd's vehicle, coalition troops fired upon the entire set of cars, killing Lloyd and his interpreter Hussein Osman in the process. After this happened, news executives at ITN found that both the Pentagon and the British Ministry of Defense were reluctant to conduct a satisfactory investigation (Azeez 2003). The Pentagon also put this philosophy into play after U.S. forces fired upon Al Jazeera's Baghdad headquarters and, later, the Palestine Hotel—which housed a number of international and U.S. journalists—killing three people in these two attacks (Ricchiardi 2003b). Rather than investigating the violation of the Geneva Conventions protecting journalists in wartime following this event, Pentagon official Victoria Clarke issued a statement reminding journalists of the dangers of reporting war outside the structures sanctioned by the Pentagon (cited in ibid.).

Though U.S. and British news organizations did pay some attention to the Lloyd incident, they paid far less attention to the death of Al Jazeera's Tareq Ayyoub in the Pentagon's bombing of the Al Jazeera headquarters, and they also ignored the many other journalists who were injured, threatened, or killed during this time (Paterson 2014). Only the white, western journalists like Lloyd garnered much attention from the Anglophone news organizations and, even in those cases, news outlets did not discuss these issues very publicly (ibid.). This oversight suggests that Anglophone news outlets possibly saw white, western journalists as more recognizably human than the "other" journalists, revealing how the mechanism of "precarity" frames even the journalists themselves as being recognizable or unrecognizable to power (Butler 2009). Indeed, this is something Hashem Ahelbarra echoed in an interview with me (April 2013). By 2003, Ahelbarra was working for Al Jazeera, and he was one of the few Arab journalists allowed to embed with coalition forces. But he felt he was poorly treated by the troops because of his heritage (ibid.). If Ahelbarra's account is true, then this suggests that the mechanism of precarity (ibid.) operates at the level of news production, framing some journalists as more recognizably human than others.

Another reason why news outlets downplayed these instances of journalistic targeting was because of the Anglophone news industry's shifting discourse on "safety culture." In 2003, a number of journalists and their news editors followed the Pentagon's rhetoric in proclaiming that embedding was a safer option for journalists in Iraq. Though hazardous environment courses were available in 2003, journalists were also offered the opportunity to go through boot camp with U.S. troops, something that was represented as a unique safety precaution available solely to embedded journalists (Lewis et al. 2006). Only 232 individual journalists actually took this offer (Clarke, cited in ibid., 47), but the symbolic meaning of the access to the boot camp is still important to note. In 2003, the English-language news industry's discourse on "safety culture" was deeply informed by the Pentagon's own rhetoric on safety—so much so, that industry commentators represented their unilateral colleagues as being reckless.

One article in the *American Journalism Review* especially drew upon this representation:

> The biggest danger is that some of our unilateral compatriots go too far, particularly television correspondents trying to compete with the vivid footage coming from their embedded colleagues and therefore taking ridiculous chances for the bragging rights of, say, entering Tikrit before U.S. forces. This adds little of journalistic value and creates peer pressure on other journalists to do similarly reckless things for no good reason. (Baker 2003)

Such a statement reveals an interesting projection on the part of embedded journalists, one that tried to paint unilaterals as being carelessly hypercompetitive. But actually, embedded correspondents were also anxious about competing with the unilaterals and international journalists who were disregarding the Pentagon. As Justin Lewis and his colleagues show, embedded reporters were especially displeased when their military units allowed unilaterals to suddenly join up with their convoy, since these journalists had already enjoyed unrestricted mobility throughout Iraq without following any of Pentagon or MOD guidelines (Lewis et al. 2006). The repeated assertion that it was safer to embed with the military covered over the fact that other journalists and media producers (both American and international) were possibly getting better stories than those who had played by the Pentagon's rules.

Despite the fact that the industrial "safety culture" favored the embedding model in 2003, industry commentators grew more critical of embedding a few years into the U.S. occupation of Iraq. It is easy to forget that the 2003 invasion of Iraq was only one distinct chapter in the story of the Iraq conflict. By 2006, U.S. forces were still occupying the nation, and they had not been successful at hiding the reality of an organized and dangerous insurgency from the U.S. public and the world (DiMaggio 2010). This insurgency was also ignoring the Geneva Conventions protecting journalists in the conflict zone, targeting both western correspondents and local Iraqi reporters. What is more, some news organizations were spending millions of dollars on Baghdad bureaus (Homer, pers. comm., June 2015) that included contracted security advisors (Bennett, pers. comm., February 2015) or armored cars (Spindle, pers. comm., July 2015), as well as local Iraqi staff who worked with the western reporters (Homer, pers. comm., June 2015; Hoffman, pers. comm., February 2015; Spindle, pers. comm., July 2015). These local staff members were seen as being crucial to western journalists' security, because they were ostensibly less noticeable and more culturally at home in Iraq than foreign reporters.

Within this context, the embedding system still existed, but it was not identical to the system that had been in place in 2003. For one thing, a number of journalists had abandoned their embeds shortly after Baghdad fell to coalition forces, either returning to their home nations or dispersing into Baghdad to report without military supervision (Romano 2003). By October of 2006, the *Washington Post* reported that there were somewhere between 11 and 24 embeds left in Iraq—a far cry from the approximately 600 with which the war had started (Keath and Reid 2006). On top of that, embeds were now expected to last for a much shorter time, where correspondents' producers would arrange a trip that may last a few days or a few weeks before the journalist could then return to Baghdad or to the United States. This was a different, more hybridized structure than the immersive, "embedding for life" philosophy first introduced by the Pentagon in 2003.

Thus, the Anglophone "safety culture" centered on the conflict in Iraq had shifted into a much larger, even more heterogeneous system, but one that still operated according to problematic hierarchies. Though the Iraqi journalists who acted as "surrogates" began to get some attention in the industry trade publications as the first decade of the twenty-first century wore on (McLeary 2006; Ricchiardi 2006), their dangerous labor was rarely addressed in the news coverage itself (Paterson 2014). It was still the white, western reporters who appeared most often within the frame. And some of these reporters did venture outside of their compounds at times. For example, CNN's Michael Holmes told me that the tide had ultimately turned against journalists in 2004, when the insurgency started making itself known to the world. Holmes and his crew were attacked by insurgents, with Holmes narrowly escaping death and his local driver and translator fatally shot (pers. comm., January 2013).

BBC correspondent Alastair Leithead, in turn, told me about his dangerous experiences reporting on Iraq in the years after the 2003 invasion:

We went from armored vehicles to local vehicles with armored plating inside so it didn't look like an armored vehicle, so you could drive around in a little van so you wouldn't stick out. . . . . Suicide car bombers targeted armored vehicles or markets in the morning. So don't go to market, don't drive an armored car, and don't go driving around in the morning. Just drive around elsewhere in a beat-up old car and you won't stand out. (pers. comm., May 2013)

Leithead's account underscores the fact that around this time, many news organizations started dissociating themselves from the large military vehicles often used in embeds, after the 2003 invasion gave way to the prolonged insurgency. In this new environment, reporters had to make tough choices about whether they should try to blend in or continue accompanying the U.S. troops that most decisively stood out. For example, as David Loyn told the *British Journalism Review*, "A shabby Toyota saloon, with a smeared windscreen fringed by woolen tassels and gray nylon curtains obscuring the rear windows, is now the vehicle of choice, leaving fleets of expensive armored vehicles to gather dust in the garage" (2007). And as Reuters's Baghdad bureau chief told the *Press Gazette*, "We have a couple of white Land Rovers, which are useless because they make very good targets. We scrapped those in favor of discreet Mercedes and BMWs. We train drivers in techniques for avoiding getting kidnapped and we have security advisors who will often travel with us discreetly in the background. We always use at least two cars" ("Reuters Bureau Chief on Reporting" 2006).

Within this precarious context, embedding was ambivalently seen as something that provided western journalists with professional security, while at the same time drawing dangerous attention from insurgents. The *New York Times's* Anthony Shadid and NPR's Anne Garrels both wrote in the November/December 2006 issue of the *CJR* that they found embedding to be an intensely disturbing experience, one that could result in emotional trauma or in the labeling of journalists as "combatants" (Shadid 2006; Garrels 2006). Some of the journalists I interviewed who embedded with U.S. troops in postinvasion Iraq told me in no uncertain terms that they felt very much in danger when escorted by U.S. troops. Holmes asserted that "you're not exactly going low-profile" when embedded with the U.S. military (pers. comm., January 2013), while the *Washington Post's* Abigail Hauslohner told me that "it was often unsettling sitting in one of their big armored vehicles, sitting in traffic and thinking, ok, is the car next to us going to explode all of a sudden, or, are we going to go over a road side bomb?" (pers. comm., February 2013). ITN's Lindsey Hilsum said that the "embedding is safer" discourse is mere propaganda, and that one of her most intense reporting experiences occurred when she was embedded with troops in Fallujah 2004 (pers. comm., May 2013). And ABC producer Angus Hines told me:

There is a nervous energy once you come off an embed. You tend to be extremely tired, and you don't realize how tense you've been on it, and you kind of suppress those feelings. You have to make a call before you go as to whether you want to go, and how you think it's going to be. . . . So you know, even though you believe that the army is going to try to keep you away from danger, bad things can happen of course. Obviously you know the story about Bob Woodruff when he was on patrol. (pers. comm., February 2013)

Interestingly, Woodruff himself seemed to identify more with the Pentagon's discourse on safety than Hines did. Woodruff told me that embedding is "really the only safe way to cover some of these parts of the world. To really be there, to see what's happening on the ground" (pers. comm., September 2013). I interviewed Woodruff on September 4, 2013 and then engaged in an email exchange with him in February of 2014—approximately seven years after the almost-fatal injury that he incurred while embedded with U.S. troops in Iraq. Perhaps it was the benefit of hindsight that inspired Woodruff's faith in the embedding system, even after he suffered such a serious wounding in the field. Or perhaps he felt that way because, after his injury, he was so often associated with the U.S. soldiers. The next section of this chapter examines the early coverage and industrial discourse on Woodruff's injury, showing how his complex and tragic experience was rewritten as a marketable melodrama. This melodrama aligned Woodruff with U.S. troops, and obscured the messier issues informing the U.S. military's prolonged occupation of Iraq.

When the IED Exploded

In his postinjury memoir, coauthored with his wife Lee, Woodruff says that ABC executive David Westin promoted him to the anchor chair at the end of 2005, as part of ABC's effort at embracing a new, "digital" future: one in which Woodruff would travel around the world to do his anchoring, while coanchor Elizabeth Vargas would work from ABC's New York studios (Woodruff and Woodruff 2007). This mobility on the part of ABC's new coanchor was meant to help the network compete with the growing array of options that younger news viewers could access online. Indeed, ABC revealed a marked interest in digital journalism around this time, attempting to populate different parts of the world with young "digital" journalists who could do everything from writing a story to shooting their own video; the network also eventually invested time and money in a digital broadcast meant to reach viewers on the internet (Samuels, pers. comm., February 2015). Woodruff's and Vargas's youthful appearance could potentially help to make ABC relevant in this new context, as could Woodruff's international "omniscience"—an omniscience increasingly being associated with the immediacy and "interconnectedness" of the web.

At the time of his promotion, Woodruff had already obtained several years' experience reporting from conflict zones. He started his career as a translator for ABC in the 1989 Tiananmen Square protests in China and, after becoming a professional reporter, he covered the 2001–2002 war in Afghanistan and the 2003 invasion of Iraq. When he returned to Iraq in 2006, it was as the new anchor of ABC's flagship nightly news program, *ABC World News Tonight*. Following in Peter Jennings's footsteps, Woodruff was known as a "marquee name," someone whose youthfulness, paired with his experience, would enhance ABC's image in a digital world where nightly news programs were perceived to be losing their influence on viewers (Wooten 2006; Romano 2006a).

On January 29, 2006, Woodruff had been in Iraq for only a few days, and he had just a few more days to go before he was supposed to return to the United States. His embed was scheduled to last for about a week. According to Woodruff, his short embed with the U.S. 4th Infantry Division was arranged for him before he even arrived in Iraq (pers. comm., February 2014). His editors and producers set up the plans to have Woodruff accompany U.S. forces on his Iraq trip while he was still in Gaza and Jerusalem, covering the 2006 Palestinian elections. Only four days after the January 25 elections, Woodruff was in Iraq. There, he encountered the IED that permanently changed his career and almost took his life.

In his memoir, Woodruff describes the morning that he and his Canadian cameraman Doug Vogt were preparing to travel with their military unit from Baghdad to the nearby town of Taji. On the way to Taji, Woodruff's military unit encountered a group of U.S.-trained Iraqi soldiers, and the Iraqi troops joined the convoy. Because Woodruff wanted to report on the progress of the Iraqi soldiers, he asked if he and his crew could ride with the Iraqis, who then took the lead position—by far, the most dangerous position in any military convoy traveling through Iraq. Not only did they ride at the front of the convoy, but eventually Woodruff and his cameraman Vogt climbed up their tank's hatch and stood in full view, hoping to record a "standup" shot for their news package. As the two correspondents stood in the hatch, the Iraqi soldier standing with them reportedly turned and told Woodruff and Vogt that they were approaching an area renowned for IEDs ("To Iraq and Back" 2008). At that precise moment, the IED exploded.

Woodruff's memoir describes how he swam in and out of consciousness before completely going under (2007). His soundman and producer—both still below, in the tank—reported later that they saw Vogt's camera fall through the hatch, covered in blood, just before the two correspondents themselves fell through the hatch (2008). Both Woodruff and Vogt were hit with shrapnel, and Vogt also suffered a broken shoulder. Woodruff was hit in the neck with a piece of shrapnel the size of a half dollar. Doctors would later tell him that the shrapnel had lodged itself against his carotid artery, and that if that artery had punctured, he would have died in Iraq (Woodruff and Woodruff 2007).

Though he fortuitously survived that dangerous wound, Woodruff's other wounds were far more critical than Vogt's, with a traumatic brain injury that would eventually lead doctors to remove a part of his skull in order to help with the swelling. As soon as the convoy was out of danger, Woodruff and Vogt were taken to the hospital at the Balad Air Base in Iraq and were later airlifted to a better-equipped military hospital in Landstuhl, Germany. From there, both men would go to the Bethesda Naval Hospital in Bethesda, Maryland, where Vogt would soon recover and where Woodruff would remain in a medically induced coma until March of 2006. It would be months before Woodruff would be capable of returning to work at ABC.

While Woodruff was incapacitated, U.S. television networks flooded the airwaves with coverage of what had happened. This early coverage of Woodruff's injury, ranging from January 29 to February 3, 2006, displayed three important themes, each of which melodramatically represented Woodruff as both victim and hero. First, the newscasts tended to remark upon the "personal" quality of this disaster, implying that Woodruff belonged not only to ABC, but also to the entire journalistic community. Second, news reports repeatedly asserted that because they were experienced war correspondents, Woodruff and Vogt had taken "calculated risks." These remarks emphasized Woodruff and Vogt's individual responsibility for their own safety in a highly dangerous profession. Third, initial coverage of Woodruff's injury attempted to align him with the U.S. soldiers in the war zone, comparing his shattered body to those of the troops who often faced IED deaths and wounds in Iraq.

When ABC first announced Woodruff's injury on January 29, coanchor Elizabeth Vargas opened the newscast by saying: "We begin tonight in Iraq as we have so many times on this newscast. But this time, it's about a colleague." The very fact that Woodruff's injury led the newscast in which he was usually an anchor pointed to the genuine emotional hit that ABC news was taking, especially since the network's longtime anchor Peter Jennings had died of cancer only months before. In the following nights, ABC anchors and reporters would invoke Woodruff's status as an ABC colleague, calling the injury a "personal" matter. Yet, other U.S. news networks did the same. In a January 29 CNN package that was re-aired especially for the Woodruff incident, Holmes asserted that though journalists often report on injuries, it is much more difficult to remain unemotional and objective when this happens to "you or someone you know." Similarly, Brian Williams declared in a January 30 newscast: "NBC sends its best wishes to people at ABC news. It is a reminder that in our highly competitive business, we are friends first and foremost." Such statements on one level reflected the shock that U.S. news employees felt over the potential loss of such a well-known journalist and friend; on another level, these assertions subtly drew upon the discourse of individualism, emphasizing personal relationships over the institutional and political issues that contributed to the incident.

This theme of personal loss was tightly linked to the theme of the "calculated risk" in the early coverage of Woodruff and Vogt's injury. When ABC's White House correspondent Martha Raddatz reported on the explosion, she included a quote from Woodruff's Baghdad producer Kate Felsen, who reminded audiences that Woodruff himself had desired to be in Iraq so that he could report the story from where it was actually unfolding. In a January 29 broadcast, CNN anchor Carol Lin remarked: "In this business of television news, in order to tell the story properly, journalists often put their lives on the line." Later in the same broadcast, Lin interviewed former Baghdad bureau chief Jane Arraf, who said that true journalists know they have to be in the field, because that is where the story is. Following this, CBS's Byron Pitts asked the Committee to Protect Journalist's Ann Cooper whether she thought that journalists should avoid war zones. She responded by asking: "What would we be left with?"

Much of the coverage following the explosion also mentioned Vogt and Woodruff's professional experience, suggesting that they were the ones who held the ultimate responsibility for their own safety in the field. After Raddatz's January 29 report on Woodruff and Vogt, for example, she and Vargas appeared on screen together, where they discussed the ABC employees' knowledge of the war zone. Vargas said that both Woodruff and Vogt were experienced "and knew very well how dangerous this assignment was." Raddatz replied: "They certainly did, and they mitigated that risk in whatever way they could. As we noted, they both had their body armor and helmets on." This invocation of both their experience and their body armor underscored the fact that Vogt and Woodruff had not acted carelessly. Yet, it also subtly placed the responsibility on the two men, portraying them as the free neoliberal subjects of melodrama. In this formulation, Woodruff especially symbolized the self-sufficient hero who had risked his life to report the truth, and who had sadly been injured in the process.

Crucially, U.S. news networks did not blame the embedding model for Woodruff's injury. Instead, network coverage focused on the instability and unpredictability of Iraq as a conflict zone, weaving in some rather ambivalent discussions of embedding alongside repeated assertions that journalists in Iraq very simply should expect the worst. ABC's Vargas noted that "embedding offers a measure of protection, but Iraq is still a very dangerous assignment." This assertion attempted to resolve the contradictions involved in the fact that an embedded journalist had just been severely wounded. Jane Arraf also tried to address this dissonance in her January 29 interview with CNN, stating that if journalists did not embed, they would run the risk of getting kidnapped or of not getting a story because of all the security precautions they would have to take. On the other hand, Arraf conceded, "there is obviously greater risk of being attacked" with the military, "as they're being attacked." Each of these assertions uneasily pointed to the irony that an embedded reporter, supposedly under the protection of the U.S. military, had been very publicly injured.

In order to grapple with the contradictions inherent in Woodruff's incident, news networks focused on the dangers heroically faced by U.S. soldiers in Iraq, a theme that would continue long into Woodruff's recovery. For example, Vargas ended ABC's broadcast on January 29 with this statement: "We are once again reminded in a very personal way, of what so many families of American servicemen and women endure so often, when they receive news of their loved ones being hurt." Similarly, NBC's Williams ended his January 30 broadcast by declaring: "While we won't be happy until Bob Woodruff and Doug Vogt are safely home and on U.S. soil, we have the very same wish for all families waiting for a loved one to return." CBS showed a picture of Woodruff that was superimposed over a graphic of an American flag. And on February 1, ABC put Lee Woodruff's personal statement on the air: "We realize that our family is going through something that thousands of military families have experienced over the last three years. . . . We should focus on the members of the U.S. military whose heroic actions [Woodruff] has reported on for years."

This coverage overtly aligned Woodruff with the U.S. soldiers whose actions he had been covering in the field. Though such commentary may have been intended to apologetically flag the fact that Woodruff was receiving

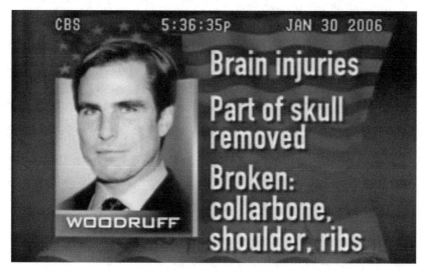

Figure 4. Patriotic coverage of Bob Woodruff's injury, airing on CBS, January 30, 2006.

more attention than the many unnamed soldiers who were wounded in Iraq, the coverage also suggested that an "independent" journalist should be viewed with as much patriotism as a U.S. soldier. In turn, the coverage invited viewers to understand the U.S. occupation of Iraq in simplistic and melodramatic terms, framing patriotic "Americans" as the most important players in the Iraq story. Though the initial U.S. television coverage of Woodruff's injury did often note that the U.S. military had overstayed its time in Iraq, this coverage repeatedly fell back on nationalistic and sympathetic discussions of the troops. From the moment he was injured, Woodruff was represented as one of these "recognizable" heroes.

The possibility of Woodruff's recovery was also a major theme in the coverage of his injury, often invoked alongside anxious representations of his broken body. Just after ABC *Nightline* showed footage of an incapacitated Woodruff on a stretcher, the show included a sound bite from Woodruff's brother David: "We're just flat out saying—he's going to be back [to work]. Because that's what he loves." The next section of this chapter examines the industry discourse on whether or not Woodruff would be able to return to work at ABC. During this later stage in Woodruff's recovery, some industry insiders debated over whether or not Woodruff was sent to Iraq simply in hopes of boosting ABC's ratings after Peter Jennings's death. Others lamented the possibility that his body and face might no longer be suitable for television. Still others worried that Woodruff would no longer be able to speak because of the damage to his brain, linking this possibility to the question of who would succeed Woodruff as the anchor of ABC's *World News Tonight*. Each of these themes illuminated the industrial imperatives that drive the celebrification and commodification of war correspondents in the twenty-first century.

Getting Back to Work

In the memoir that she coauthored with her husband, Lee Woodruff writes: "One of the greatest frustrations with a head injury is that while the person might seem just fine to others, things are profoundly changed inside. These patients—with significant but outwardly subtle damage—were called 'the walking wounded'" (Woodruff and Woodruff 2007). Lee Woodruff's statement revealed a major fear that she personally experienced during her husband's recovery: the possibility that the internal damage would outlast the external damage, transforming Woodruff into a fundamentally different person. Yet, Woodruff's outward injury was also not so subtle, at least, not at first: "Anyone who saw ABC's co-anchor lying immobile, his head grossly swollen and his face blasted by shrapnel, would never have believed this was a man who might one day return to work" (ibid.).

The question of how Woodruff's injury would impact his work continually surfaced in the "behind the scenes" commentary on Woodruff's incident. Some of this discourse suggested that Woodruff had never been more than a pretty face, implying that without that beauty his career was over. For instance, in a February 4 edition of *B&C*, J. Max Robins invoked a series of articles written by the *New York Times*. According to Robins, these articles had suggested that Woodruff's 2006 presence in Iraq had been a mere "ratings strategy," and that as an anchor, he did not have the necessary skills to report from a conflict zone (2006a). To this, Robins responded:

> In an industry that prizes cosmetics, anchors and correspondents with Hollywood looks too often feel the need to parachute into harm's way to prove they're more than just pretty faces. Please don't misinterpret what I'm saying. I share the dismay that many at ABC News feel about the *New York Times* headline. . . . Still, I can't help but wonder: Was Woodruff motivated by the same need shared by so many of his brethren, including his late pal [David] Bloom, to establish himself as the real deal, beyond great cheekbones and a terrific head of hair? (ibid.)

In this passage, Robins ultimately bolstered the views propagated by the *New York Times*, emphasizing Woodruff's "great cheekbones" and "terrific head of hair" in order to question his professional ability to report from the site of conflict. Robins's description of Woodruff's physical appearance, alongside his remark that the television news industry "prizes cosmetics," operated in a way that aligned Woodruff with the consumerist, celebrity culture so often lambasted by public intellectuals. Indeed, this article subtly feminized Woodruff *because* of his previous physical beauty, implying that anyone with such a perfect exterior must be a poser in the professional field of conflict correspondence. Not only did this statement contradict the ten years of experience Woodruff had acquired in various conflict zones; it also subtly blamed Woodruff himself for the incident in Iraq, asking whether he was "motivated by the same need shared by so many of his brethren . . . to establish himself as the real deal."

Despite this cynical outlook on Woodruff's skills as a reporter, ABC had considered Woodruff a franchise for a long time. As early as 2003, ABC producer Paul Slavin said: "I don't need a bureau in Afghanistan, but I am sending Bob Woodruff. That is a more efficient use of resources" (cited in Fleeson 2003). ABC correspondent Jim Wooten also said that the network's "relentless reduction of its foreign staff" kept Woodruff parachuting into war zones, something that turned him "into a prominent name on the network's marquee" (Wooten 2006). With this statement, Wooten suggested that in the first decade of the twenty-first century, one person was now expected to stand in for an entire news bureau, pointing to the huge amount of work that was increasingly being placed on the shoulders of individual reporters. Woodruff's fame grew out of his exhausting labor as a conflict correspondent, someone who was expected to do the work that an entire staff would have done in earlier eras.

Later in 2006, ABC news editors told the *American Journalism Review* that the post-Jennings *World News Tonight* format was meant to draw upon Woodruff's experience: "It wasn't built because we all of a sudden wanted to have two people sitting next to each other at a desk. The program was built on two people who complemented each other, were terrific reporters, who could travel around the world" (Smolkin 2006). Yet, Woodruff's injury had upset these plans, leaving ABC to figure out whether Vargas should continue on her own or whether the network should take a different route. Almost every time an industry commentator reported on the status of Woodruff's recovery, focusing either on his outward appearance or on the damage to his linguistic capabilities, that commentator would also mention that there was still no word on when Woodruff would be back in the anchor chair. This continual reference to the anchor chair overtly underscored the linkage between Woodruff's broken body and his role as a major franchise for

ABC, despite the fact that his injury had happened precisely as a result of that professional role.

Instead of discussing this uncomfortable truth, journalists and editors focused on the financial troubles that the news networks were suffering—especially homing in on the conglomerates' direct involvement in the shuffling of anchors across the Big Three's morning and evening programs (Robins 2006b; Romano 2006a). Woodruff was also repeatedly invoked in these discussions, if only to briefly explain why ABC's original plans to increase its status with viewers had fallen through. In these instances, Woodruff's injury was directly linked to the faltering news economy and to the U.S. networks' bottom line, an issue that anxiously informed the perpetual questions about when Woodruff would return to the air. ABC executive David Westin repeatedly gave interviews on the issue, always keeping his language rather vague.

When ABC finally decided to permanently give the anchor chair to Charlie Gibson, Westin told *Broadcasting and Cable* that this decision granted ABC "some much-needed stability" (cited in Romano 2006b). In an interview with *B&C*'s Allison Romano, Westin made it sound like this instability was solely due to what he called the quite "personal" losses of Jennings and Woodruff, remarking that the personal nature of Woodruff's injury had especially made it difficult to know when to fill the anchor chair ("Try, Try Again" 2006). Yet, in another article, Romano noted that the decision to give the job to Gibson came just after the *CBS Evening News* had beaten *World News Tonight* in total viewers for the first time in five years (2006b). *B&C*'s Robins drew attention to that issue as well, stating: "You don't have to be Einstein to know that Gibson wouldn't be going to *World News Tonight* if the ratings weren't slipping" (2006c).

Within this precarious financial context, ABC began constructing a new version of its melodramatic narrative on Woodruff's injury. The network began promoting Woodruff's return to the network as a reporter, rather than an anchor, capitalizing not only on his talents as a correspondent but also upon his personal survival story. In June of 2006, ABC's nightly newscast ended with Gibson reminding viewers about Woodruff's injury, replaying that same footage of Woodruff standing in the hatch of the Iraqi tank just before the explosion. Gibson then announced that Woodruff had visited the newsroom that day and showed video of him giving a speech to all the ABC employees. In the speech, viewers could hear Woodruff—speaking clearly and without hesitation—telling the ABC staff that he had thought of them while he recovered, hoping to get back to doing the work he loved. The video then showed Woodruff walking down a hallway, blowing a kiss to the camera, and proclaiming: "Man, it's good to be here!"

Crucially, Woodruff was represented in this way a few weeks *after* officially losing the anchor chair, suggesting that Woodruff himself was excited to return to ABC and work as a correspondent. On one level, this showed Woodruff's very real commitment to his network and to his identity as a journalist, an identity that many of my interviewees have said they value very deeply. On another level, this coverage linked the personal with the professional, presenting Woodruff's physical and mental recovery as being interwoven with his professional dedication. In fact, Woodruff's recovery was subtly represented as another kind of heroic labor, in the sense that his injury and miraculous healing could repeatedly serve as an interesting story to put on the evening news. For a journalist, then, the term "the walking wounded" takes on a different tone. Once Woodruff's outward appearance began to heal, he could help ABC tell his own story, partially because he would now always be marked by his highly publicized experience. As the "walking wounded," Woodruff could perpetually reenact a melodramatic narrative of patriotic sacrifice and recovery. According to John Kinder, this narrative of patriotic sacrifice and recovery was also linked to U.S. soldiers who had miraculously recovered from injuries incurred in the "war on terror" (2015).

The patriotic nature of Woodruff's own recovery narrative became clearer as ABC prepared for his to return to the air as a reporter. On January 29, 2007, Gibson noted the anniversary of Woodruff's injury. While Gibson spoke, viewers were shown the images of Woodruff before the explosion, intercut with much more recent images of Woodruff giving speeches and—importantly—working on a documentary featuring U.S. soldiers who had also suffered brain injuries in the field. Gibson's discussion of Woodruff ended with the promotional assertion: "It will be great to have him back on the air next month." Later in February, the promotion of Woodruff's return began again, anticipating his February 28 debut. On the evening of February 26, Gibson told audiences that Woodruff's documentary would air the next night. He also took viewers on a step-by-step tour of Woodruff's recovery.

This report began with Gibson's pronouncement: "I want to show you a CT scan of Bob's skull, taken during the five weeks he was unconscious." As Gibson spoke, the screen cut to the medical image of Woodruff's internal injuries, presenting viewers with the now "invisible" wounds that would, nevertheless, mark the rest of Woodruff's career. Gibson also noted that part of Woodruff's skull was missing, because doctors had wanted to give his brain enough room to swell. As Gibson explained that each of the dots on the right

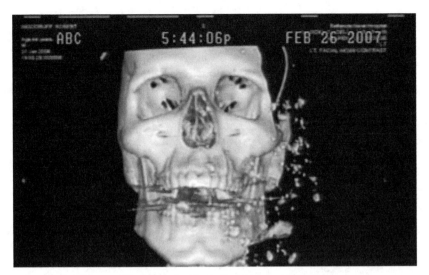

Figure 5. The CT scan of Bob Woodruff's skull, airing on ABC, February 26, 2007.

side of the image represented the shrapnel that had pierced Woodruff's face and neck, the camera slowly zoomed in on the CT scan, inviting viewers to scrutinize the injuries more closely.

By airing the image of Woodruff's CT scan, ABC turned the raw material of Woodruff's body into the object of the viewers' gaze, subtly reminding them of what Woodruff had suffered in order to tell ABC's viewers the story of Iraq. Kinder suggests that this discursive strategy also happens in the popular U.S. discourse on wounded soldiers arguing that in the post-9/11 world, the public increasingly witnesses the wounded war veteran "overcoming" his or her injuries. This propagates the utopic myth that there are no permanent casualties in war (2015, 1). What is more, Kinder states that in the global War on Terror, the U.S. public has "grown intimately acquainted with the latest generation of body-mending technologies . . . designed to help veterans return to a productive life" (ibid.). ABC's representation of Woodruff's injury treated viewers to a glimpse of these "body-mending technologies," most especially when Gibson reintroduced Woodruff to the viewers by showing the images of Woodruff's wounded skull.

After showing this image of Woodruff's CT scan, ABC then offered viewers a visual timeline of Woodruff's full recovery. Viewers saw a still image of Woodruff with two of his children, his head noticeably misshapen. Gibson again invoked the missing portion of Woodruff's skull and noted that this photo was taken only two days after Woodruff awoke. Next, the screen cut to an image of Woodruff with a shorn head and some noticeable scars, but with his skull rebuilt. And lastly, viewers saw a picture of Woodruff in a suit, interviewing a U.S. soldier and surrounded by a camera crew. In regard to this image, Gibson said: "And now Bob, looking like his old self, reporting for tomorrow night's broadcast!"

This reintroduction of Woodruff to ABC's newscast functioned in two important ways. First, the report attempted to prove to ABC's viewers that Woodruff was physically healed from the highly publicized wounds he had suffered and that he had not paid the ultimate price in his effort at anchoring from a war zone. Second, this report constructed a timeline for viewers that began and ended with Woodruff's embodied labor for the network. Gibson opened the report by reminding the audience that Woodruff would be back on the air the next day, and he closed the report with an image of Woodruff working on the next day's story. In between those two points, Gibson took audiences through the process of Woodruff's physical recovery, a recovery that was itself a marketable story for ABC.

Gibson's invitation for viewers to peer into Woodruff's injured skull also operated on a rhetorical level. It was, in a sense, an invitation to view Woodruff as the "walking wounded," as someone who had been internally injured but who had ultimately survived the horrors of war. No longer an anchor, Woodruff did his first postinjury report on the traumatic brain injuries suffered by U.S. soldiers in Iraq, a story that subtly drew upon his own personal narrative in order to lend credit to the narratives of the countless unnamed soldiers who faced the threat of IEDs on a daily basis. Indeed, when Gibson introduced Woodruff's report on February 28, a huge banner floated on the screen, the words "Home Front" emblazoned upon it. Gibson then told audiences that Woodruff, who suffered injuries in Iraq, would now be reporting on those with similar injuries. In this sense, ABC's coverage of Woodruff's recovery represented Woodruff as a melodramatic victim-turned-hero. The plights of the myriad other journalists who had been hurt or killed in Iraq were not mentioned in this coverage, nor were the thornier political questions about the U.S. invasion and prolonged occupation.

Conclusion

Throughout its coverage of Woodruff's injury, ABC—along with the other U.S. networks—had avoided much criticism of the soldiers themselves, celebrating their "heroism" in the field and their willingness to risk their own injuries for their country. ABC's mostly favorable portrayal of the soldiers on the ground was precisely the type of coverage that early critics of embedding had portended. In fact, Woodruff told Gibson in a February 27, 2007 interview that "you just feel so tight with [the soldiers]," emphasizing the interconnections between their experiences and his own. Such a statement was indicative of the continued goodwill that U.S. networks showed toward U.S. troops in 2006, even as they began to report—rather apolitically—on the possibility of the U.S. military's withdrawal from the region (DiMaggio 2010).

Woodruff's harrowing injury and long recovery brought a number of crucial issues into sharp relief. Chapter Two analyzes the Pentagon's rhetoric of safety that underwrote the treatment of correspondents in Iraq, pointing to the hypocritical (and illegal) targeting of unilateral journalists as a silencing strategy that the Pentagon exacted upon those who did not play by the rules. The attack on the Al Jazeera headquarters, alongside the murder of unilaterals like Terry Lloyd, flouted the Geneva Conventions protecting journalists as civilians in wartime, no matter how "accidental" the Pentagon claimed them to be. This created a profoundly precarious environment for conflict correspondents covering the 2003 invasion of Iraq, as well as the insurgency that followed.

Yet, this chapter also shows that the purportedly safer practice of embedding did not prove to save ABC's famous anchor from bodily harm. Instead, Woodruff's proximity to military troops facilitated his nearly fatal injury, confounding the generally accepted logic that embedded journalists were trading professional freedom for greater safety in the field. Indeed, many of my interviewees have asserted in hindsight that embedding with U.S. troops in postinvasion Iraq or in other conflict zones can ultimately be a terrifying experience precisely because of the resulting conflation of the journalist with the military. Though embedded correspondents are technically viewed as civilians under the current Geneva Conventions (Geiss 2010), they are increasingly recognized as the "enemy" by various political groups who contest the U.S.-led "war on terror."

Chapter Two also illuminates another issue: in post-9/11 war reporting, the mainstream, English-language news organizations tend to place their white, western reporters most firmly within the frame, representing them as the heroes of melodrama. ABC followed this strategy as a response to Woodruff's injury. Yet, as Woodruff's case shows, as late as 2006, this focus on specific war correspondents as heroes ultimately resulted in the omission of other important issues. U.S. networks were not asking the tough questions that their viewers needed answered; instead, they were aligning themselves and their correspondents with the military men and women whose presence in Iraq had outlasted all of the original predictions. In that dangerous environment, U.S. networks were also capitalizing upon the dangers in which their correspondents placed themselves, crafting stories out of near-death experiences that could have been prevented. This strategy continued in the news coverage of Woodruff's tragic injury, situating him at the center of an already vexed discourse that further contributed to the dangers that war correspondents face in the field.

At the time of his injury, Woodruff was a very famous figure in the Anglophone news industry, and his celebrity made it easy for news organizations like ABC to craft a highly Anglocentric view of the war in Iraq. Yet, western news organizations also drew heavily upon the often-uncredited work of Iraqi stringers after the 2003 invasion, especially as the insurgency made it more dangerous for identifiably "western" reporters to travel to the places they wanted to go. These stringers faced a unique set of dangers, since they were routinely targeted by both the insurgents and the coalition forces operating in Iraq. This increased vulnerability—inevitably linked to local news employees' more complicated cultural affiliations—is sadly a common story. Historically, local news employees have rarely received credit for the work they do. They have also received very little safety training or equipment from the western news organizations that hire them. Yet, these local news employees working for western news outlets often face an intense level of peril, partly because of the split cultural identities they are necessarily forced to perform. The next chapter of this book examines the plight of two such journalists covering the Iranian Green Revolution of 2009.

3

The "Exile's Eye"

Maziar Bahari and Nazila Fathi's
2009 Expulsion from Iran

I would leave Tehran in two days. I immediately started
the countdown, but at the same time, I felt guilty for
doing so. I didn't want to look forward to leaving my
country. I didn't want to go into exile. . . . But I couldn't
stay in Iran.

—Maziar Bahari, 2012

I do not know when I will get to go home again, and
with every year that passes my children grow further and
further away from the country of their birth. So, too, do
[my husband] and I. But if the opportunity presents itself,
I would like to return to Iran. I would like to see, one
more time, the sun shining off the Alborz mountains and
glimmering on the surface of a Tehran swimming pool. In
my heart of hearts, I long to swim in those waters again.

—Nazila Fathi, 2014

When Maziar Bahari and Nazila Fathi hit the streets of Tehran to cover the
2009 election protests, they were both navigating a precarious site of conflict
that was, nevertheless, familiar to them. Unlike the hordes of foreign reporters who streamed into Iran's capital in the early summer of 2009, Bahari and
Fathi knew Tehran on a personal level. Both born in Iran, Bahari and Fathi
were "natives"; despite the fact that they had, at separate points in their lives,
obtained dual Canadian citizenship, these journalists both thought of Iran
as their home. Yet, their strong connection with Iran was complicated by the
fact that both Bahari and Fathi also worked for western news organizations.
For years, these journalists had balanced their ties to Iran with the Anglo-

phone news industry's negative attitude toward Iranian politics, especially in the years following the September 11 attacks on the World Trade Center. After 9/11, the U.S. rhetoric driving the "war on terror" eventually spilled outside of Afghanistan and Iraq, inspiring a keen sense of paranoia about numerous other conflicts that were unfolding around the world. Not only did this politicized discourse address militarized conflicts like Israel's 2008–2009 attack on Gaza, but it also attached itself to political protests like the Iranian Green Revolution, especially when these protests became violent. Because the Iranian demonstrators were protesting the reelection of president Mahmoud Ahmadinejad, who they claimed had rigged the 2009 election battle against his reformist opponent, Mir-Hossein Mousavi, Anglophone news organizations took special interest in the uprisings. Ahmadinejad had long rankled the U.S. government with his plans to expand Iran's nuclear energy capabilities, while Mousavi appeared to U.S. news commentators as someone more in line with "American" democratic values.

Bahari and Fathi themselves contributed to the English-language news coverage that bolstered the western suspicion of Iranian religious and political leaders in the years following 9/11. Working primarily with *Newsweek* as a local stringer and later a contract freelancer (Dickey, pers. comm., December 2015), Bahari helped to write a number of stories that addressed the vexed relationship between U.S. and Iranian leaders ("Moving Forward" 2001; "Iran Connection" 2002; "Scaring the Ayatollahs" 2003). This continued in the summer of 2009, when Bahari began covering Iran's presidential elections ("Mohammad Khatami" 2009; "Iran Turns against Its President" 2009). Fathi also participated in constructing news coverage that was critical of the Iranian government. She started out as a news fixer and then a stringer for the *New York Times*, and by 2009 she had become a contract correspondent for the publication (Fathi, pers. comm., July 2015). Like Bahari, Fathi's stories reflected the tension between U.S. and Iranian interests ("Iran Won't Join US Campaign" 2001a; "Bush's 'Evil' Label Rejected" 2002; "UN Nuclear Inspections Chief" 2003). Her coverage of the 2009 uprisings also revealed a critical view of Ahmadinejad's regime (Worth and Fathi, "Ahmadinejad Stages Huge Campaign Rally" 2009; Fathi, "Iran's Top Leader Dashes Hopes" 2009).

Yet, Fathi and Bahari also contributed to a very different type of news coverage between 2001 and 2009. Alongside the political stories on Iran's relationship with the western world, both reporters wrote a number of pieces that illuminated the social complexity and the cultural beauty of Iran. An avid cinephile and filmmaker, Bahari partnered with journalist Carla Power to write about the Iranian cinema scene ("Freedom for Film" 2001), and he also made his own films about his home country (*Football, Iranian Style*

2001b; *And Along Came a Spider* 2003). Fathi wrote about everything from soccer ("Iranian Soccer Fans Celebrate" 2001b) to the feast of Yalda ("Iranians Welcome Winter" 2001c) to women's rights ("Beckham's Kid Sister" 2004; "Iranian Women Defy Authority" 2005). In both cases, these journalists shared their insiders' knowledge of Iran with English-language viewers and readers, offering fresh perspectives on the nation that had long been portrayed as backward and dogmatic by the West (Moallem 2005).

The ambivalence of Bahari and Fathi's own coverage points to a larger ambivalence that this chapter explores in detail. The chapter begins with a broader discussion of the Anglophone news industry's attitude toward "local" journalists, showing that the very terms *local, native,* and *multinational* are often inadequate when describing the cultural experiences of these diverse media workers. As scholars have long argued, "culture" itself is far from some homogenous and static thing but is instead heterogeneous and constantly changing (Appadurai 1989 and 2010; Hall 1996; Rosaldo 1993). In addition, the term *native* is arguably an imaginary construct, binding various groups and individuals to some "authentic" identity that ultimately does not reflect the porousness of cultural experience on a collective or individual level (Appadurai 1989; Narayan 2003). Still, such reductive labels are sometimes applied by people in the Anglophone news industry, as well as by other actors based at the site of conflict, and these labels can concretely limit the agency of the journalists to whom they are assigned. Thus, I do not entirely jettison these terms here, but I do use them critically and cautiously. In doing so, I hope to expose the contradictions entangled within these concepts, while also highlighting the inegalitarian hierarchies that limit the professional and personal mobility of the journalists labeled as "local" or "native."

On one level, journalists like Bahari and Fathi might culturally identify with their home nations, struggling to ensure that western news organizations do not misunderstand or ignore the complexity of the "foreign" regions they cover. Yet, this identification with the home nation also marks "native" journalists as "other" to their own employers, sometimes resulting in lower pay, fewer bylines, and shoddier efforts at protection in precarious environments (Cottle 2016).

On another level, not all of the journalists deemed as "nonwestern" are simplistically "local" to the sites at which they help U.S., Canadian, or British reporters work. A number of these journalists are multinational, in that they grew up in western nations or traveled there at pivotal moments in their lives. They may speak English fluently, and yet, they may also speak the local languages and identify with cultures that differ from those found in the United States or Britain. These journalists can simultaneously identify with both their "home" nations and their foreign employers and news audiences, celebrating the professionalism that major English-language news media ostensibly embody and embracing western cultural traditions that mark them as "other" to their own people. What is more, their identification with the West—either through the simple act of working with a western news organization, or through the more complicated process of becoming a dual citizen, affiliated with a nation like Canada or the United States—can also place journalists like Fathi and Bahari on dangerous footing with the communities and governments located at the site of conflict.

Chapter Three examines the tension between locally based journalists' *own* multilayered identifications and the *imposition* of certain identities upon these journalists from the outside. I especially trace this two-pronged phenomenon in relationship to its entanglement within "new" digital practices. As Hamid Naficy asserts, the contradictory experience of exile is increasingly "mediated by one or another of the media," (1993, 3) and this is true for journalists as well as for those who merely consume media texts. Naficy says that for those who are either psychically or physically displaced, the use of digital media can provide a sense of "discursive emplacement"; yet, online practices "involve highly complex and cathected psychological and political economies that are, on one hand, fraught with anxieties, affects, associations, and politics of all kinds, and with intriguing possibilities for liberatory diasporic and feminist multicultural practices, on the other" (2013, 4). Rather than simplistically linking the "exile" to "home" through the utopic promise of "interconnection, digital media practices ambivalently contribute to (and, in some cases, are born of) the notable tension between the subject's own multivalent cultural performances and the imposition of certain identities upon those subjects by external forces.

Following this, Chapter Three also includes a discussion of Bahari and Fathi's experiences in Iran 2009, illuminating the complex ways in which these journalists' identities were performed (and imposed), not only on the "ground," but also on social media networks. The growing popularity of social media was a major talking point for Anglophone news outlets covering the Green Movement, especially since the pro-Mousavi protesters were using the still relatively new social media platforms to tell the world about the government crackdown on their demonstrations. Social media also played a major role in Bahari and Fathi's reporting strategies, providing ways for them to track what was happening across Tehran and to maintain contact with colleagues around the world. Yet, Bahari and Fathi also found their social media practices being used against them. Bahari's imprisoners invoked his use of social media—and his online connections with western colleagues—in order to incriminate him as a "western" spy. And though Fathi celebrated social media after she fled from Iran, asserting that it helped her to stay connected with the people from her homeland, it was, according to Fathi, this virtual connection that caused Fathi's editors to disassociate her from her "on the ground" status as a "local" reporter.

Chapter Three argues that "local" and "multinational" journalists must engage in shifting, yet strategic, performances of their cultural identities in order to navigate the different agendas of their western employers and audiences and their "home" communities. These strategic performances sit in tension with the larger cultural narratives in which locally based journalists are entangled. Bahari's emphasis of his western identity ultimately landed him in Evin Prison, where members of the Basij imposed a particularly xenophobic understanding of "westernness" upon him. At the same time, news organizations in the Anglophone world also associated Bahari with some rather simplistic notions of westernness as they sought his release from prison. While this strategy did help to secure his safety, it also contributed to Bahari's ultimate exile from Iran, pointing to the specific risks that "local" and "multinational" journalists often take in the process of reporting for Anglophone news outlets.

As in Bahari's case, Fathi found herself in danger because of her association with a western news organization. And like Bahari, Fathi eventually fled Iran, without much hope of ever returning. But unlike Bahari's case, Fathi's story did not appear in the 2009 Anglophone news coverage of the Iranian uprising. Her persecution was largely omitted from the frame, until she published her own story in the form of a memoir (Fathi 2014). Thus, both of these cases raise important questions about which journalists are considered "valuable" enough to operate as the heroes of the melodramatic Anglophone news narrative. Bahari was represented in this way, but he was also temporarily "westernized" in the process. Fathi was not represented at all, until her own memoir shed light on what she had suffered in Iran. Bahari and Fathi's experiences ultimately reveal the dangerous ambivalence that the Anglophone news industry displays toward "native" or "multinational" news employees, ambivalence that can threaten these journalists on physical psychological, and professional levels. Never quite "westerners," but also not "local," their journalistic labor can incriminate them on all sides, making it difficult to find a place in the world.

"Local" Journalists, Working for Foreigners

Cultural theorist Trinh T. Minh-ha writes that "home" is itself often ho-
mogenized and naturalized in the exile's mind, though it is something that
can never be perfectly retrieved (1994). In turn, Naficy asserts that "exile is
a process of becoming, involving separation from home" and "a period of
liminality and in-betweenness that can be temporary or permanent" (1993,
xvi). Such liminality leads one to see "the entire world as a foreign land,"
which makes possible "an originality of vision" (Said 2000, 148). Many of the
so-called "local" journalists that I interviewed also destabilized the notion of
a "pure" cultural identity, revealing their own "originality of vision." This is
despite the fact that not all of these journalists were exiles in the traditional
sense. Some of them were born in Egypt, Palestine, Jordan, or Lebanon, or
their families were born in these nations. But because they worked with
western news organizations, they had to straddle different cultural identities.
Other interviewees were born in certain nations but grew up elsewhere, such
as Britain, the United States, or even in a different Middle Eastern nation
than the one with which their families most identified. In each case, these
journalists destabilized the notion of the "pure" cultural identity.

For example, the late Lebanese American war correspondent Anthony
Shadid is mostly remembered as an "American" reporter, but his widow Nada
Bakri told me that Shadid was always searching for ways to connect with
his Lebanese heritage and to bring the complicated story of the Levant more
firmly into Anglophone news reporting (pers. comm., July 2015). Another
interviewee, Luna Safwan, worked in Lebanon where she had been born and
raised, but she emotionally identified with Syria while also celebrating her
interactions with English-language foreign journalists as a lesson in journalistic professionalism (pers. comm., June 2015). A few other interviewees
had grown up in Lebanon and were working for foreign news organizations,
but their families fled Palestine at different points in the Israeli-Palestinian
conflict. Because of this, they sometimes felt like outsiders in Beirut, even
though most of their friends and colleagues thought of them as Lebanese.
And Fathi herself very much identified as an Iranian, but also as a Canadian,
since she and her husband had obtained dual citizenship earlier in life (pers.
comm., July 2015).

In light of this complexity, some of my interviewees stressed the advantages
of performing multiple cultural identities in their work as journalists. Nour
Malas, a Syrian American working for the *Wall Street Journal* told me: "Our
Middle East bureau, we're all hyphenated Americans. . . . All of us are, and

I think that's a huge advantage, because we have the language skills. We're partly native" (pers. comm., June 2015). In a similar vein, an Egyptian journalist covering the broader Middle East for the *Guardian* told me that his Egyptian heritage makes it possible for him to gain access to sources with different "Arab" identities:

> Egyptians are always lucky in the sense that people tend to look at Egypt as a kind of Arab ideal. And so everybody projects their political beliefs on you. . . . The Sunnis think you're Muslim Brotherhood. The Christians think you're pro-Sisi. The extreme Syrian nationalists think you're Nasserist. . . . So I found it a little easier, and it kind of fed into the idea that I was able to talk to all points of view. (Kareem Shaheen, pers. comm., June 2015)

Lebanese American freelancer Sulome Anderson told me about her tendency to emphasize her "Arab" heritage or her "American" heritage, depending on the situation:

> With certain people, I'm like, "no, I'm an Arab like you. I understand." And it's true, I do, I understand the rules. The unspoken rules, things like, you don't shake hands sometimes. . . . But with other people, I pretend to be completely American, and I don't speak any Arabic. . . . It's really great when I pretend not to speak or understand any Arabic, because I understand what they're saying to each other, and they don't know it. (pers. comm., June 2015)

In each of these cases, the journalist working for an Anglophone news organization did not entirely identify as "western" or "foreign." Yet, neither did these journalists entirely identify as "native" or "local." Instead, they viewed their competing cultural identities as performances in which they could strategically engage, in order to do better journalistic work. Accentuating certain cultural attributes at certain moments helped these journalists obtain information that not every war correspondent can easily obtain. The ability to understand a variety of languages and to interface with a variety of people helped these journalists to cover stories that would be less accessible for a white reporter born and raised in New York or London.

Yet, the journalists I interviewed for this specific chapter worked closely with white foreign correspondents or bureau chiefs who typically hailed from nations like the United States, Canada, or Britain. In some cases, the working relationships between these foreign journalists and my interviewees were healthy, respectful, and even educational. For example, a Palestinian journalist working in Gaza said of her foreign colleagues: "They know sometimes even more than me. I've worked with professionals. They know

Gaza by meter. They know everything. They know all the officers, so yeah, it's very helpful" (Abeer Ayyoub, pers. comm., September 2015). Safwan added that western journalists tended to be more "professional" than Lebanese journalists, pushing harder for objectivity (pers. comm., June 2015). And numerous interviewees said that they remain friends with certain foreign journalists who worked with them in the past. This sentiment was echoed by many of the Anglo journalists and editors I interviewed, with ABC's Ray Homer suggesting that local journalists become like family to the foreign correspondents (pers. comm., June 2014) and Philip Bennett of the *Washington Post* emphasizing the importance of building trust between local and foreign journalists who work together (pers. comm. February 2015).

On the other hand, some of my interviewees also said that certain foreign correspondents and news editors take a more rigid, hierarchical approach to working with "local" or "multinational" journalists. One Egyptian journalist working with ABC during the Iraq war said that Peter Jennings himself told her that her "Arab-sounding" name was a problem for U.S. viewers (Hoda Abdel-Hamid, pers. comm., April 2013). In turn, a Jordanian journalist working with Anglophone news outlets in Beirut said he had scored some of his best assignments because he did not have a markedly "Arab" accent (Nabih Bulos, pers. comm., June 2015). Sulome Anderson flatly told me: "The shitty thing about local journalists is that they are not treated the same. They're not given the same weight. . . . A lot of them don't have the opportunity to get the credit they deserve" (pers. comm., June 2015).

This is either because Anglophone news organizations do not often feel the need to give locally based journalists a byline, or because a byline actually puts the journalist in danger of being targeted by local governments or militant groups. Sometimes, though, the issue of "getting credit" is less about the byline and more about receiving the same professional respect that foreign correspondents receive. Shaheen told me that foreign news outlets tend to believe that the work of Arab journalists does not merit the same kind of trust associated with western journalists. Freelance reporter Anna Lekas Miller named the problem even more overtly, asserting that white male correspondents from the United States have a much easier time getting foreign reporting work with mainstream, Anglophone news outlets, despite the fact that they often know very little about the cultures on which they are reporting (pers. comm., May 2015).

The distrust, and sometimes the outright racism, of Anglophone journalists toward nonwhite, locally based people goes back at least two centuries. For example, postcolonial scholar David Spurr identifies a longstanding trope of "debasement" in colonial journalistic discourse, "where the qualities as-signed to the individual savage—dishonesty, suspicion, superstition, lack of self-discipline—are reflected more generally in societies characterized by cor-ruption, xenophobia, tribalism and the inability to govern themselves" (1993, 73). During the Golden Age of Anglophone war reporting, correspondents would often report on the plight of "natives or foreigners" without showing much sympathy: in fact, representing them as animals or servants (Knight-ley, 2004, 46). This representation continued during the World Wars, when British war correspondents represented the conflicts in colonial territories as "exotic 'spectacles' almost always victorious—written up in the breathless register of war correspondence somewhere between exotic travelogue and ripping *Boys' Own* yarn" (Carruthers 2011, 52–53).

Anglophone journalists have also long revealed a marked distrust of "lo-cal" and especially "nonwhite" people who play a role in journalistic practice. Indeed, mainstream U.S. war reporting has been a mostly "white" profession since its inception, with African American war coverage often being ignored, and with African American war correspondents being relegated to working solely for the black press (Hamilton 2011). Besides barring journalists of color from working in the mainstream news profession, Anglophone war journalists also devalued the testimony of nonwhite, nonwestern sources in the field. For instance, in the nineteenth century, *Daily Mail* correspondent George Warrington Stevens said that he "vowed to state nothing on any authority unless I saw it myself or heard from a European who had seen it" (cited in Knightley 2004, 57). This suggested that non-Europeans could not be trusted as credible sources. Apparently, neither could non-Anglo journal-ists be trusted. An Associated Press correspondent wrote this 1912 complaint to his editors, from his post in Mexico City:

> One of the greatest difficulties encountered in covering news throughout the republic of Mexico is the almost complete absence of men with any newspaper training or news sense, as viewed from an American standpoint. Mexican cor-respondents, who appear to serve well enough Mexican newspapers, invari-ably miss the point of a story, or bury it in such a mass of verbiage that one is left in doubt as to what actually occurred. If not this, then their reports are so biased by their prejudices that they are likely to represent their personal views. (cited in Hamilton 2011)

This attitude continues to surface in the twenty-first-century coverage of the "war on terror," with white, western journalists all too often suggesting that "local" journalists are unprofessional, overly emotional, or generally less desirable than Anglo reporters born outside the Middle East. Typically, foreign news bureaus based in the Middle East offer lower-paying jobs called "news assistantships" to local journalists, jobs that entail a great deal of translating, setting up interviews, and even writing, but which do not promise much money or cultural capital. One such news assistant for the *LA Times* in Beirut even told me that local news sources treated him with less respect than his white colleagues, because they read him as being the "brown" interpreter and not a journalist (Bulos, pers. comm., June 2015).

The hierarchy between Anglo journalists and "local" journalists becomes especially problematic when considering the ways in which this hierarchy informs the Anglophone news industry's growing safety culture. In some respects, the attention to the plight of local journalists has improved in this area, especially after so many locally based reporters were enlisted to help news organizations cover the war in Iraq. Bennett told me that the *Washington Post* helped some of the Iraqi reporters to flee the country (pers. comm., February 2015), and ABC's Homer said that the U.S. television networks did the same (pers. comm., June 2015). By the Green Revolution of 2009, organizations like *Newsweek* were certainly willing to campaign for the release of Iranian-Canadian journalists like Bahari. Yet, as of 2016, locally based journalists still appeared to have very little access to proactive safety preparation (Cottle 2016).

While a few of the journalists I interviewed for this chapter stated that in special cases, certain news outlets had sent them to a safety training course or given them a flak jacket, this appeared to be a rare practice. Some of my interviewees said that certain news outlets might provide them with body armor and insurance for the duration of their working arrangement. But many of the locally based journalists I interviewed said that if they wanted body armor, insurance, or hazardous environment training, they had to pay for it themselves. Ayyoub had not yet undergone hazardous environment training at the time when she was working with the BBC in Gaza, for example (pers. comm., September 2014), and Egyptian journalist Mostafa Sheshtawy told me that he had once been shot because his western colleague was arguing with the Egyptian police. Her news organization did not even pay his medical bills (pers. comm., July 2015). Crucially, Sheshtawy told me that the local journalists who assist foreign reporters are themselves an element of Anglophone safety culture—they are supposed to know the terrain so well that they can protect the visiting correspondent. The local journalists' own safety is also their own responsibility, specifically because they ostensibly already know the dangers on the ground (ibid.).

The vast majority of the journalists I interviewed for this chapter echoed Sheshtawy's claim that "local" journalists are expected to protect the visiting correspondent, and not the other way around. This points to a disturbing double standard in the Anglophone war reporting industry, where local or multinational journalists' "native" identities are imposed upon them as evidence that they are already protected and, thus, that they do not have a place in the industry's growing safety culture. Yet, this attitude does not account for the dangers that locally based journalists often face simply because they are affiliated with western media. Just as certain news organizations might treat these journalists as less deserving of health insurance or safety training than U.S., British, or Canadian reporters who grew up in the West, so too might local governments and militant groups doubt the cultural loyalty of journalists who work with western news organizations. "Local" or "multinational" journalists are continually accused of espionage, and they are sometimes punished for the cultural insensitivity that foreign journalists might display during their short visits.

The precarious balancing act between appeasing the local government and appeasing western news correspondents and editors defines the labor of many "local" and "multinational" journalists who work with mainstream, Anglophone news outlets. This is even more the case in the age of social media, where locally based journalists' complicated cultural performances can be tracked online as well as on the ground. I now turn to a discussion of Bahari's specific experiences in Iran, showing how his complicated social media practices were invoked by the people who imprisoned him. To one of his colleagues at *Newsweek*, Bahari was an Iranian "who spoke great English and was great company" (Dickey, pers. comm., December 2015). Yet, to his captors, Bahari was potentially a western spy. Bahari thought of himself as both Iranian and Canadian, a war reporter who had covered Iraq and who had lived in Montreal and London (2012). This multilayered identity would lead to his 118-day captivity in one of Iran's most notorious prisons and, eventually, to his permanent exile from the land where he was born.

Bahari "On the Ground," and Online

In the early summer of 2009, Bahari was living with his pregnant fiancée in London, after recently traveling back from Tehran where he had been covering the events leading up to the impending presidential election (Bahari 2012). Watching the election unfold from a distance, Bahari knew he had to go home again:

> As much as I wanted to be with Paola in London, reading the pregnancy books piled near our bed, I knew that I had to get back to Iran to report on the historic elections just days away. I needed to witness for myself the choice my nation was about to make. There was so much at stake. (ibid., 3)

Though Bahari had lived in Canada and the U.K. for years, unlike the foreign journalists flocking to Tehran at this time, he had a personal investment in this story. It was, after all, the story of his home nation, a place that had enchanted and frustrated him throughout his life. Though Bahari often traveled to Iran to cover its events, he also said that since he'd left to go to university in Canada, he had never really wanted to live in Iran again (2012). His father and his sister had both been imprisoned and tortured by previous regimes, all for speaking out about their beliefs (ibid.).

The politics of Iran were tightly interwoven with Bahari's family history, something that few of his American or Canadian colleagues could claim. Yet, it was also the presence of the foreign journalists flooding the Tehran airport that made Bahari feel he was right to return to Iran instead of staying in London. He described the atmosphere as "electric," filled with foreign correspondents who could also share this story with the world (ibid., 9). But as the correspondents from English-language organizations and other international news outlets moved through the Imam Khomeini International Airport the night that Bahari arrived in Iran, they did not yet know they would be covering an uprising at all. Unaware of how things would turn out, Bahari celebrated the opportunity to cover what he hoped would be the election of a new, reformist president: Mir-Hossein Mousavi. Excited about the days ahead, he went to his mother's house and prepared to spend the next week talking to the people at the polling stations (ibid. 2012).

Bahari's 2012 memoir outlines his first few days of covering the elections and the resulting demonstrations, which were met with a violent crackdown from Iran's Revolutionary Guard and Basij forces. This memoir, published a few years after Bahari's release from Evin Prison, provides a number of rich examples of how his complicated cultural identity impacted his reporting. On the one hand, Bahari's account points to his status as a cultural "insider," a journalist born and raised in Iran. For example, he was immediately able to comprehend why Mousavi's supporters wore the color green: "Green has long been associated with Islam; it signifies that Islam is a religion of peace. Mousavi's supporters wore green T-shirts and wristbands and carried green banners and flags. 'We will build a green Iran,' was their slogan, meaning a country at peace with itself and the rest of the world" (ibid., 15).

Figure 6. Mir-Hossein Mousavi greeting a sea of demonstrators—and cellphones—in Iran during the 2009 Green Revolution. Image by Hamed Saber.

What is more, Bahari's "local" identification inspired him to keep working, even when other journalists were being censored. Very quickly, the Iranian regime began to push foreign journalists away from sensitive areas or to ban them from covering the demonstrations that followed the controversial reelection of Ahmadinejad. Because of this, many of these foreign correspondents either stayed in their hotels or left the country, relying on social media posts to find out what was happening with the protests. Yet, when the government organization in charge of the media required that foreign journalists report only from one specific polling site on the day of the election, Bahari ignored this decree: "I had never thought of myself as part of the foreign press. I was an Iranian, so I planned to visit as many polling stations as I could" (ibid., 47). He continued to think this way even when the government banned journalists from covering the postelection demonstrations:

> I knew that many reporters would be afraid to disobey the ban. But I felt differently. Given my knowledge of Iran, my contacts in the government, and my sources in the foreign media, I was in a unique position to report on the disputed election and the chaos that followed. (ibid., 63–64)

In each of these situations, Bahari's "local" identity overrode his western identity, driving him to cover an increasingly dangerous story so that he could add his unique perspective to the international coverage of the protests. However, Bahari's affiliations with western media also sometimes inhibited him from covering the elections and demonstrations as freely as he would have liked, pointing to the complex ways in which locally based journalists' multilayered identities are also imposed upon them by outsiders. For instance, when he went to one of the polling stations that did not allow foreign journalists, he was accosted by local police who were unsure whether he was an Iranian or a foreigner (2012).

Bahari was also blocked from entering the Ministry of the Interior, where the votes were being counted, because officials associated him with the foreign press. And his decision to give his footage of Basij forces firing on protesters to the U.K.'s Channel Four News automatically put him on the Revolutionary Guard's bad side, causing a few of Bahari's friends to warn him that the Guard was now watching him closely (ibid.). Bahari had originally asked Lindsey Hilsum of Channel Four to run his footage without crediting him, something with which Hilsum later told me she and her team had complied (pers. comm., April 2015). But the Basij figured out that Bahari shot the video, and this contributed to the Guard's growing opinion that he was a spy for the West (ibid.).

Key to this reductive perspective on Bahari's identity was his journalistic use of social media, which overlapped with the demonstrators' own digital practices:

> When I got home, I tried to find out what was going on in different parts of the country by contacting some of my friends on Facebook. Despite the government's effort to block Facebook, many Iranians used Freegate, a filter buster developed by Chinese dissidents to circumvent government censors; they used Facebook and Twitter to communicate with the outside world and with one another. In fact, Iran had the largest community of bloggers outside of the United States and China. There were more blogs in Persian than in any other language except English. The Iranian government's long-standing monopoly on information was being challenged not only on the streets but also in cyberspace. By this time, Facebook was the most reliable source of information. (ibid., 70)

The fact that Bahari's insider perspective made him trust social media more than the official discourse is interesting, considering the Anglophone news industry's own highly ambivalent stance toward social media in 2009. As new technological practices developed over the first decade of the twenty-first century, numerous industry commentators also noted that the Anglophone news industry was still struggling to maintain its relevance and its funding in the age of YouTube, Facebook, and Twitter (Brown 2009; Hagerty 2009; Hewlett 2009; Palser 2009a).Thus, financial and technological anxiety continued to inform the Anglophone news industry's insider discourse, as well as its coverage of events like the 2009 Green Revolution. Anglophone journalists and editors obsessed over social media, discussing everything from how to effectively use Facebook and Twitter in professional news reporting (Gazze 2009; Podger 2009; Strupp 2009b) to the rise of the digital citizen journalist (Doyle 2009; Delano 2009; Gaber 2009; Moffat 2009; Palser 2009b). As it had in earlier years of the twenty-first century, this discourse drew upon the notion of the digital sublime (Mosco 2005), sometimes representing social media as a deeply suspicious and uncontrollable entity, while at other times celebrating social media in utopic terms.

For Bahari, using social media platforms like Facebook could keep him closer to the demonstrators on the ground than could Iranian television. Facebook could also keep him connected to his western colleagues, some of whom were covering the protests from a distance—especially after western reporters were told to leave the country. Yet, Bahari's use of Facebook also worked against him because of the Iranian regime's deep distrust of the West. This distrust long predated the invention of social media and intricately affected the purportedly utopic properties of social media that technological determinists celebrated throughout the Green Revolution of 2009.

A group of men came to his mother's house on June 21, 2009, and took him to Evin Prison. Bahari would later learn that they were members of the Revolutionary Guard. He stayed in prison for a total of 118 days and, during that time, he was constantly accused of being a spy for the United States, due to his affiliation with *Newsweek* (Bahari 2012). Bahari's interrogator went through his emails and Facebook posts, demanding that he provide information on every person who had posted on his wall or tagged him in a photo. The interrogator seemed especially interested in Bahari's social media friends with "western" names (ibid.). This suggests that Bahari's use of digital media to negotiate his layered cultural identity sat in tension with the Revolutionary Guard's own notion of Bahari's identity—a notion that was also directly linked to his use of social media. Within the Guard's framework, Bahari was narrativized as a spy for the United States because of his affiliation with a U.S.-based news outlet and because of his online connections with western social media users. Invoking Bahari's use of social media as incriminating evidence, the Revolutionary Guard crafted a narrative that placed the purportedly duplicitous Bahari at the center.

Because of his complex cultural identity, Bahari served as the "villain" of one melodrama while simultaneously being written as the "hero" of another—the melodrama being propagated by the Anglophone news industry. Oddly enough, Bahari was released in large part because of the very "western" connections that had also landed him in Evin Prison. As Bahari himself later asserted, he was lucky to be a well-known filmmaker working with major outlets like *Newsweek* and Channel Four (ibid.). He was also lucky to possess dual citizenship, rather than merely being at the mercy of the Iranian government. As soon as Bahari's editors at *Newsweek* learned of his arrest, they sprang into action: obtaining a lawyer, talking to both the U.S. and Canadian governments, and ultimately launching a campaign to put pressure on the Iranian regime (Dickey, cited in Schmidt 2014; Dickey, pers. comm., December 2015). As *Newsweek* executive Christopher Dickey later said:

> If Maziar had been abducted by a terrorist group, that might have been a slightly more ambiguous situation. But this was a state actor, a member of the United Nations, a country that wanted to be taken seriously. So you knew you had some kind of leverage. You had leverage through governments. (cited in Schmidt 2014)

Newsweek emphasized Bahari's western—and specifically, Canadian—ties, making him more politically and socially recognizable to the Anglophone and European states that already held a great deal of power over Iran's international reputation. This political and social "recognizability" is central to Butler's notion of framing, where some subjects are represented as being more valuable than others (Butler 2004). On a more collective scale, this interplay between the "recognizable" and "unrecognizable" attaches to entire populations, suggesting that some groups of people are worth cultivating and saving, while others are not (Butler 2009). Thus, while *Newsweek*'s use of melodrama certainly represented Bahari as a heroic and yet victimized individual, this narrative had wider social ramifications. The subtle message was that a "western," Canadian journalist was more salvageable than an Iranian journalist.

This type of framing drove the industrywide campaign for Bahari's release. Canada's two most widely circulated newspapers, the *Toronto Star* and the *Globe and Mail*, especially drew upon this strategy. From their very first reports on Bahari's arrest, to their final reports of his release, both papers overwhelmingly referred to Bahari as "Canadian" in their headlines, dropping his dual Iranian

citizenship until further down in the story (Colvin 2009; "Maziar Bahari Canadian Scapegoat" 2009; Hume 2009; "Regime Detains Canadian Citizen"
2009; Ward 2009). Once these articles addressed Bahari's Iranian ties, they
also explained that he had obtained Canadian citizenship while studying at
Concordia University in Montreal. Bahari's education would then sometimes
be followed by the invocation of his international notoriety as a professional
filmmaker ("Don't Forget This Detainee" 2009; "Iran vs. the Media" 2009) or
his "even-handed" reporting style (Campion-Smith 2009). The references to
his "even-handedness" and his "professionalism" were strategic as well; they
were meant to signal that Bahari was a western journalist instead of a less trust-
worthy "local" journalist. In this formulation, Bahari was "one of us," rather
than a nonwestern "stranger" who could not be trusted.

Bahari's white, western fiancée became an important figure in the campaign, partly because of her vocal efforts at getting Bahari released, but not
least of all because she was pregnant. Since Paola Gourley was half-Italian, the
Newsweek team used the story of her pregnancy to inspire Italy's then-prime
minister Silvio Berlusconi to weigh in on the situation, despite Italy's good
relationship with Iran (cited in Schmidt 2014). As Dickey later reminisced:
"There's this beautiful woman, who's pregnant, whose pregnancy is troubled,
whose child may be born with its father in jail, and that was something that
nobody wanted headlines about. And anytime anybody backed off, they got
headlines about it" (ibid.). Bahari himself put things even more bluntly at
the end of his memoir, when he spoke about *Newsweek's* campaign:

> The only problem was that after the election, hundreds of people had been
> arrested. *Newsweek* had to find a creative way to convince people that my
> story was worthy of extra attention. Paola was the difference. Paola's efforts
> while visibly pregnant helped make my story interesting to the international
> media. (Bahari 2012, 294)

In order for his imprisonment to seem "interesting" to the international
media, Bahari had to be associated with his white fiancée, who was pregnant
with a "western" child. Thus, *Newsweek* wove Bahari's white, half-European,
half-British wife into the narrative that called for his release. So, too, did the
Toronto Star and the *Globe and Mail*. The *Globe* invoked Gourley's pregnancy complications and represented her as "pregnant and ailing" (Hume
2009; Verma 2009). The *Star* followed suit, portraying Gourley as teary-eyed
and "counting days . . . until her baby is born" (Ward 2009; Campion-Smith
2009). One article mentioned that Gourley had been taken to the hospital
"after she began bleeding due to stress" (McLean 2009). Despite the fact that

hundreds of other people had been arrested in the wake of the 2009 Green Movement, Bahari's campaigners decided that in order to make him stand out, they needed to appeal to the priorities of an "international"—namely, a white, European, and Anglophone—audience. The presence of a white, pregnant body in this narrative, alongside the repeated invocation of Bahari's value as a journalist for Anglophone news outlets and his political status as a Canadian citizen, drew heavily upon the more recognizably western elements of Bahari's cultural identity.

While the Anglophone news industry engaged in a vocal campaign to secure Bahari's freedom, little was said during this time about what proactive safety measures had been taken on Bahari's behalf. When I asked Dickey what role Bahari's Iranian citizenship might have played in his arrest, and whether or not this was discussed before Bahari was sent to Iran to cover the 2009 elections, Dickey said: "There was really no question of Maziar NOT going back to Iran, although we knew things could get tense" (pers. comm., December 2015). He also asserted:

> Maziar moved in and out of Iran as he pleased in order to get the stories he thought were compelling, and we usually agreed about what those might be. . . . Maziar cultivated many friends in various influential positions in Iran, and felt that they would be able to protect him, but he knew it was always a bit of a tightrope walk, and we worked closely with him to protect his identity when he felt there might be a problem. (ibid.)

In this statement, Dickey subtly referenced the larger industrial notion that "local" journalists can take care of their own safety, by virtue of their "localness." This sat in tension with the more public representation of Bahari as a western journalist, pointing to the deep ambivalence that the Anglophone news industry displays toward local or multinational reporters. Because Bahari was well-acquainted with Iranian culture, and because he had a network of friends in Tehran, *Newsweek* assumed that Bahari could handle himself, rather than pursuing more cautious proactive measures to keep him safe in a situation where his cultural identity could place him in unique danger. And though both *Newsweek* and Channel Four helped secure Bahari's release, Bahari was forced into exile after he left Evin prison. He was later tried and sentenced in absentia for "propagandizing against the system" and "conspiring against the security of the state" (2010), an outcome that made it even more unlikely he could ever return to the place where he was born.

Even in the most literal kind of exile, Bahari continued using digital media as an expression of his complicated cultural identity. In 2013, Bahari launched IranWire, a platform that was meant to blend Iranian citizen journalism with professional news reporting. In 2014, he launched the Journalism Is Not a Crime campaign, complete with a website meant to expose the abuse of journalists working in Iran. Thus, despite the fact that Bahari's use of social media had been "fraught with anxieties, affects, associations, and politics of all kinds," these digital media practices revealed "intriguing possibilities for liberatory diasporic" actions as well ((Naficy 2013 [1999, 4). Iranian journalist Nazila Fathi also encountered the potential and the problems with the exilic use of digital media. I now turn to a discussion of her experiences in Iran 2009, and the exile that followed.

Fathi, "On the Ground," and Online

By the time she covered the 2009 demonstrations in Iran, Fathi had been working with the *New York Times* for more than 15 years. Because she had studied English during her college years in Tehran, Fathi first worked as an interpreter for western reporters visiting Iran in the 1990s. Eventually, she graduated up to the position of stringer for the *Times*, and later negotiated a position as a contract correspondent, paid on a monthly basis (Fathi 2014; pers. comm., July 2015). Fathi's 2014 memoir, *The Lonely War*, explains how this relationship began, emphasizing her fascination with the power of international journalism and the reporting techniques of the foreign correspondents with whom she worked. In this memoir, she highlights her enthrallment with the global reach of western journalism, as well as with western journalists' interest in Iranian politics.

For example, Fathi describes working with *Times* correspondent Judith Miller and the satisfying feeling of having government officials look her in the eye during the interviews she helped Miller translate (2014). According to Fathi, this was atypical for Iranian men at the time, because of different cultural notions about the relationship between men and women. Fathi also describes being "bitten by the journalism bug"—a concept often used by Anglophone war reporters when they are trying to explain why they love their job. Like her western colleagues, she was so exhilarated by journalistic work that it became a top priority. Through examples like these, Fathi's memoir reveals how her early work with mainstream, English-language news outlets led her to identify with western reporting cultures, teaching her to ask challenging questions of a repressive government (ibid.).

Alongside this identification with western news reporting, Fathi's memoir also reveals the unique ways in which her "local" identity remained crucial to her. Several times in the book, Fathi asserts that Iran was her country, and that she wanted to see it prosper. She also reveals her extensive knowledge

of Iranian culture and politics, a journalistic advantage with which few Anglophone reporters could compete. For example, Fathi's ties to the Iranian
people made it easy for her to understand Iran's long-standing tension with
the United States:

> Many people believed the US government had interrupted the course of Iran's
> democratic development. Democracy had been born at the time of the Con-
> stitutional Revolution, and it survived amidst external and internal threats,
> even under the reign of Reza Shah. Mossadeq's government had been the
> country's first democratic government that stood up to the British exploitation
> of the country's wealth. But the United States had helped the British crush
> Mossadeq and had empowered the shah, and in so doing had set Iranian
> democracy back on its heels. (ibid.)

While U.S. and British news reporters have long had access to historical
information about these events, Fathi actually lived through some of the
ramifications of this foreign meddling, making her "local" perspective all the
more valuable. Because she had an insider's perspective on the intricacies of
Iranian politics, Fathi's Iranian identity looms large in her memoir and in
much of her news coverage for the *New York Times*.

Over the years that she worked with Anglophone news organizations,
Fathi's identification with her "home" culture was also exploited by external
actors. Soon after she started working with the *New York Times*, Fathi was
summoned to a meeting with the Iranian Intelligence Ministry. At this meeting, a government agent chided her for working with western—and especially,
U.S.—news outlets who had supported Iraq in the 1980s conflict against Iran:
"'You know that Iran fought a war for eight years with a country that western
powers armed,' he said in a monotone. 'These reporters may want to mis-
represent Iran to undermine the regime. The ministry needs to be vigilant'"
(ibid.). Thus, Fathi found herself at odds with her own government because
of her work with the foreign press. The sense of enmity between the Iranian
government and western political powers permeated even her own interactions with reporters on the ground, causing Iranian officials to demand that
she register with the government organization in charge of the foreign media
and report back to Iranian officials on what the foreign media were doing
(ibid.). These incidents reveal that Fathi's Iranian identity was also imposed
on her by the regime itself, leaving little room for her to completely identify
with the western news outlets for whom she worked.

Yet, Fathi also saw some possibilities in this new arrangement with the
Iranian officials:

The Intelligence Ministry may have distrusted foreign journalists, but I knew that they—and I, to a degree—also served the government's interests. By assisting reporters, I was helping to introduce the outside world to the human face of the Iranian people, thereby changing the international perception of Iran. . . . There was life beneath the surface; there were ordinary people all over the country who longed for freedom and dignity just as people did in any other part of the world. (ibid.)

This statement points to the positive potential of Fathi's multilayered cultural identity. Though her own government demanded that she exploit her western colleagues in order to bolster the regime, Fathi recognized that she had the chance to introduce western news audiences to a more nuanced and human representation of Iran. On top of this, Fathi saw that even these government officials recognized that potential, which was part of the reason that they continued to allow her to work with foreign journalists in the first place. Instead of acting as a strictly local journalist, then, Fathi was being given the chance to be both local and foreign, to bridge the cultural divide between the Iranian people and the people of the western nations that she felt had long misrepresented Iran in their mainstream news reports.

This was a valuable, if not precarious, position for Fathi to inhabit, and she was allowed to operate in this way for a number of years. Even so, Fathi's memoir opens with a harrowing account of facing the regime's surveillance, because she had continued to cover the 2009 protests after the regime banned reporters from covering the story. At the beginning of the memoir, Fathi describes the cars full of men who sat outside her apartment every day, sometimes following her down the street. Fathi also notes that one of her friends had recently warned her that her name had been given to snipers (ibid.).

Only government forces would tail you so brazenly. They'd already arrested thousands of protestors and hundreds of former government officials, activists, and independent reporters, including my sources. I speculated they were after me because I had defied a ban: the government had ordered me, along with every other reporter working for the foreign media, not to cover the protests. My colleagues with the *New York Times* who had flown into Iran to cover the elections had left. . . . I continued to go out and write stories every day. (ibid.)

In this passage, Fathi points to the intense "tug of war" game unfolding between the Iranian authorities and the foreign media at this particular point in Iranian history. In 2009, the Iranian government saw the U.S. news industry as the propagator of an incorrect cultural narrative that represented the

Iranian government as the "villain" and the demonstrators as both heroes and victims. Unfortunately, Fathi was caught in the middle: banned from reporting by her own government but expected to continue reporting for her employer—most especially because the vast majority of foreign journalists were forced to leave Iran once the regime became suspicious of their coverage. Though Fathi took a few proactive steps to ensure her own safety—writing a letter of explanation to her editors, should she be arrested, and telling them on the phone that she was under surveillance—there is no mention in Fathi's memoir of the *Times* editors taking any proactive safety measures on Fathi's behalf (ibid.). This points to the problem invoked by many of the other journalists I interviewed for this chapter, where locally based or native journalists are not privy to the benefits of the mainstream, Anglophone news industry's growing safety culture, because their "native" insight is assumed to be its own kind of safety preparation.

Fathi told me in a 2015 interview that she had not encountered a great deal of proactive safety preparation at any point in her time working with western news outlets (pers. comm., July 2015). Yet, by 2009, Fathi was a contract correspondent for the *New York Times*, and she was also the primary person covering Iran from the ground. Perhaps because of her newly increased value to her news organization, Fathi told me that the paper did not want her to flee from Iran with her family:

> The *Times* didn't want me to leave, because I was the only person on the ground. A lot of people had been kicked out. . . . I felt I couldn't do anything, and then when my house came under surveillance, I just told the *New York Times* that I was not going to stay. I was completely stressed out by then. (ibid.)

Compellingly, Fathi's editor told me something different. Susan Chira, former foreign desk editor for the *New York Times*, asserted that Fathi's safety was Chira's top priority at that time (pers. comm., November 2016). Chira said that she continually asked Fathi if she needed to leave Iran during the 2009 uprising, but Fathi herself went back and forth on the matter: "It was a very fluid situation, very difficult to gauge" (Chira, pers. comm., November 2016).

It is impossible to verify which of these two accounts is correct, since both of my interviewees are looking back upon a stressful experience that occurred several years ago. Memory itself can be a fluid and creative process. What these competing accounts do undoubtedly illuminate is the very real emotional strain that Fathi experienced due to her status as the "only person on the ground" for a western news organization whose Anglo reporters had been told to leave Iran. This emotional strain came as a result of Fathi's own understanding of her precarious liminality—as an Iranian, she felt she was vulnerable to the regime's anger, and as a "native" *Times* employee she felt she was expected to face that anger and get the story anyway.

Industry commentators did not appear to recognize the dangers that Fathi faced during this time. Fathi was only mentioned in one of the trade articles on the 2009 protests, while U.S. journalists, such as *New York Times* editor Bill Keller, were lauded for traveling to Tehran and covering the demonstrations (despite their quick exit once the regime started cracking down on journalists) (Strupp 2009a). This oversight was reflective of a larger issue in the industrial discourse more generally: the tendency to represent the coverage of the Iranian protests as a story with only three primary actors: the beleaguered foreign press, the censorious Iranian regime, and the digital activists using social media to get around the regime's crackdown on the flow of information. This triad all but ignored the presence of professional Iranian journalists who were risking their lives to report from the streets of the city they called home.

For example, Barbara Palser of the *American Journalism Review* wrote in the late summer of 2009 that "the situation in Iran was a perfect setup for spotlighting the strengths of Twitter, Facebook and YouTube, particularly when the professional media are hobbled. . . . Amateur content took center stage" (Palser 2009b). This utopic celebration of social media made no mention of the professional Iranian journalists who also continued working, despite the government crackdown. In turn, *Broadcasting and Cable's* John Eggerton quoted U.S. President Barack Obama as proclaiming that "despite the Iranian government's efforts to expel journalists and isolate itself, powerful images and poignant words have made their way to us through cell phones and computers" (cited in Eggerton 2009). By using this quote, Eggerton celebrated the demonstrators' use of social media and aligned it with western interests. But again, there was little mention of the Iranian professionals who were doing similar work. Joe Strupp of *Editor and Publisher* asserted that "The post-Iran election protests in June also showed how both news outlets and citizens bypassed government shutdowns to get information out," linking citizen journalists and the foreign press together through their use of social media (Strupp 2009b). His article did not, however, draw any connections between professional Iranian journalists and professional western journalists, despite the fact that they been working together long before the 2009 uprising.

Strupp's linkage between foreign journalists and citizen journalists is interesting, considering the Anglophone news industry's somewhat paradoxical tendency to ambivalently question the value of citizen journalism during the first decade of the twenty-first century (Doyle 2009; Hinton 2009; Moffat 2009; Palser 2009b; Palmer 2012). Throughout this time, industry discourse had often portrayed citizen journalism in a rather negative light, likely because the Anglophone news industry was itself struggling to remain relevant (and fiscally solvent) in a digital age (Brown 2009; Haggerty 2009; Hewlett 2009; Palmer 2012; Palser 2009a; McKie 2009).). In order to grapple with this contradiction, Anglophone trade publications accentuated the censorship that foreign journalists especially faced in Iran in 2009, censorship that ostensibly necessitated the rise of the citizen journalist. This discourse made little mention of the Iranian journalists who also had to deal with an array of challenges. For instance, the U.K.'s *Press Gazette* mentioned the expulsion of the BBC's John Leyne ("Iranian Election 2009) and the brief arrest of the BBC's John Simpson ("Iranian Authorities" 2009), while Canada's *Ryerson Review of Journalism* discussed how members of the foreign press had been "confined to their hotel rooms" (Tang 2010). The implication was that since the "real professionals" could not work in this climate, brave citizens were using their smartphones to get the message out instead. Yet, this discourse ignored the bravery of the Iranian journalists who also faced the ire of the regime to get the message out.

If they were mentioned at all in the mainstream, English-language news discourse, Iranian journalists were typically given one or two lines in the article. They were also often lumped together with the bloggers and activists who were being persecuted by the government during the demonstrations ("Iran Elections" 2009; McNally 2009; Vaughan 2009). This odd maneuver suggests that Iranian journalists were not always viewed as being separate from the amateur media producers who also covered the protests of 2009, pointing to some of my interviewees' assertions that western journalists do not always view "local" journalists as true "professionals." What is more, Iranian journalists usually went unnamed in these reports. Bahari was the major exception, but he was always named in the context of his affiliation with *Newsweek*. There was no mention of reporters like Fathi who kept covering the protests even after the foreign press had receded. Judging from the discourse, one would never know how heavily the Anglophone press depended upon journalists like Fathi to cover the 2009 uprisings.

This suggests that the English-language news industry did not value the labor of some of its locally based employees as much as it valued its Anglo reporters and the citizen journalists who dominated the industrial discussion of the uprising. Fathi's precarious positioning did not significantly surface in the official U.S. news coverage of the Green Revolution. Fathi did a few short interviews with CNN during the uprisings, as well as with PBS, and she was listed as a writer or contributor for a number of *Times* stories on the demonstrations. Yet, unlike Bahari, Fathi's own experiences of danger were not woven into the news story itself. Fathi was not even mentioned by the Canadian newspapers that had taken such an interest in Bahari's arrest, until she arrived in Toronto after fleeing Iran. This omission of Fathi from the frame raises questions about which journalists are considered most valuable to the Anglophone news industry, and thus, most recognizable to power (Butler 2004, 2009).

The *Toronto Star* wrote one single story about Fathi's eventual exile to Canada, stating that she had silently been reporting from Toronto since she left Iran (Cohn 2009). Fathi was also allowed to write a story about her own experience for the *New York Times*, a story titled "The Exile's Eye" (2010). In that piece, Fathi explained how she received dual Canadian citizenship while working on her master's degree from 1999 to 2001 (ibid.). Central to this piece was Fathi's description of the emotional and existential precariousness of her situation, a precariousness that hit her as soon as she boarded the plane to leave Tehran: "More than anything, I feared falling into what Iranian journalists call 'the exile syndrome'—my understanding of Iran would be frozen in the moment of leaving, and I'd be unable to keep up with events on the ground" (ibid.). Thus, Fathi voiced a fear that is relevant to the broader experience of exile: losing her cultural connection to the country where she was born.

Yet, Fathi's article did describe one strategy that helped her to combat this "exile syndrome"—her strategic social media practices, which helped to keep her abreast of events in Iran:

> For me, that was like a new dawn: rather than being cut off, I had made contact with another Iran—a virtual one on the Internet, linking reformers abroad to bloggers and demonstrators still inside the country, and to reporters and sources outside. In fact, by following blogs and the cellphone videos seeping out of Iran, in some ways I could report more productively than when I had to fear and outwit the government. (ibid.)

Through her use of social media, Fathi was able to stay connected to the country with which she deeply identified. It could be argued, then, that while Bahari's use of social media revealed the larger social constraints that can limit the exilic subject's navigation of mediated landscapes (Naficy 1999), Fathi's use of social media pointed to the "intriguing possibilities for liberatory diasporic . . . practices" (ibid., 4).

Despite this potential, Fathi also ran up against the larger social constraints that limit the exilic subject's navigation of mediated landscapes, social constraints that shape and inhibit even the most utopic of technological practices. Fathi told me that once she arrived in Toronto, the *New York*

Times eventually tried to relieve her of her services (pers. comm., July 2015). Fathi said she was able to stay on board and cover Iran from Toronto—for about a year. Once the *Times* got a new foreign editor, Fathi says that the publication told her that her services were no longer required because the *New York Times* did not want Iranian coverage from a person based outside of Iran (pers. comm., July 2015). When I asked Fathi's former editor about this claim, she said that Fathi had continued to work with the *Times* for at least a year after she left Iran, "offering knowledge and analysis, all of which was invaluable" (Chira, pers. comm., November 2016). But after some time had passed, it became difficult for the *Times* to find a place for Fathi: "At that point, from my perspective, she was going in a new direction. . . . Her job was to cover Iran for us. You can't cover Iran indefinitely from outside of Iran" (ibid.). Chira could not remember whether Fathi had simply been terminated or whether the decision had been more complicated. Another editor who worked with Fathi said that he also could not recall the details, though he did say that "the preference in enlisting a stringer or contract writer to cover a place abroad is to engage someone who is in fact living in the country" (anonymous, pers. comm., November 2016).

Chira told me that she was aware of the risks that Fathi faced in her work, and how challenging it must have been to reinvent her life after fleeing Iran. "It's an existential crisis when you leave your country and the job you had didn't exist in the same way" (Chira, pers. comm., November 2016). Speaking a few years after these events, Fathi put her own feelings in no uncertain terms: "It was more than a job. It was a life, you know? Me, my husband, we'd lost the life that we had built in Iran because of the job that I did for the *New York Times*" (pers. comm., July 2015). In her memoir, Fathi describes how her children started learning English within a week of arriving in Canada. She also describes the nightmares that followed her journey from Iran:

> I dreamed again and again that I was back in our apartment in Tehran, scrambling to find something precious to take with me. But before I could find anything, the government forces began banging on the door. I would wake up sweating and breathless, and ask myself why I would even consider going back. But I knew the answer: I had left part of me behind without saying good-bye. (2014)

In this passage, Fathi expresses the deep emotional strain that her sudden departure from Iran inspired. Forced to live in a new nation, but also forced to keep looking back to the nation with which she felt she had unfinished business, she had truly inherited the "exile's eye"—a way of seeing the world in pieces that are difficult to put back together again. While Edward Said has famously argued that exile causes one to see "the entire world as a foreign land," which makes possible "an originality of vision" (2000, 148), Fathi's case shows that this vision is no less painful or fragmented for the person who experiences it.

Luckily, it was Fathi's memoir that at least partially helped her to make sense of everything that had happened and to move forward: "I decided to reinvent myself. I wrote the book, partly because it was very self-therapeutic, and partly because I thought it would help me start building a career here, or in the States" (pers. comm., July 2015). Through the use of her journalistic craft, Fathi was able to write her own narrative, one that could help her work through the emotional and cultural strain of her exile from Iran. She was also able to produce a new body of work that could help her to continue making a living as a writer in North America. Despite the fact that so few Anglophone news outlets had included Fathi and her Iranian colleagues in their narrative of Iran, Fathi wrote her own version of the story. Her memoir was both the story of Iran, and the story of Fathi herself.

Conclusion

Trinh argues that "exile, despite its profound sadness, can be worked through as an experience of crossing boundaries and charting new ground in defiance of newly authorized or old canonical enclosures" (1994, 16). Both Fathi and Bahari have "crossed boundaries" and "charted new ground," since they have spent their post-Iran years publicly interrogating Iran's contentious relationship with democracy while still touting the beauty of Iran's culture and its people. Yet, both Trinh and Said argue that exile is a collective, rather than a simply individual experience, and it is an experience that exceeds language. Rather than stopping at a celebration of the literature of exile, we must understand the social and political aspects of this phenomenon (Trinh 1994; Said 2000), aspects that only seem to be intensifying in the twenty-first century.

While Fathi and Bahari have both contributed to a more cautious and nuanced discourse on the experiences of the "local" journalists who face the threat of exile because they work with Anglophone news organizations, there is still much to be addressed on this issue. As my interviewees asserted, the English-language news industry has long devalued the labor and the safety of its locally based reporters. Though Anglophone journalists and editors began to discuss the safety of war reporters more often as the first decade of the twenty-first century wore on, this attention to safety was (and still is) geared more toward the protection of Anglo staff reporters, rather than the protection of the reductively termed "native" journalists who can ostensibly take care of themselves. The industrial tendency to overlook the safety of journalists like Fathi points to the insidious ways in which the logic of precarity bleeds into the production cultures of war reporting, rather than simply surfacing within the news coverage. If white, western journalists are more worthy of receiving both proactive and reactive assistance with safety, then it appears that the mainstream, English-language war reporting industry does not ethically recognize the value—indeed, the humanity—of its locally based employees.

Chapter Three has also suggested that there is a need for a more careful consideration of the ways in which the experiences of journalists like Bahari and Fathi are (or are not) narrativized by Anglophone news organizations. In Bahari's case, news outlets represented his incident through the use of a melodramatic narrative that emphasized his western identity while subtly jettisoning his Iranian identity—despite the fact that Bahari's Iranian heritage had helped *Newsweek* to garner a wealth of rich news coverage. In Fathi's case, Anglophone organizations barely narrativized her story at all. Fathi's experiences were left outside the frame, until she told her own story. This story ambivalently grappled with Fathi's western affiliations, as well as with her Iranian heritage. She wrote this story partly to heal, but also because she hoped it would help her get more work in the English-language news industry that continues to show a marked ambivalence toward its nonwestern news employees.

There is another identificatory issue that inspires deep ambivalence in the English-language news industry, and this is an issue with which Fathi herself has long been acquainted: the attitude toward gender and sexuality in the conflict reporting business. The next chapter of this book examines gender and sexuality in the profession of war correspondence, focusing specifically on the 2011 sexual assault of CBS correspondent Lara Logan. Since she was covering the Egyptian uprisings in Tahrir Square when the assault occurred, Logan's incident swiftly became linked to large discussions about the alleged "hypermasculinity" and "predatory" nature of Egyptian men. This was a dubious discourse that entangled itself within the conversation on how to deal with gendered dangers in the conflict zone. Not only did Logan's assault raise questions about the treatment of (mostly white) female war reporters; it also raised troubling questions about the intersection of gender, race, and ethnicity in the professional practice of conflict correspondence.

4

The "Intimate Threat"

Lara Logan's 2011
Sexual Assault in Egypt

"[With rape], the physical wounds heal. You don't carry
around the evidence the way you would if you had lost
your leg or your arm in Afghanistan."

—Lara Logan

On February 11, 2011, CBS conflict correspondent Lara Logan was sexually assaulted in Cairo's Tahrir Square, hours after President Hosni Mubarak had resigned ("CBS News' Lara Logan Assaulted" 2011).[1] Logan had arrived in Egypt that day, unlike many other journalists who had been deployed to Cairo at the beginning of the 2011 protests that successfully ousted the U.S.-supported Mubarak. After reporting from Tahrir Square for a few hours, Logan was swept into what an official CBS statement later identified as "a dangerous element amidst the celebration," "a mob of more than 200 whipped into a frenzy" (ibid.). According to the CBS statement, this "mob" beat and sexually assaulted Logan, before a group of Egyptian women and some Egyptian soldiers eventually rescued her.

Once CBS released its statement, news organizations, social media sites, and industry trade publications quickly began to talk about Logan's experience, in some cases subtly implying that Egyptian protesters had assaulted Logan; yet, many other professional (and citizen) journalists were also attacked in Tahrir Square, and in these cases, even U.S. news outlets more overtly blamed plainclothes regime police, rather than the crowd (Amar 2011). Competing representations of this event flooded the internet. Some commentators blamed Logan herself for the sexual assault she had suffered, invoking her long-standing reputation as a "War Reporter Barbie" (Dimiero 2011; Lalami 2011; Mirkinson 2011). Some commentators instead blamed the people of Egypt, invoking Islamaphobic stereotypes in a way that situated Logan as a passive, feminine victim of a predatory (and racialized) masculinity (Schlussel 2011).

Meanwhile, a number of female journalists stepped forward and asserted that sexual assault is a danger that women especially—not exclusively, but especially—face in this line of work, turning Logan's experience into a platform for debate about the safety of female conflict correspondents (Barrett 2011; Ricchiardi 2011). Whatever people said, one thing seemed evident: CBS's official statement on Logan's assault had not successfully served as the authoritative frame through which to understand what had happened. In the age of Web 2.0, accounts of Logan's experience were circulating out of CBS's control, careening across multiple media platforms. A few months later, Logan appeared on the network's famous program, *60 Minutes*, in what appeared to be an effort at regaining control of her own very intimate narrative.

Chapter Four explores Logan's assault in Cairo and her subsequent interview with *60 Minutes*. I first give a brief overview of the historical gendering of conflict correspondence in the Anglophone news industry, showing that the idealized model of conflict correspondence envisions an implicitly masculinized subject who can freely transcend and traverse the site of conflict in order to harmoniously communicate with a larger network of distant studios and audiences. Not even male correspondents can easily live up to this ideal when reporting from the space of the conflict zone. Yet, the female correspondent troubles this ideal even further, as the role of the mobile and "transcendent" subject has so often been denied women who have historically been sexualized, commodified, or relegated to a static, reproductive role (Massey 1994). Thus, female war reporters operate within a professional culture that perpetually contradicts itself where gender is concerned.

I next examine Logan's own gendering throughout the first decade of the twenty-first century, tracing the ways in which she had been cast in the sometimes-conflicting roles of "sexual object" and "self-sufficient employee" even before her incident in Cairo. Once Logan was assaulted, her *60 Minutes* interview focused more on representing her as a maternal figure, in a melodramatic effort at simultaneously portraying her as a feminized victim, objectified and contaminated by a racialized "other," *and* as a self-sufficient news employee who was personally responsible for her own well-being in the field. Though Logan's incident did raise awareness about the danger of sexual assault in the conflict zone, her interview with *60 Minutes* propagated a melodramatic narrative of white womanhood that obscured the experiences of nonwhite women (and the Egyptian protesters more generally) from the frame.

Gender in Anglophone Conflict Correspondence

Female journalists have been covering wars for over 100 years. Margaret Fuller covered the Italian patriot movement for the *New York Herald Tribune* as early as 1847, for example (Hamilton 2011). In the early twentieth century, correspondents like Peggy Hull gained the admiration of U.S. military officials in the first World War "by marching where the troops marched, sleeping on the ground in a poncho, and yet keeping her blond, brown-eyed femininity" (Knightley 2004, 135). During the Spanish Civil War of the 1930s, "accounts written by women were often given considerable prominence in national newspapers, despite the lack of seniority of their authors" (Deacon 2008, 69). World War II was covered by the likes of Gwen Dew, who saw herself as being "indebted to the State Department for permission to return to the Far East as an accredited correspondent at a time when this was almost an impossibility for a woman" (1943, vi). And Dickey Chapelle, a female photojournalist from Wisconsin, is perhaps just as famous for the photograph of her death in the Vietnam war zone as she is for the pictures she captured throughout her career.

Female war reporters have been around for at least a century, but the industrial discourse addressing their work—and their mere existence—has been riven with contradiction. In the first half of the twentieth century, female conflict correspondents faced the constant distrust of their colleagues, but they also found that editors might emphasize their gender in order to lure more readers (Deacon 2008). Though the commodification of the female war reporter has a history of its own, history has more typically viewed war reporting as a staunchly "masculine" profession. Military officials, news editors, and male correspondents fought to keep women out of the war zone during the World Wars (Chambers, Steiner, and Fleming 2004), while the English-language news industry more generally represented its war correspondents as manly figures who sexually *desired* women, or who expected women to wait for them at home (McLaughlin 2002; Hamilton 2011). For instance, Frederick T. Birchall, who worked for the *New York Times* during the first half of the twentieth century, once reportedly said that "foreign correspondents should be eunuchs," after crashing his car because he was engaging in sexual foreplay with a woman seated next to him (cited in Hamilton 2011). Decades later, John Burrowes dedicated his 1984 memoir "to reporters everywhere—and the women who have to suffer them" (cited in McLaughlin 2002, 20). In this type of discourse, women were represented strictly in relation to their feminine "difference," cast as either passive objects or unruly sexual deviants who contributed to the chaos of the conflict zone. Conversely, men were represented as active agents, more capable than women of traversing the spaces of war.

When the news industry addressed the women who worked as war reporters, the discourse focused on questions of marriage and family, or on questions of traditional gender performance. For instance, a colleague of *New York Post* correspondent Dorothy Thompson said that she "was Richard Harding Davis in an evening gown" (cited in Hamilton 2011), accentuating the incongruity of a war reporter wearing a dress. On the subject of marriage, *New York Herald Tribune* correspondent Marguerite Higgins felt compelled to tell her friends that she did not plan to marry "until I find a man who's as exciting as war," (cited in Knightley 2004, 369) while Martha Gellhorn's failed marriage to Ernest Hemingway haunted her work at every turn (Deacon 2008). Gellhorn eventually banned her friends from discussing the marriage at all, a request they did not always observe (Buford 1978). Female correspondents were walking contradictions, in other words, and the industrial discourse of the twentieth century struggled to resolve the accepted notion of female passivity with the notion of the active, "masculine" war correspondent.

As the twentieth century progressed, these circumstances did not drastically improve. Former freelance reporter Janet Key told me of the challenges she faced in her career as a female war journalist: An editor at UPI told her that he would send a woman abroad "when hell freezes over," and the *Cincinnati Enquirer* suggested that she be their "gardening reporter" (pers. comm., April 2013). Key finally got her start as a war correspondent after spending days in the *New York Times*'s morgue files, researching everything the paper had ever published about Northern Ireland. Because she was able to impress a *Times* editor with her expansive background knowledge on the topic, he sent her to cover the conflict unfolding in Belfast in the late 1960s and early 1970s (ibid.). This didn't stop her bureau chiefs from complaining that the *Times* had sent a woman to work with them (ibid.).

During the Lebanese Civil War in the 1980s, then-freelancer Liz Sly continually overheard male reporters mocking even the well-established women in their profession. "The climate was so sexist then, and a young female freelancer like me was somebody to be hit on, but not somebody to be taken seriously," Sly told me in an interview (pers. comm., June 2015). One reporter offered to help Sly edit a story she was writing, but when she arrived at his hotel room for their meeting, he was naked and expecting sex. Sly ran from the room and found someone else to help her. She then became more cynical, learning how to get by on her own and prove that she could do the same work that men could do—despite male correspondents' tendency to think of women as sexual objects (ibid.).

Some of my interviewees have noted that this paradoxical understanding of women in war reporting continued to pervade the conflict reporting industry in the early years of the twenty-first century. For instance, freelance reporter Sulome Anderson described how a male correspondent once commented on her "nice rack" (pers. comm., June 2015). Another male correspondent infantilized her, accusing her of playing at "war reporter" so she could feel closer to her father—the Terry Anderson who was kidnapped during the Lebanese Civil War (ibid.). Both of these experiences reveal the contradictory attitudes toward women reporting in the war zone: one suggests that these women are there for the male correspondents' sexual pleasure, while the other implies that women are too different—too weak, too childlike—to work as war journalists.

Similarly, freelancer Jessica Dheere described her work covering the 2006 July War in Lebanon, suggesting that she struggled to "erase the notion of that foreign correspondent that we all have in our heads . . . the man, it's always the man" (pers. comm., June 2015). This masculinist image of war correspondence deeply affects the younger correspondents who are first starting out:

> There are too many idiots who show up in Syria wanting to be war correspondents . . . that kind of "bro" mentality. You know, like this "dude bro" in a war zone. . . . It's kind of like this dick-swinging mentality, like: "I just got shot at this many times, and I went to Syria, and I went here and there and got shot." (Anderson, pers. comm., June 2015)

The key to this gendered performance is that the war reporter lives to tell the story—ultimately transcending the "chaotic" space of war so that "he" can brag about his survival later on. Yet, as Anderson and many of my other interviewees noted, war is not easy to survive. Still, war correspondents feel the urge to demonstrate their ability to do so, and this urge is distinctly gendered.

BBC reporter Caroline Wyatt commented upon such dangerous idealism:

> "I suspect that sometimes there is an element of needing to prove yourself as a man. Sometimes, I think that can come across on camera. . . . Programs want their guy showing what kind of danger he's in on the frontline with bullets running past him. (pers. comm., May 2013)

Wyatt's assertion points to the ways in which the traditional ideal of the intrepid male war reporter, dodging bullets and living to tell about it, is still so embraced by news editors that it haunts real journalists in the field, making them take serious risks in order to live up to the masculinist image. Her statement also illuminates the economic imperatives attached to the gendered performances in which war reporters engage. From Wyatt's perspective, television news editors especially prefer to place their correspondents in danger, showing their audiences salacious footage that suggests the melodramatic manliness of the reporters in the field.

Despite this ideal, Wyatt suggests that male correspondents constantly struggle to live up to the myth. Freelancer Josh Wood suggested that this idealized model resonates with men at a young age: "You're 22 and you're hyped up on testosterone and [you] want to go see war and all that stuff. . . . Being a young man, I think there's a certain war gene" (pers. comm. June 2015). Correspondent and documentarian Sebastian Junger also voiced this problem, remarking that he intentionally chose to start reporting from the conflict zone, because up until that point, "I didn't feel like a man" (pers. comm., February 2013). As someone who had grown up in a privileged suburb, Junger conflated war reporting with masculinity, certain that in successfully facing "the adversity that . . . any young man needs to face [in order] to be fully formed," he would finally embody true "manhood." Yet, later in Afghanistan, Junger experienced the difficulties of the conflict zone in a way that the dauntless war hero is not supposed to mention: "It's a physically intimidating environment, and I got an unbelievably severe case of dysentery, and I was extremely sick. Quite a bit of the assignment I did while running a really high fever."

Each of these stories points to the fact that the "mobility" and "agency" of the implicitly masculine war correspondent has been a difficult performance for *all* correspondents to pursue, not just for women. Former BBC correspondent and current psychotherapist Mark Brayne argues that the problem is more systemic than individualized: the war reporting culture "has to be a macho culture, it has to be a tough, 'let's get the story done' culture" (pers. comm., February 2013). Brayne told me that this drive toward "getting the job done" is a psychological coping strategy and a professional survival technique; yet, this strategy can also make it very difficult for correspondents to seek help when they find themselves affected by the spaces in which they work (ibid.). "Macho culture" demands that correspondents continue to place themselves at risk to "get the job done," and, as my interviewees suggested, to do so in a way that trivializes or ignores the particular perils of the job.

This "macho culture" stands in stark tension with the growing "safety culture" of the news industry. Indeed, one of the perils that correspondents face in the field is the risk of sexual assault, a threat that haunts male journalists as well as female journalists (Wolfe 2011). As recently as the first decade of the twenty-first century, the burgeoning "safety culture" of the news industry did not significantly address the gendered and sexualized elements of the risks that war reporters face. As the response to the 2011 Logan incident revealed, female correspondents have traditionally kept silent on the issue of sexual harassment or assault in the field for fear that their so-called "personal" issues would make them seem less objective and self-sufficient to their male bosses and colleagues (Matloff, cited in Barrett 2011, Brodbeck 2011; Ricchiardi 2011). A number of my female interviewees, as well as correspondents interviewed in the industry trade articles expressed this fear, and many of them were also quick to assert that sexual assault does not happen very often since women are no more vulnerable in the field than men.

For example, one camera woman who works for a major news network told me that she disapproved of Logan's *60 Minutes* interview because it might cause people to think that all women correspondents have experienced this trauma (pers. comm., December 2012). Freelancer Holly Pickett declared that both male and female correspondents face the same safety issues, and the goal is to deal with these issues in a calm and knowledgeable way (pers. comm., July 2013). And in an article published in the *Ryerson Review of Journalism*, correspondent Stephanie Nolen asserted: "I think it's really dangerous to frame this as a conversation about the vulnerability of women in this job, when I don't think women are any more vulnerable than men" (cited in Remy 2012). In each of these cases, the female correspondent downplayed the idea of a uniquely "feminine" vulnerability that might cause their editors to remove them from conflict zones in which women journalists have long fought to be taken seriously.

As part of this struggle, twenty-first century female correspondents have operated in a contradictory professional culture that sometimes commodifies their feminine "difference," while at other times demanding that they act as if they are no different than men—even when it means remaining silent about sexual harassment and assault. The imperatives of this "macho culture" have in turn normalized the studied obfuscation of particularly gendered and sexualized experiences from industrial discourse—experiences that affect both men and women. The Committee to Protect Journalists had not conducted any significant research on the issue of sexual assault in the field until after Logan was attacked in Egypt (Simon, pers. comm., April 2015), for example, and at that time, there were reportedly very few segments on sexual assault in the vast majority of the hazardous environment courses offered to war correspondents (Remy 2012). Even after Logan was assaulted, the writers at the *American Journalism Review* called the executives at a number of news organizations, asking them what they planned to do to address the issue of sexual assault in the future: none of them had an answer (Ricchiardi 2011). This points to the systemic problem that war reporters especially faced in the early twenty-first century, one in which their own profession could not conceptualize the intimate threats they encountered.

Instead, Logan's assault inspired a proliferation of discourse on the steps that specifically female reporters should personally take to avoid sexual assault in the conflict zone. At first glance, this appeared to be a major step forward for the mainstream, Anglophone news industry's "safety culture." After all, people were finally talking about the danger of rape in war reporting, a subject which, up until 2011, had still been largely taboo. Even so, there were some problems. While this discourse did finally bring the question of sexual assault to the forefront of journalistic discussion, it also coded that threat as an obstacle that female correspondents must overcome on their own, without any significant change in industrial policy. The responsibility for avoiding sexual assault was swiftly offloaded onto the correspondents themselves, suggesting that these individuals were also somehow to blame for their own sexual attacks. Not only did this trend point to preemptive "victim blaming" on the part of the news industry; it also distracted industry commentators from pushing for deep structural changes in industry security policies, instead demanding that female correspondents do what they always claimed they could do to begin with: take care of themselves.

Female war correspondents were encouraged to display the same self-sufficiency and agency that was expected of their male counterparts, even as the no longer taboo discussion of rape coded them as being more "vulnerable" than men. For example, news commentators embraced the notion of female self-defense courses, while former war correspondent and current academic Judith Matloff published a list of "do's" and "don'ts" for female war reporters in the field (2011). She recommended:

- Wear a wedding ring, or a band that looks like one.
- Travel with a male companion.
- Dress like a frump . . . (slows down attackers).

This sampling of pointers on how to "minimize the risk of sexual assault" reveals the paradoxical experiences of women trying to work within the confines of the industry's "macho culture" in the first years of the twenty-first century. The advice to wear a wedding ring suggested that as long as female correspondents appeared as though they were someone else's property, they could avoid being assaulted. If these female reporters eschewed traditional "western" gender performance as well—by "dressing like a frump"—they could then stave off an attack that would happen more quickly if they were dressed in the sexualized clothing that might admittedly get them more airtime in the world of corporate, Anglophone television news. Of course, making the choice to dress like a frump would bolster the idea that female war reporters were "asking for it" when they got raped, because their sexual vulnerability was also a problem of sexual desirability (for which they, and not the men they encountered, were supposedly responsible). In turn, if they "travel[ed] with a male companion," they would likely be safer, according to Matloff. But that choice would also suggest that they could not be self-sufficient—anathema to the war correspondents working in the neoliberal age.

Logan serves as a central example of this contradictory conceptualization of the female war correspondent in mainstream Anglophone war reporting. Before her assault in Tahrir Square, Logan was often described as *both* a successful inhabitant of macho culture—possessing skill, mobility, and agency—*and* as a sexualized woman intruding in a masculine space. As I will show, the industrial emphasis on Logan's femininity in the first decade of the twenty-first century was also tied to her commodification. The figure of a woman in a war zone continued to ambivalently fascinate editors as it had during the Spanish Civil War (Deacon 2008), eventually leading news commentators to pronounce Logan a "global celebrity" (Torregrosa 2015). Yet, central to Logan's persona was the notion of her feminine difference, the mark of "otherness" that she could never quite evade.

Barbie Goes to War

Even before her sexual assault in Egypt, Logan was famous for her work in the most dangerous of conflict zones. She was a highly visible news correspondent, primarily because of her coverage of the conflicts in Afghanistan and Iraq. Yet, before her attack, industry commentators constantly made reference to Logan's physical beauty. Shortly after she became CBS's chief foreign correspondent, a media analyst for *Newsweek* emphasized the purported difficulty "for an attractive blonde woman to earn her news chops" (Meadows 2006, 82). According to *Newsweek*, the soldiers Logan shadowed "constantly tease[ed] her because her backpack [was] weighed down with beauty supplies," pointing to the overt feminization of Logan at the hands of popular commentators (ibid.).

Industry trade articles also referenced Logan's consumption of beauty products in the field, juxtaposing her supposedly excessive consumerism with her professional experience: "I know it sounds like Barbie goes to war," Logan herself is quoted as saying, "But I don't care. At this stage, after all the work I've done, that's really what you're saying? Come on. I'm not a pretender" (cited in Guthrie 2009). In a similarly paradoxical fashion, Logan's boss Sean McManus once said that history would remember Logan for her hard work in dangerous places (cited in Guthrie 2008). At the same time, the CBS executive also tended to remark upon Logan's "star value," marveling that "some people just jump off the screen" (cited in Steinberg 2005). This reference to Logan's "star value" points to her feminized commodification, which sat uneasily alongside Logan's effort at acting as a transcendent subject, actively navigating the conflict zone.

Entangled within such commodification was Logan's sexualization: references to her blonde hair, her attractive face, and her swimsuit model body (Steinberg 2005; Greppi 2007; Guthrie 2008). This sexualization was especially exacerbated after Logan was involved in a widely publicized sex scandal. In 2008, tabloids reported that Logan had started seeing a defense contractor working in Iraq and that he was married to someone else (Barrett 2008). CNN's Howard Kurtz discussed the "news" on a few different episodes of his show, *Reliable Sources*, while the tabloid headlines spoke of steamy love triangles (ibid.1). In these cases, Logan was constructed as a duplicitous femme fatale, hungrily consuming married men and lacking perspective on her own personal choices.

Perhaps for this reason, Logan's boss McManus took it upon himself to issue a statement on Logan's behalf, reminding the public that, "in 15 years, Logan is going to be judged on the quality of her work, not her personal life" (cited in Guthrie 2008). McManus's remark invoked another, contradictory tendency in the industry discourse on Logan, which represented Logan as an experienced reporter who had long been traveling to war zones and asking tough questions of powerful military men. Where one commentator might talk about Logan's attractiveness, for example, another might mention her award-winning coverage and her skill for always getting the story—and some industry pundits did both in the same breath (Higgins 2005; Steinberg 2005). Because of this, McManus attempted to harness both strands of discourse and keep them under control.

Yet, McManus's statement also points to something else: CBS's willingness to appropriate Logan's notoriety, however negative. This makes sense, considering the fact that CBS had long been suffering from poor ratings, with Logan's career being deployed as a key strategy for rebranding what was increasingly seen as a news network for the elderly (McClintock 2003; Offman 2003; Learmonth 2006). Following this, alongside McManus's assertion that the public should focus on Logan's hard work, he also remarked: "It's a fact of life when you have a public job, your personal life is covered," implying that Logan's "personal" life was actually a part of her job, rather than separate from it. This view led to McManus's celebration of Logan's "star value," her status as a hot commodity as well as a voracious consumer of lipsticks and men. Rather than directly censoring Logan, her CBS boss instead harnessed her mystique, capitalizing on her "feminine" qualities while also expecting that she navigate the spaces of conflict with the tirelessness of any male correspondent.

These contradictory roles were especially illuminated when it came to light that Logan would be having a baby with the man she had supposedly "stolen" ("Lara Logan Pregnant" 2008). As journalist Yvonne Ridley has noted: "Male journalists never get stopped in the war zone or an area of conflict and asked, 'What are you doing here? What about your children at home?'" (Ridley 2003). Ridley's assertion points to the problematic double standard that female correspondents experience, where they must engage in implicitly "masculine" and "feminine" gender performances simultaneously. Such tension underscores much of the discourse around Logan's mobility before her attack in Cairo. For example, in a 2010 interview on her trip to Afghanistan, Logan described a shootout in which she ran for cover: "You know, usually, I would have run for the cameraman, but once you have two little babies at home, you have a different perspective on things" (Silvio 2010).

With this statement, Logan performed the traditional role of mother even as she told the story of endangering her maternal body by inhabiting the traditionally "masculine" space of war. She resolved this tension by drawing upon the more contemporary figure of the "working mother"—one who has procreated according to traditional norms, but who also acts as a self-sufficient and hardworking member of society. Logan's performance of the "working mother" motif attempted to diffuse any potential negativity directed at her, since it suggested that she was a dedicated, responsible worker, but also a conscientious mother. Still, the very fact of having to run for cover from bullets reminded the public that Logan's particular career involved the precarious labor of traversing a conflict zone, a space in which her body and her life would always be in danger.

This contradictory performance highlights the collision between more traditional gender roles and the intensifying expectations for conflict correspondents in the first decade of the twenty-first century. At this unstable time, celebrities like Logan were expected to shoulder all of the responsibility for themselves and their networks in an increasingly unpredictable environment.

During this decade, when news bureaus had closed around the world, celebrity reporters acted as the branding faces of their news outlets, linking their news studios to the conflict zones that they could no longer cover on a regular basis. Such a phenomenon underscored the assertion in *Broadcasting and Cable* that news networks depended upon "their warzone reporters to keep the war from getting relegated to the back burner," (Guthrie 2008) as if there were not an entire staff of news researchers and supervising producers, constantly deciding what did and did not appear on the air. This phenomenon also led to CBS executive Paul Friedman's complaint that CBS's war coverage faltered at one point simply because of Logan's pregnancy (cited in ibid.). Rather than examining the increasingly impoverished strategies for reporting war in an era when conflict was fluid, digitized, and seemingly without end, CBS executives made Logan bear that entire burden along profoundly gendered lines.

Logan had long been discussed as someone who took full responsibility for the news product, her "relentless knack for gaining access to dangerous places" (Steinberg 2005) allowing her to "go into any warzone, no matter how dangerous" and always "come . . . out with a story" (Fager cited in Higgins 2005). This celebration of individual responsibility, so typical of the neoliberal age, has been mentioned by some of Logan's colleagues as an important element of her celebrity persona—part of what gave her access to the "boys' club" of professional conflict reporting (Wood, pers. comm., February 2013; Hilsum, pers. comm., May 2013). Yet, when Logan was sexually assaulted in Tahrir Square, CBS began to portray her in a rather different light: as the feminized victim of a racialized and "predatory" environment. This melodramatic narrative attempted to obscure the industrial and political pressures that female war correspondents faced in the twenty-first-century conflict zone. It also served to cast suspicion on the political intentions of the activists and citizen journalists who helped to produce the space of Tahrir Square for a global public.

Logan in Tahrir Square

CBS's melodramatic representation of Logan's assault in Tahrir Square must be understood within the broader context of news outlets'—and especially U.S. television networks'—larger effort at covering the 2011 uprisings in Egypt. During these uprisings, the question of financial resources haunted U.S. television executives. They had famously been grappling with budget reductions, lower ratings, and foreign bureau closures throughout the twenty-first century. Thus, when writers at *Broadcasting and Cable* asked news executives how long they would maintain a presence in Egypt to cover the 2011 events, they all rather anxiously asserted that they would stay as long as the story demanded it, implying that the length of these particular events in Cairo would determine the length of their presence there (Grego 2011a, b).

As far as the news executives were concerned, the upside of covering the 2011 revolution was clear. CBS's McManus saw the coverage of Egypt as a way of rebranding CBS as an organization that cared about foreign news: "People talk a lot about the fact that networks don't cover foreign news as much as they should, and they're closing the bureaus . . . [but] if you look at the kind of coverage that all of us have done for the last week, to say that there isn't a commitment to foreign news or that the networks aren't in a position to cover it is just silly" (cited in Morabito 2011a). In turn, ABC, NBC, CBS, and CNN all remarked upon the pivotal role that Egypt was playing in building their network brands. CNN executive Tony Maddox noted an increase in his network's ratings during the Egyptian uprisings, and the network even saw an increase in the sale of mobile applications during that time (Morabito 2011b; Winslow 2011). Because of these potential opportunities, news executives felt that sending recognizable faces into Tahrir Square was decisively worth the investment.

As part of this effort at revitalizing what they perceived to be the decline of their networks before 2011, news executives vacillated between grand assertions of the importance of their correspondents' safety, and even loftier discussions of their correspondents' "natural" tendencies to put the story before their own well being. For example, during the Egyptian uprisings, McManus remarked:

> Listen, they are journalists and they are reporters, and they have this innate sense that they want and need to go to the heart of the story. And even if at the heart of the story there is obvious danger, so many of them will just rush in because they think that's what their job is, and quite frankly, it isn't even something that a lot of times they think about, it's just their instinct to go to where the story is. (cited in Morabito 2011a)

This assertion suggested that the Anglophone news industry's burgeoning safety culture had not made much headway by the time 2011 rolled around. Despite the explosion of discourse on journalistic safety in the conflict zone, major news executives were still conceptualizing their war correspondents as neoliberal individuals who were ultimately responsible for their own safety.

Repeatedly, news executives invoked the desires of their people on the ground in order to justify continued coverage of an event that was growing dangerous for the journalists. Toward the end of the 18-day uprisings, professional journalists came under attack by people whom they identified as plainclothes police or Mubarak supporters. CNN's Anderson Cooper was physically assaulted in the Square, and another team from Fox News ended up in the hospital. British editors also complained that their journalists were being censored and attacked. Though news outlets were fairly careful to make the distinction between the attackers and the anti-Mubarak demonstrators, they also drew upon their correspondents' physical endangerment in order to bolster the brand they were placing on their lucrative coverage of Egypt: for instance, after Cooper discussed his assault on the air, his CNN boss Maddox remarked that it was "a compelling piece of television" (cited in Morabito 2011b).

Besides drawing upon these "compelling" professional reports, people around the world could also learn about what was happening in Tahrir through the use of social media. In the short time between the Iranian Green Opposition of 2009 and the Egyptian revolution of 2011, the use of social media to report on international events had become even more of a norm. As ABC's Alexander Marquardt told me, it was common during the Egyptian revolution to begin one's day by scanning Twitter, in hopes of figuring out where reporters would most be needed (pers. comm., January 2013). By this point, reporters were also expected to maintain a robust presence on Twitter and other social media sites, so that their voices could directly compete with the voices of the Egyptian protesters who were telling their own stories. Anglophone news reports brought protesters' tweets directly into their newscasts and drew heavily upon their own reporters' presence online as well.

Yet, as the CBC's Susan Ormiston told me, it could be exhausting and even perilous to try to inhabit the digital space of protest and the material space of Tahrir Square simultaneously: "Your head's down, you're trying to get your thumbs on those keys, and the mob is closing in. It's very dangerous" (pers. comm., May 2013). Ormiston noted the dissonance between the correspondents in Tahrir Square and editors back at headquarters, who had no concrete sense of the threats their correspondents faced as they navigated the protests. Remarking on this precariousness, many of my interviewees stopped short of criticizing their editors and instead blamed the "crowd" in Tahrir Square. These correspondents displayed a marked ambivalence toward the "crowd," an ambivalence that also surfaced in the industry trade discourse. On the one hand, the "crowd" was a term used to reference the demonstrators who opposed Mubarak and demanded that he resign. On the other hand, the "crowd" also referred to plainclothes police, pro-Mubarak thugs, and the miscellaneous "criminals" accused of mysteriously infiltrating the demonstrations. Sometimes the correspondents or trade articles would make the distinction between the two, and other times they would not. In this sense, both the activists and the regime police were sometimes conflated into one monolithic mass of unpredictable and threatening people. This discourse often drew upon the "Arab street" metaphor, which Terry Regier and Muhammad ali Khalidi identify as an overwhelmingly negative trope that "constructs Arab public opinion in a stereotypical, inaccurate, and pejorative fashion" (ibid., 11). Consequently, Paul Amar argues that this negative metaphor informed many U.S. news portrayals of Tahrir Square, represented as "a space constantly bursting with predatory sexuality and not disciplined enough to articulate either coherent leadership or policy" (2011, 301). Amar asserts that this degrading term haunted western portrayals of Tahrir Square even before Logan's assault. He explains that the earlier physical attack on CNN's Anderson Cooper drew upon the "Arab street" trope, though still temporarily shifting the focus to the possibility of plainclothes regime police attacking journalists instead of protesters (ibid.). Yet, Amar asserts that Logan's assault brought the "Arab street" metaphor back into plain view and—at least temporarily—resolved some of the ambivalence in U.S. reporting on Egypt:

> Media reports did not consider that the harassers could have been plainclothes paramilitaries or subcontracted thugs sent by State Security. . . . The predatory culture of Muslim men became the talking point. No reporters followed up on the fact that Logan had been rescued by a group of Egyptian young women political activists and twenty male military officers. Were these subjects not also representative of Egypt, "Muslim culture," and the revolution? (2011, 301)

This degrading portrayal of the men in Tahrir Square hinged upon the related portrayal of Logan as a "vulnerable" maternal figure who had been enveloped by the alleged hypermasculinity of the "Arab street." Such a representation not only points to the decisively racist attitudes toward Egyptian men in U.S. news coverage of Tahrir; it also illuminates the fact that female correspondents constantly negotiate the contradictory representations of their labor and their persons more generally.

Such contradictions surfaced in CBS's April 2011 interview with Logan ("Lara Logan Breaks Her Silence" 2011). Most of the Anglophone trade publications had reported on Logan's assault, typically referring to her hard work as a star correspondent in the field and shelving the earlier references to her days as a swimsuit model. When industry commentators did try to criticize Logan for carelessness in Tahrir—either for cultural insensitivity or for being a bad mother by even going to Egypt (Dimiero 2011; Lalami 2011; Mirkinson

2011)—the majority of industry pundits struck back with vehemence, citing Logan's experience in the field as reason enough for her journey to Cairo. Yet, Logan herself had not publicly addressed the incident until it was announced that she would do two interviews: one with the *New York Times* (Stelter 2011), and one on her own network's *60 Minutes* program ("Logan Breaks Silence" 2011). After this announcement, industry trade discourse largely celebrated Logan's decision to "speak out" about what had happened to her.

Logan certainly did not do all the talking in the *60 Minutes* interview that aired on her own news network. Instead, she often appeared in the video as an object of scrutiny, carefully contained within CBS's larger frame. The interview semiotically constructed Logan according to two logics: First, the video portrayed Logan as victim of a hypersexualized environment, whose maternal, white femininity had been "adulterated" by a racialized "other." This maneuver distracted from previous portrayals of Logan as a sexual object and an unruly consumer, casting her instead as an archetypical maternal figure. Rather than a naive Barbie or a femme fatale who was "asking for it," the *60 Minutes* interview constructed Logan as a mother whose (white) body had been violated.

Second, the CBS interview attempted to facilitate Logan's belated transcendence of the site of Tahrir Square, constructing her testimony as a moment in which she could take control of her own experience as a "free" and self-sufficient news employee. This was especially evident in the interview's rhetoric concerning the notion of "breaking the silence," where Logan was meant to individually speak out for other women in her industry. On both registers, CBS used Logan's testimony as a mechanism through which to obfuscate the industrial oversights that had long ignored the threat of sexual assault in the field. Instead, the *60 Minutes* interview blamed the supposedly violent "Egyptian male" for Logan's experience and rendered that figure as "other" to Logan, to CBS, and to CBS's public.

The *60 Minutes* segment opened with CBS anchor Scott Pelley sitting against a dark screen, a still photo of Logan's unsmiling face hovering in the background. Pelley addressed his audience, asserting that Logan was "an experienced reporter," but that the night of Mubarak's resignation "became her most hazardous assignment." The CBS anchor then explained that dozens of journalists had been attacked throughout the revolution, "often by agents of the regime." Yet, Pelley said that on the night of February 11, a "mob" turned on Logan and "singled her out in a violent sexual assault." Using these words, Pelley's opening monologue reflected the ambivalence that the Anglophone news industry had already displayed on the subject of

Figure 7. The opening shot of the CBS 60 Minutes interview with Lara Logan, posted on CBS's website on May 11, 2011.

violence in Tahrir Square, slipping from a discussion of Mubarak "thugs" to more generic discussions of "crowds" and now, "mobs." It may be arguable that Pelley meant his audience to understand the "mob" as a group of regime police; but if this was true, then why was the somber photo of Logan floating behind Pelley overlaid with images of smiling Egyptian demonstrators, celebrating Mubarak's fall? This visual rhetoric ran beneath Pelley's vague wording, revealing the slippage between "demonstrator" and "predator."

Pelley's initial reference to Logan's professional experience had an important function, as the *60 Minutes* video obsessed over Logan's status as "working mother," a phrase that almost operated as a paradox in this case. On the one hand, Pelley said that Logan had been recuperating from the attack with her husband and two small children. On the other hand, Pelley said that Logan was "returning to work," implying that she might once again end up in a conflict environment, endangering her maternal body. This tension was at least temporarily resolved when Pelley stated that Logan had "decided to tell the story of what happened—just once—here on our broadcast." Such a statement revealed that Logan's melodramatic testimony was part of her labor for CBS, and that she had personally decided to do this work. In other words, she had taken full responsibility for telling her story, even as that maneuver provided new material for CBS to broadcast. Thus, Logan embodied a paradoxical position, simultaneously cast as both the victim and the neoliberal hero of melodrama.

When Logan first appeared on-screen, she embodied the "self-sufficient" role, smilingly telling the story of how she and her team drove straight from the airport to Tahrir Square on the night of February 11. Video of Logan and her team running through heavy traffic rolled beneath Logan's voiceover: "I'm anxious to get to the Square, I've got to be there, because this is a moment in history that you don't want to miss." With this statement, Logan echoed a sentiment that many of my interviewees also expressed: the desire to be present at the site where history is perceived to be unfolding. Often, conflict correspondents voice this feeling as an explanation for why they do such dangerous work, revealing that the need to "be there," is part of the performance of individual passion and responsibility so integral to conflict reporters' production cultures. The professional reporter's physical presence at the pivotal event is also perceived to be an important part of navigating the site and harmoniously communicating with the correspondents' larger environment. Following this logic, the video soon showed Logan standing in the middle of the celebrating demonstrators, her voiceover asserting that "everyone's [being] very physical." The interview then cut back to Logan on camera, saying that this was "a real moment of celebration."

It is difficult to tell which parts of Logan's actual testimony were edited in the interview, since the video so often cut away from Logan in the studio and focused on images from February 11. Whatever the case, Logan's assertion that the celebrating protesters are "very physical" and her remark that this was "a real moment of celebration," revealed more of the same ambivalence toward the Egyptian demonstrators that Pelley displayed in the beginning. Though Logan appeared to be making an effort at recuperating the larger event at stake—the initial success of the 2011 revolution—the *60 Minutes* video was structured so that this statement became submerged within the melodramatic narrative. Logan's pronouncement that the celebrators were being "very physical" foreshadowed what was to come, and generated the conflation of the "physical" protesters and the "mob" that would soon assault her.

After reporting from the Square for about an hour, deploying a favorite U.S. narrative ("This is about freedom!")—Logan told Pelley that her team's camera battery began to die. This remark was supplemented with flickering video of Logan, still surrounded by people, telling her team that their local fixer—mentioned only by the name "Baha"—told her that he was nervous, and that they needed to leave the square. Pelley, on camera, asked Logan: "He's Egyptian, he speaks Arabic, and he understands what the crowd is saying?" Logan immediately responded: "I was told later they were saying, 'Let's take her pants off.'" Then Logan described the suddenness with which the "crowd" began assaulting her. There was no mention of the regime police that had targeted reporters throughout the revolution. Instead, Logan went from being immersed within a group of demonstrators to being attacked by a "mob," with no explanation of how this transition occurred.

Despite the fact that Logan's local fixer received only a brief mention, his presence in the *60 Minutes* interview illuminates a few important issues. First, though Logan had always been one of CBS's branding "faces," this "behind-the-scenes look" at the process of conflict reporting reveals that she was also compelled to rely on local news employees just to understand what the people around her were saying. In other words, CBS parachuted Logan into an Arabic-speaking country without requiring that she possess any familiarity with the language or the culture. This was an extremely dangerous oversight, because one of the conflict correspondents' primary safety tools is the ability to "read" the crowd. For instand, CNN's Hala Gorani and ABC's Lama Hasan were in Tahrir Square during the 2011 uprising, and both depended upon their knowledge of Arabic to navigate the shifting agendas of the various people they encountered there.

Yet, Logan could not "read" the crowd, instead relying on a local fixer to do this work for her. Many of my interviewees have stressed how common this is, especially in an industrial era when foreign bureaus—and their much more culturally savvy correspondents—have been disappearing. Though there are still some operational foreign bureaus, stocked with reporters who live in the country and understand the culture, they have increasingly closed in the years following the corporate conglomeration of media organizations. Because of this, parachute journalism has become the norm, and the fixer has become the necessary cultural interface between U.S. and British correspondents and the people on whom they report.

Even so, fixers rarely get acknowledged for their work. Some news organizations say that they leave the option of acknowledging the fixer's labor up to the correspondents themselves, while others cite vague policies in which the fixer can be credited only if he or she has "significantly" contributed to the story (Bossone 2014). Logan's fixer appeared in the *60 Minutes* video merely as a narrative feature, moving the story forward for CBS viewers. We never heard him speak, nor did we ever learn his full name. We only heard Logan and Pelley's own interpretation of his words, an interpretation that they used to bolster their portrayal of the "crowd." In this sense, Logan continued to operate as the branding "face" of CBS's coverage in Egypt, dubiously covering over the crucial labor of local media employees.

Virtually ignoring the valuable information that Logan's fixer could have provided, neither Logan nor Pelley explained why the attack happened so randomly. The only factor that Logan mentioned was the fact that her team's camera battery started to malfunction. Viewers were more dramatically reminded of this when Pelley narrated over the flickering video that now showed only the Square full of demonstrators, facing away from the camera. There was no way for viewers to know if this video was shot at the same moment in which Logan was assaulted, or if this was simply file footage of the protesters celebrating their victory. The *60 Minutes* video implied that the video was taken as the camera battery was dying, with Pelley's voiceover saying: "As she was pulled into the frenzy, the camera recorded her shout." Viewers then heard Logan's voice scream, "Stop!" before the video abruptly faded to black.

This was the decisive point in the *60 Minutes* interview when the construction of Logan as a "self-sufficient professional" was joined with the contradictory construction of Logan as a "victimized mother" figure. Crucially, viewers did not witness Logan's assault with their own eyes. Because of this simple technological failure in Tahrir Square, Logan could re-create the moment only through her testimony, simultaneously acting as speaking subject and victimized object in the process. The technological failure of Logan's camera was an important part of the media text, facilitating Logan's positioning as someone who was paradoxically speaking about her own silencing, about her

Figure 8. The black screen shown on CBS 60 Minutes to signify the moment the camera battery allegedly dies during Logan's reporting in Tahrir Square.

own objectification. Much of the rest of Logan's interview occurred within the space of the *60 Minutes* studio where Logan verbally re-created the assault on her own body for her viewers. She described how she screamed and screamed, thinking that this would cause her attackers to stop, or cause someone else to intervene: "And it was the opposite. The more I screamed, it turned them into a frenzy."

Oddly, at this moment, Pelley's voice narrated over Logan's own voice, though the video still showed the two of them sitting together in the studio: "Someone in the crowd shouted that she was an Israeli, a Jew. Neither is true, but to the mob it was a match to gasoline. The savage assault turned into a murderous fury." Pelley's voiceover functioned in two distinct ways: First, it revealed that even though Logan was being portrayed as a self-sufficient news employee, speaking out for her colleagues, her voice was still tightly contained within an implicitly masculinist frame. Pelley was actually the first person to speak in the *60 Minutes* segment, while Logan's passive image acted as a backdrop to his words. Then, when Logan began to discuss the most delicate part of her testimony, Pelley spoke over her, asserting that "the crowd" had attacked Logan partly because they thought she was affiliated with Israel.

This remark directly linked the "crowd" to the larger political framework of the "war on terror," suggesting that enemies of Israel were enemies of the United States. Pelley's remark also bolstered a broader logic operating within

Figure 9. Lara Logan recounting her assault in Tahrir Square from the space of the 60 Minutes studio.

the *60 Minutes* interview: the logic of precarity (Butler 2009). Because this video framed the people in Tahrir Square as a monolithically unrecognizable "enemy," the precariousness of life itself was reorganized into a hierarchical focus on which lives were most recognizable and which lives were not worth protecting and cultivating. In the world of the CBS interview, the demonstrators in Tahrir Square were potentially the same as Mubarak's plainclothes police; what is more, the inhabitants of the Square were associated with the "enemy" in the global "war on terror." In turn, Logan herself was associated with the whiteness and the westernness of those whom the Anglophone news industry had long been representing as most recognizable to power.

The *60 Minutes* interview revealed CBS's efforts at containing and channeling Logan's experience—using it to portray the Egyptian demonstrators in a politically unfavorable light—while still positioning Logan as the "free" hero of melodrama, fully responsible for her own experiences in the field. As an experienced and self-sufficient conflict reporter, she ideally needed no one's help; as a "passive victim," she ostensibly proved that Egypt's revolutionaries must be carefully watched as they entered a new political stage. This last point was underscored by Logan's next assertion on camera: "And when my clothes gave way, I remember looking up and seeing them taking pictures with their cell phones. The flashes of their cell phone cameras." With this statement, the *60 Minutes* segment overtly aligned the Egyptian demonstrators with the "mob" that assaulted Logan, associating the potential digital record of her attack with the technology most associated with the Egyptian revolutionaries in 2011—the cell phone camera. Though the cell phone had also been celebrated throughout the uprising as a potentially liberatory tool, the *60 Minutes* interview with Logan subtly aligned this digital technology with the more dystopic side of the digital sublime, invoking the "depth of evil" that this technology can ostensibly "conjure" (Mosco 2005, 24).

Rather than simply demonizing digital footage, however, this part of the CBS video also points to a crucial claim made by postcolonialist feminist scholars, before and after 9/11: the white, female body has long been deployed as a justification for U.S. warfare, as well as for U.S. meddling in international affairs (Grewal and Kaplan 1994; Mohanty 2003; Riley, Mohanty, and Pratt 2008). Though the Egyptian uprising of 2011 was not a "war" by traditional standards, it was a moment of political dissent that had direct ramifications for U.S. diplomacy in the Middle East. This is why U.S. coverage, both on CBS and otherwise, initially decried the impending ouster of Mubarak, lamenting the loss of a U.S. ally in the region.[2] The demonstrators' highly visible ability to digitally distribute their own coverage of their uprising further antagonized U.S. news networks, who simultaneously marveled at their digital productivity and described it in terms of a "spreading" virus, invoking the discourse of the "digital sublime" (Mosco 2005).[3] Within this context, the 60 Minutes segment forced Logan's white, feminine body to operate as a justification for U.S. intervention into Egyptian affairs, subtly suggesting that the protesters had not only violated Logan's body—thus, "proving" their depravity and their need for a president like Mubarak—but also that the digital image of Logan's body might be circulating along the very same channels that demonstrators had been using to tell their own story of the 2011 protests.

This digital violation—itself entirely unprovable—was made to appear even more damaging as the 60 Minutes segment emphasized Logan's role as a mother. As Logan described the moment when her attackers pulled her completely away from her security advisor, she recounted how angry she felt with herself for giving up: "I can't believe I just let them kill me. That that was as much fight as I had. That I just gave in. And I gave up on my children so easily." Pelley responded to this by remarking: "Your daughter and your son are one and two years old." This exchange firmly cast Logan in the role of "mother," suggesting that her once scrutinized and commodified sexuality was now aligned with her reproductive function—a function tainted by a racialized "other." Indeed, Logan described her body that night as "filthy, black with dirt, from going down into the filth," drawing upon racialized diction to suggest that she had been defiled.

CBS's discourse drew upon a long-standing tradition of racialization in colonialist journalism (Spurr 1993), as well as representing Logan's body as being "geographically marked" as a "site of conflicting projected identities" (Rogoff 2000, 144). In this sense, CBS's gendered discourse was tightly linked to colonialist attitudes toward race. Logan's white body was contrasted with the "blackness" of the street and of the "mob," suggesting an explosion of western anxiety over the infiltration of the white body's borders. In the CBS video's configuration, the protesters were not allowed the privilege of disseminating ideology within their own rational public sphere. Instead, they comprised a "murderous fury" on the "Arab street," a "street" that CBS mapped over the space of Tahrir Square and over Logan's body.

Still, one element of Logan's experience should have confounded CBS's impoverished effort at demonizing Tahrir, though this element was submerged within the narrative. Logan mentioned that she was eventually saved by a group of Egyptian women who put their arms around her until some Egyptian soldiers intervened. While Logan did say that she was overjoyed to have received this help, she also remarked that she knew she had a chance at survival "because now it was about their women." Logan then declared that sexual harassment is "endemic" to Egyptian culture, and Pelley echoed this statement in his own closing voiceover, layered over a generic long shot of the celebration in Tahrir Square: "That night, her attackers faded into the crowd. It's not likely anyone involved will be brought to justice. We may never know with certainty whether the regime was targeting a reporter or whether it was simply and savagely, a criminal mob. It is true that in Egypt in particular, sexual harassment and violence are common." Whether or not these statements held any truth, the Egyptian women's intervention barely fell within the frame. When it did receive attention, this intervention was immediately reframed as further proof of the purportedly sinister nature of Egyptian men. There was no room in CBS's configuration for the agency of the female activists in Tahrir Square, pointing again to the Anglophone tendency to frame some lives as more recognizable and valuable than others (Butler 2004, 2009).

The *60 Minutes* interview ended with Pelley back on camera, asking Logan why she had decided to speak out about her experience. Logan replied that she did so because her female colleagues claimed that she had broken the silence on the dangers that women journalists face in the war zone. Logan then explained that women often do not report sexual assault "because you don't want someone to say, 'well, women shouldn't be out there.' But I think there are a lot of women who experience these kinds of things as journalists, and they don't want it to stop them from doing their job." The segment closed on this statement, suggesting that Logan's testimony had allowed her to thoroughly and officially take charge of her own incident and "break the code of silence" that had dominated the news industry's safety culture up until that point.

Yet, nowhere in this video was there any suggestion that the Anglophone news industry was even partially to blame for what happened to Logan. There was no analysis of the gendered history of war reporting, nor was there any deliberation on the systemic problem of ignoring gendered violence in English-language war reporting. Instead, Logan drew upon the rhetoric of individualism and self-responsibility, saying that no female reporter wanted to be barred from doing her work. With this statement, Logan echoed the larger industrial tendency to focus on the "free" individual rather than on the larger industrial structures in need of reform. In turn, the *60 Minutes* interview offered only one true culprit for Logan's sexual assault: the men on the "Arab street."

CBS, along with many other western news outlets, offered only one impoverished frame through which to view the question of sexual assault in Egypt, as well as the larger questions engendered by Mubarak's resignation. Even as Mubarak's regime police were accused of tampering with various journalists' diverse representations of Tahrir Square during the uprising, networks like CBS also belied the diversity of perspectives that informed this space in 2011, attempting to streamline the global public's knowledge of Tahrir Square down its own traditional channels. As freelancer Shawn Baldwin told me, the Square was "where everything was really happening" (pers. comm., February 2013). Baldwin said that Tahrir was an incredibly saturated space, constructed collaboratively by an international array of professional journalists, and by the demonstrators themselves.

U.S. networks were only a few of the many professional news outlets covering the Egyptian uprisings. As one anonymous camerawoman told me, most people in Tahrir initially thought she was from Al Jazeera when they saw her working, pointing to both the Arabic-language and English-language networks' high visibility during the revolution (pers. comm., December 2012). Al Jazeera's motto—"voice of the voiceless"—was repeatedly invoked by U.S. trade publications throughout the uprisings, as was the quality and dedication of AJE's news reports. This was especially interesting considering the vexed relationship between Al Jazeera and U.S. news networks after September 11, 2001 (Samuel-Azran 2010). Tahrir was also flooded with journalists from Russia, China, Turkey, and numerous other nations, each representing the uprising in a distinct way.

On top of this diverse professional presence, many of the Egyptian activists were reporting on the event in their own right, struggling to post accounts of the protests on Twitter, Facebook, and YouTube. Though CBS deployed Logan's assault in a manner that suggested most of these activists were men, there were also a number of women participating in the revolution from its very beginning ("Egyptian Women Protesters" 2012). This did not stop after Logan's assault. Months later, several Egyptian women were attacked and molested by military figures still in control of the Egyptian government (Zayed 2011). One of these attacks was caught on cellphone video and revealed a soldier stripping an Egyptian protester down to her blue bra, an image that became iconic for the initial post-Mubarak movement (ibid.). In light of the fact that this image went viral, it seems all the more difficult to situate Logan's assault as the prime example of the "endemic" obstacles that Egyptian women face. The "blue bra woman"—an iconic figure that traversed multiple communicative channels—instead came to represent this notion, while also representing the complexity and the tenacity of the longer-term revolution in Egypt.

Conclusion

After her appearance on *60 Minutes*, Logan announced that she did not plan to do any more interviews, declaring: "I don't want this to define me" (cited in Poniewozik 2011). Such a remark underscored Logan's own knowledge of the way in which her testimony could be used against her. By becoming the victimized hero of melodrama, Logan's work could be defined by the sexual assault she had endured. Logan's hesitance to continue "speaking out" points to the resilience of the gender problem in twenty-first-century conflict reporting. Rather than adequately addressing this problem, the CBS *60 Minutes* interview with Logan drew upon long-standing representations of gender in order to construct a lucrative melodrama. In CBS's formulation, Logan was both a maternal victim and the self-sufficient neoliberal subject. In an effort at distracting from earlier portrayals of Logan as a commodified sexual object, CBS emphasized Logan's status as a maternal figure who also displayed the neoliberal tenets of self-sufficiency and individual responsibility. Logan acted as both a "pure, maternal victim" and as a "self-sufficient individual" whose passion for the story trumped the risks she might face.

By representing Logan as a self-sufficient subject who could narrativize her own objectification, CBS avoided any effort at examining the larger systemic failures that contributed to Logan's experience. In turn, CBS also used Logan's experience as a launch pad for an incredibly Islamaphobic representation of the Egyptian activists. Chapter Four illuminates the anxiety underscoring the U.S. coverage of the 2011 uprisings in Egypt, where U.S. news organizations ambivalently cast the protesters (who were also, in many cases, citizen journalists) as volatile "crowds" full of "dangerous elements." This ambivalence reached a fever pitch in CBS's *60 Minutes* interview with Logan, where the protesters were rhetorically conflated with the people who had attacked her. CBS's maneuver drew upon the "Arab street" metaphor in order to blame the figure of the "Egyptian male" for Logan's assault, as well as placing the responsibility for protection onto Logan herself. Crucially, this maneuver cast the Egyptian protesters as unrecognizable, suggesting that they were somehow less significant than Logan herself. In turn, the numerous Egyptian women who face sexual assault were obscured from the frame.

The next chapter similarly examines the systemic failures that can lead to the endangerment of conflict correspondents, but in this case I focus on the industrial, technological, and political imperatives that result in the ultimate danger: the correspondent's death. Turning to the early days of the civil war in Syria, I investigate the 2012 death of veteran correspondent Marie Colvin, analyzing her very last reports from the field. These reports became doubly lucrative for news outlets after Colvin died, because they endowed the correspondent's participation in the construction of journalistic "liveness" with the decisive authority of death itself—of the correspondent's dedicated willingness to risk everything in order to tell the story. Chapter Five explores these issues, in an effort at better understanding the exploited labor of the "living dead."

5

The "Living Dead"

Marie Colvin's 2012 Death in Syria

"War is about those who are killed, limbs severed, dirt
and rock and flesh torn alike by hot metal."

—Marie Colvin

On February 22, 2012, Syrian forces launched a mortar attack on the Baba
Amr district of Homs, killing a number of civilians and rebel troops as well as
two journalists covering the nation's civil war.[1] One of these journalists was a
French photographer named Remi Ochlik. The other was the famous conflict
correspondent Marie Colvin, who had just spoken with Britain's Channel 4
News, CNN, and the BBC in a series of televised interviews the night before
her death. Colvin was a veteran conflict reporter, known primarily for her
work with London's *Sunday Times*. Perhaps because of this notoriety, CNN
and other news networks obsessively replayed Colvin's final report from
the field, once word got out that she had been killed in Syria. Through this
constant replay of her testimony, these networks drew upon Colvin's labor
even after her physical body no longer existed. Colvin's final contribution to
"the story" of Syria continued after her individual end, signaling the slippage
between the conflict correspondent as storyteller and as cultural sign, made
to speak beyond her own intentions.

Before she died, Colvin tried to tell the story of the people in the Sunni
Muslim district of Baba Amr, where forces loyal to the Alawite Syrian president Bashar al-Assad were said to be massacring civilians. It was difficult
for journalists to verify this accusation according to professional standards
(Mawad 2012; Morabito 2012; Sengupta 2012). Though a steady stream of
grisly amateur footage had made its way onto YouTube in the months preceding Colvin's visit to Homs, the news organizations that drew upon these
images also displayed a great deal of ambivalence toward the figure of the

activist-turned-citizen-journalist. On the one hand, these digital activists provided major news networks with a great deal of enthusiastic—and un-paid—labor. On the other hand, they had not been trained as professional journalists, and they were clearly not reporting from an objective stance. Be-cause of this, professional journalists relying on the amateur footage tended to offer one simple warning: "We can't verify this information."

Despite the continual use of this disclaimer, the reliance upon eyewitnesses unaffiliated with the news organizations inspired a profound anxiety among industry pundits, who touted the training and the experience of the profes-sional correspondent as a counterpoint to the "unpredictability" of the citi-zen journalist, and of social media more generally (Ackerman 2011; Marash 2011; Pintak 2011; Silverman 2011; Gray 2012). Indeed, the Anglophone news industry discourse and the news coverage of the Syrian conflict tended to situate the "independent" professional as the figure most capable of verifying the "amateur" content streaming out of places like Syria. Colvin decided to act as this independent, professional witness at the precise moment when the few journalists who had made it into Syria were fleeing the battered city of Homs (Conroy 2013).

Colvin spent her last night reporting on the death of a Syrian baby, a death that her interviews with CNN, the BBC, and Channel Four implied she had witnessed firsthand. Yet, a memoir later released by Colvin's photographer Paul Conroy (2013) suggested something rather different. Conroy's memoir gave the impression that Colvin had actually "witnessed" this death on a laptop screen located inside the media center where she and Conroy were stationed (ibid., 195). According to Conroy's memoir, a Syrian activist showed the video of the dying baby to everyone in the media center. If Colvin wit-nessed the baby's death on a laptop screen, rather than in person, then this also suggests that Colvin might have had no more access to that specific event than did the news viewers who saw the footage. Indeed, Conroy's memoir told of the peril he and Colvin faced in leaving the media center at all. Whether or not Colvin witnessed the baby's death first-hand, three major English-language news networks interviewed Colvin as if she were their own eyewitness in the field, capable of verifying the video of the baby, as well as all of the other amateur videos upon which they had overwhelmingly relied.

The networks awarded Colvin this authority because she and her photog-rapher were the only professional English-language journalists known to still be physically present in Homs. Since the early months of the uprising, Assad's regime had barred reporters from crossing Syrian borders without a government-issued visa, a decision that had resulted in very few journalists' attempts at smuggling themselves inside. CNN correspondent Arwa Damon managed to get into Baba Amr but left shortly after Colvin arrived, due to intelligence that Assad's forces were planning a ground invasion in the same neighborhood where the media center was situated (*Anderson Cooper 360*, February 21, 2012). The BBC's Paul Wood also successfully smuggled himself into Homs several days before Colvin got there, but he and his team left the city just as the shelling intensified (pers. comm., February 2013). Most journalists instead reported on the uprising from the nearby borders with Lebanon and Turkey, or—if they had been lucky enough to secure visas—under the tight supervision of Assad's intelligence officers in Damascus.

Despite the fact that Colvin and Conroy could rarely leave the media center to do any reporting, the physical presence of a veteran English-language conflict correspondent in Homs instantly became a hot commodity, with Colvin getting a number of interview requests (Conroy 2013). Though Colvin and Conroy debated whether or not it would be safe to do a broadcast from the media center, she eventually decided to give the interviews (ibid.). The next morning, Assad's forces shelled the media center in an attack that Conroy believed was deliberate and well-executed (ibid.), killing Colvin and Ochlik in the process. Immediately, the news networks began replaying Colvin's testimony from Homs, continuing to draw upon her precarious labor, despite the fact that she no longer lived.

Though many of the English-language news organizations celebrated Colvin as a valiant witness who paid the ultimate price in order to professionally report the "truth" to the world, the video interviews in which she participated especially betrayed a decisive bias toward the Syrian opposition, using Colvin's final interview as further proof that Assad was the sole villain in this story and that the opposition was a unified group simply seeking democracy. There was no significant exploration of the various players in the Syrian conflict. Instead, the reports used Colvin's death to bolster the melodramatic narrative that demonized one side of the conflict while avoiding any critical assessment of the other side.

Chapter Five investigates Colvin's death in Syria, first exploring the grim political economy that has long demanded the Anglophone war reporting industry's heavy dependence on the deaths of "others." At one level, the conflict correspondent encounters and narrativizes these deaths, navigating a site that is often very literally comprised of dead and dying bodies, in order to transform those material deaths into a marketable story. Sometimes these deaths are represented as being recognizable to power, and thus, worthy of the news audiences' grief (Butler 2004, 2009). Yet, at other times, these deaths are aligned with the nonhuman, associated with "the enemy." To complicate things further, the conflict correspondent risks his or her own individual death, working under conditions that constantly suggest this death is imminent. In order to construct the melodramas that are so lucrative to news organizations (Dobkin 1992), the conflict correspondent faces the threat of his or her own death as well.

This was the case for Daniel Pearl in 2002, and it remained a problem when Marie Colvin traveled to Syria in 2012. As the first decade of the twenty-first century drew to a close, the industry's burgeoning safety culture had yet to adequately address the death-driven economy of war reporting. Following this, Chapter Five focuses on the spurious ways in which both the Anglophone industry trade journals and Colvin's own news organization, the *Sunday Times*, narrativized her death after the fact. Each of these entities tied Colvin's death in Syria to a melodramatic narrative on "good guys," "bad guys," and abstract notions of sacrifice, rather than thinking carefully about better ways of proactively protecting war correspondents in the field. Perhaps unsurprisingly, television news networks did no better in representing Colvin's death. Chapter Five closes with an analysis of Colvin's final interviews with CNN, the BBC, and Channel Four News, illuminating those interviews' dependence on the televisual strategy of "liveness" to reanimate Colvin's labor and continue verifying the amateur footage on which these networks had long relied. Colvin ultimately functioned as the "living dead," a conflict correspondent still working for the Anglophone news industry even after she had succumbed to the ultimate danger in the field.

Death in the Political Economy of Conflict Correspondence

It is easy to misrecognize the long-standing usefulness of death to the conflict reporting business, as this usefulness gets obscured by lofty industry discourse on the importance of bearing witness. World War II photojournalist Gwen Dew invoked this discourse in her 1943 memoir, when describing her encounter with a dead body in Hong Kong:

> On the corner lay a mass of something which had been a man. I took a picture, not heartlessly, nor without thought of the smiling Chinese this had been—but with the hopes I could show people in America what war means when it hits next to you. (1943)

Though Dew emphasized the importance of "showing people in America what war means," her decision to photograph the dead body of a cultural "other" was also rooted in the Anglophone war reporting industry's interest in luring more news readers with graphic stories of carnage. As early as the Civil War, "a large New York newspaper could sell five times its normal circulation when it ran details of a big battle" (Knightley 2004, 23). During this time, newspaper's "special artists" drew pictures of dead or dying bodies, along with salacious scenes of fighting (Katz and Virga 2012). During World War I, British newspapers were also anxious to cover the fighting because they had a very clear sense that they could sell more papers that way—by using the word "battle" in headlines (ibid.). After Dew's time, this impulse continued, most especially with the rise of television news reporting in Vietnam. Television reporter Richard Lindley said of his editors during this time: "At first they were satisfied with a corpse. Then they had to have people dying in action" (cited in Knightley 2004, 451).

Yet, accompanying this drive to capture and publish images of the dead, there was also the long-standing tradition of censoring those images—either through the coercion of the military, or through news editors' own self-censorship. The British military fiercely censored photojournalists during the World Wars, for example, (Knightley 2004), and in Vietnam, Anglophone editors displayed a great deal of ambivalence on just how *much* death they should show their audiences. U.S. television networks during Vietnam worried that their sponsors would not want their products associated with graphic images of death, and "as a matter of policy, networks did not show casualties who could be identified by viewers" (Hamilton 2011). By the time of the Persian Gulf War, American pool journalist Kenneth Jarecke took a graphic picture of a dead Iraqi, and no one in the United States would publish it; the photo was instead published in a British newspaper, and there was a public uproar (Knightley 2004).

Throughout the history of war reporting, Anglophone news organizations have vacillated between showing graphic images of death and censoring those images, depending on the historical circumstances. When audience members have been called upon to consider the death of a group or of an individual, this invitation has more typically occurred via the deployment of what Barbie Zelizer calls the "about-to-die" image: an image meant to symbolize a subject's possible death or an image meant to serve as a reminder that the subject died shortly after being filmed (2010). This strategy obscures the fact of death from the image's viewers. It also obscures the fact that conflict correspondents themselves must continually encounter the reality of death in order to do their work.

Many of the correspondents I interviewed said rather bluntly that they had "seen a lot of messed up stuff," over the years, suggesting that the dead and dying are an integral part of the war reporter's environment—obstacles to be navigated, as well as proof that the correspondent is truly "present" in the field. For example, CNN correspondent Michael Holmes told me:

> I've seen a lot of dead people. I've seen a lot of burning bodies, I've seen a lot of hacked up bodies, and smelled a lot of dead people. Including in the case of our translator and driver, seeing them basically killed in front of us. And in other places seeing a lot of dead kids. And I just think some people can have one experience of that and they will never do it again. Other people can return and go through those sorts of things, and not be unimpacted, but are able to process it differently in a way that allows them to continue that kind of work. (pers. comm., January 2013)

With this statement, Holmes implied that "seeing dead people," was one of the most foundational elements of being a conflict correspondent, and that the most successful correspondents find a way to come to terms with the potential trauma of processing these sights. Yet, the gruesome memory of these encounters stays with the correspondents long after they have left the conflict zone. For example, freelance journalist Judith Matloff described in detail a mass grave she saw years before in Rwanda, where "a dog ran off with a femur bone. And a church was filled with the bones and skulls of 5,000 humans, some with flesh still attached" (pers. comm., June 2013). Similarly, ITN's Jonathan Miller recounted the time that he and his crew were in a village in East Congo, where "every house that we went into was full of dead people. They'd just been shot and the soldiers who'd done it were in the hills up above us, looking at us and pointing their guns at us" (pers. comm., May 2013). Miller told me that this was "one of the most terrifying situations" he had ever experienced (ibid.).

Despite the emotional intensity of bearing witness to the deaths of others, conflict correspondents have long been charged with going to places where death is central to the events that are transpiring—places where most people cannot, or will not, go. The conflict correspondents' role as eyewitness is key to the construction of journalistic authority, in other words, and this authority cannot be separated from the news industry's political economy:

> News organizations most often use eyewitnessing to accomplish the reportage of events that cannot easily be confirmed, challenged, or tested but are made more credible by virtue of a correspondent's on-site presence. Eyewitnessing thus is valuable in marking journalism's credibility and authenticity,

particularly when audiences have no first-hand knowledge of what is being reported." (Zelizer 2007, 411)

Perhaps this is why correspondents like Al Jazeera English's Zeina Khodr foreground their experience with witnessing the deaths of others when also foregrounding their authority as professional journalists. Khodr told me that she could easily tell whether or not the YouTube video from Syria was legitimate, based on the way the dead were arranged in the frame (pers. comm., February 2013). Perhaps this is also why a colleague of freelance correspondent Sulome Anderson bluntly told her: "Listen, when you see piles of little dead children all piled on top of each other, it stops being about giving a voice to the voiceless. I do this because I'm good at it, and because I like to fuck the competition" (Anderson, pers. comm., June 2015).

The encounter with death is unfortunately entangled within the competitive nature of the Anglophone news industry. Getting to the front lines, capturing images of the "bang-bang," as many of my interviewees have called it, and constructing stories that communicate the extreme nature of war—these tasks are often invoked as the most lucrative for conflict reporters. Yet, Anglophone conflict correspondents must also engage in a rather precarious balancing act. As professional eyewitnesses, they must *link* the networks' readers and viewers to the deaths being reported, *without* necessarily showing those deaths—and hopefully, without getting killed themselves. Why else would industry trade journals discuss the need to get correspondents into Syria, "in order to make a better connection for viewers" (Morabito 2012)? The presence of the correspondent within the frame assures the news audience that there is an element of individual human agency in the stories being told.

For instance, one *Broadcasting & Cable* article that ran shortly after Colvin's death declared: "Journalists bring a face and a story to war, with a capital W, by bringing it down to the lowercase scale of the many individual lives it destroys" ("More than Numbers" 2012). This "glimpse of human agents behind the headlines" bolsters the belief "that editorial products are made by people with the power and freedom to impart information in any way they choose," rather than being at the mercy of complex economic, political, cultural, and technological agendas (Machin and Niblok 2006, 41). Despite their enmeshment within these complex networks, correspondents appear to viewers as individual subjects, recognizable figures who can guide viewers toward a better understanding of death in wartime.

The conflict correspondent's labor partially hinges upon the creation of a vicarious firsthand experience that has historically depended upon the journalist's physical presence in the conflict zone (Zelizer 2007). The obsession with getting correspondents into Syria exemplifies this drive to provide news audiences with professional eyewitnesses who can give firsthand accounts of what is happening. For example, in an article published just after Colvin's death, *Broadcasting and Cable* asserted that "every network would rather get in-country to report the story first-hand" (Morabito 2012). *B&C's* editors reiterated this notion when commenting upon the dangers involved in correspondents' "being the world's eyes and ears in troubled times and places" ("In the Line of Duty" 2013). In other words, having professional correspondents on the ground potentially guarantees a more incisive sensory connection for distant viewers, who usually cannot inhabit these dangerous spaces on their own.

As Zelizer notes: "A journalist's authority often derives from the fact that the public cannot verify what he or she has done" (1999). In a sense, the public also cannot verify what the journalist has smelled, heard, or seen while physically present at the site of death and destruction. The embodied quality of this logic informs one *Columbia Journalism Review* article published after Colvin's death: NPR correspondent Deborah Amos cited the need to "feel it . . . smell it, and . . . see it" (cited in Mawad 2012). Such sensory details have long been considered a fundamental element of a story's professional texture (Zelizer 2007); the correspondent's living body must smell, feel, and especially *see* a war zone that can, at any moment, kill that body.

Even before she died, Colvin herself was represented in the trade publications as someone who relied heavily on embodied personal experience to help her connect her readers to the war zone. Sherry Ricchiardi of the *American Journalism Review* quoted Colvin as saying: "My own experience tells readers more about what is happening than merely attributing every quote. The people I meet and my reactions to them—that is part of the story" (cited in Ricchiardi 2000). After Colvin's death, Ricchiardi included a quote from Colvin that suggested the precarious nature of doing this type of work: "You get so cold, hungry, and dirty. You exist on a few bites of stale bread, and drink water out of mud holes, but, no matter what, you don't walk out on the story" (Ricchiardi 2012). These quotes both point to the embodied nature of the war correspondent, whose immersion at the dangerous site is the correspondent's source of capital and the very thing that makes it difficult for the correspondent to do her job.

This embodied authority has been attached to the figure of the war correspondent since the very first civilian war correspondent, William Howard Russell, accompanied British troops into battle during the Crimean War in the mid–nineteenth century (Knightley 2004). Russell's presence "on the ground" was crucial to the authority he enjoyed, and this embodied authority continued to drive conflict correspondents closer and closer to the dangerous action in the second half of the nineteenth century as well (Korte 2009). The physical presence of the conflict reporter in the war zone also resonated throughout much of the twentieth century, with the likes of Edward R. Murrow, whose radio show "Hear It Now" appealed to news audiences' senses in order to suggest that professional war reporters were physically inhabiting the conflict zone, telling the truth about what they saw.

By the turn of the twenty-first century, though, conflict correspondents were no longer the only ones distributing information, images, and sensory details from conflict zones. Because of this, news organizations no longer enjoyed the same monopoly on the lucrative business of linking the public to the distant deaths of others. Instead, newsroom technologies began to converge at a more intense rate than in previous years, necessitating that news employees be capable of working across multiple media platforms (Singer 2008). In this context, news work became "increasingly diversified, outsourced and multitasked, with individuals working across media and news organizations, often from afar" (Zelizer 2009, 5). One element of this phenomenon was the increased effort at harnessing the productivity of digital activists and citizen journalists who captured visual and aural content that news organizations could no longer always get for themselves. Unpaid digital activists working for particular political causes overwhelmed the internet with graphic images of dead friends and family members, images often used by the professional news outlets that simultaneously belittled them.

For example, when CNN and the BBC both aired the still photos of 13-year-old Hamza Ali al-Khateeb's corpse, after Assad's forces had allegedly tortured and killed him, both networks issued a disclaimer about the graphic nature of the image. They also chose to blur the image in certain places (*Anderson Cooper 360*, May 30, 2011; "Could Death of Syrian Boy" 2011). CNN's John King went so far as to lament that Al Jazeera had shown the image of al-Khateeb without blurring out the gory details, implying a moral difference between CNN, Al Jazeera, and even the activists who originally posted the video. Both CNN and the BBC also attested that because this image was "all over YouTube," it was impossible to verify. Ultimately, the BBC and CNN used citizen footage of a reportedly dead boy—blurring the visual content that both networks felt was realistic enough to censor—while at the same time disavowing the credibility of citizen journalists' own accounts of their encounters with death. The network's double standard points to Zelizer's argument that "the eyewitnessing provided by private citizens has been critiqued for shortcomings that have always plagued eyewitnessing, but without the sanctioning provided by conventional journalism to contextualize and mitigate those same shortcomings" (2007, 423).

This double standard informed the news organizations' ambivalent attitudes toward the question of verification during the early days of the Syrian civil war. At this time, citizen journalists affiliated with the opposition were willing to work without payment, supplying major news brands with the images of death that they very often could not get themselves. Most U.S. news outlets did not have a foreign bureau or even what news executives duplicitously call "an editorial presence"—i.e., the ability to parachute a correspondent into a particular region from a nation relatively close by—in Damascus when the Syrian uprising began (Marash 2011). The BBC had at least one reporter, Lina Sinjab, in Damascus when the protests broke out, and Al Jazeera had a Damascus office. Yet, even Al Jazeera employees were eventually forced out of the country and the borders were closed to other journalists (Khodr, pers. comm., February 2013).

In this climate, Anglophone news organizations drew upon three types of labor: 1) digital activists in Syria, 2) freelance reporters willing to sneak into Syria without insurance or professional backing from a big news network, and 3) news staffers who either reported from the Turkish-Syrian border or who smuggled themselves inside. Colvin fit into this last category, while her photographer Conroy fit into the more precarious category of "freelancer." Yet, even with the backing of the *Sunday Times*, Colvin was not immune to the ultimate danger involved in war reporting. Her death raised questions of what exactly the "backing" of a major news organization really entailed. Most of the trade articles focused on her individualism and on her drive to report from the most dangerous war zones even though it gave her editor a number of "sleepless nights" (Ricchiardi 2000). None of these trade articles mentioned any example of Colvin's editor categorically ordering that she stay away from such regions or refusing to run her material should she venture into a dangerous zone without permission.

In fact, many of the correspondents I interviewed who were working in 2011–2012 implied that the Anglophone news industry's growing "safety culture" engendered some staunchly contradictory discourse during this time. Editors and news directors would tell reporters not to travel to dangerous places like Syria, but then they would still run their stories if they chose to go anyway. ABC's Alexander Marquardt told me:

It's always going to be the case where people will tell you not to do something, but if you get it, they're certainly going to use it. I mean, if I come back with footage of bullets ringing all around me, hitting the walls next to me, of course ABC's going to use that, I mean I would want them to, I put my life on the line for them to use it. But there's absolutely no way ABC's going to tell me to go in and get some, that's ridiculous, they tell me the opposite: stay away from that. So I have no pressure to go out and do that thing for my editors, whereas freelancers certainly have self-imposed pressure to go out and get the best stuff because it's a much, much tougher market out there. (pers. comm., January 2013)

Compellingly, in this statement, Marquardt made a distinction between staff reporters and freelancers, suggesting that as a staff correspondent for ABC he did not face the same obstacles that freelancers did. Yet, his statement certainly revealed that he, like any freelancer, would be told to avoid risking his own death, and then would still be rewarded for that very risk. Marquardt also illuminated the insidious ways in which conflict correspondents internalize the rhetoric of war reporting, declaring that he decisively wanted the network to use his story if he risked his life reporting it. The narrative of willing sacrifice took on a decidedly neoliberal tone in this statement, where the purportedly "individual" decision to risk one's life for a story was also an "individual" assessment of the potential benefits.

Crucially, Marquardt was talking about the paradoxical elements of the industry's safety culture as it existed at the *end* of the first decade of the twenty-first century, suggesting that not much had changed since the individualizing discourse on Daniel Pearl's death in 2002. By 2012, this individualizing discourse was no less powerful, despite the fact that the paradoxical nature of the industry's safety culture was larger than any individual journalist or editor. Instead, both the news editors and their correspondents were caught within a professional framework that was diffusely driven by a precarious political economy. For example, former CBC editor David Nayman told me:

No one can be ordered to go and cover a story. If anybody has qualms or reservations, then they have the right to say no. Now, arguably some people will say, well, that's a career killer. If you say no, then you're never going to be promoted and you're never going to get a chance to do anything. And I suppose that's the risk anybody takes in any career, but no one can be forced to go somewhere. The reality is that very, very few reporters will refuse. (pers. comm., March 2015)

Nayman's statement echoed many other editors' rather odd belief that the brunt of the power rests with the news correspondent more so than with the news editors and executives. ITN's Charlie Beckett also implied this, confessing that he could not imagine contacting veteran correspondent Lindsey Hilsum in the field and saying: "Don't forget to tell us where you are!" (pers. comm., February 2015). Such remarks suggest that editors are ambivalently caught up in this practice of offloading safety responsibility onto the correspondents themselves.

Some editors do try to gain control of the relationships they build with these reporters. For instance, foreign editor of the *Guardian* Jamie Wilson said: "If I had doubts about somebody and I wasn't sure that they were going to follow the rules—if I wasn't sure they were going to do that, I would be very unwilling to send them, and I would make that clear to them" (pers. comm., March 2015). And speaking specifically of freelancers, a former editor at the *New York Times*, John Geddes, told me:

> Most of our freelancers overseas have relationships with either the correspondent in the area, or with the foreign desk. And the foreign desk is expected to come to some assessments. Where do I put them? How do I keep them out of danger? We're very rigorous in trying to not—we never use freelancers as cannon fodder. Put them into areas of danger that we weren't willing to put our own employees in. That would be wrong. (pers. comm., February 2015)

Of course, there are major differences between freelance war reporting and staff reporting like Marquardt's, differences that largely center on whether or not the news organizations will insure the correspondents or pay for their safety training or travel expenses. Former *Toronto Star* reporter, Andrew Mills, told me that staff or contract correspondents tend to take bigger risks in the field than freelancers do because they're better protected (pers. comm., April 2013). In this vein, former freelancer Don Duncan said that he drew the line at reporting from Syria starting in 2013, because many news organizations refused to make any agreements with him until he bought his own insurance; and they still did not always pay his way into the dangerous environments he visited (pers. comm., January 2013).

Similarly, freelancer Ben Gittleson told me that he also did not feel comfortable going to a place like Syria without the expensive hostile environment training that news outlets expected him to fund on his own (pers. comm., February 2013). A number of freelancers have refused to cover the Syrian conflict in more recent years, because they do not have the structural support from the news outlets that could help them stay alive. Others have continued their efforts at covering that story, only to be kidnapped or killed. The 2014 deaths of freelancers James Foley and Steven Sotloff in Syria attest to the unique dangers that freelance correspondents continue to face—dangers that have led numerous news editors, including those at the *Sunday Times*, to more recently refuse any footage or stories from freelancers who travel to Syria on their own (Rodgers 2013). Yet, other editors still rely on freelance labor, citing the economic landscape of the industry:

> The media relies on the freelancers more than people realize, I think. And we celebrate their work, and we have to treat everyone with the same amount of respect when it comes to security. There are discussions throughout the industry going on about this. And again, I think it will develop over time, you know, who gives them protective gear? Are they supposed to have their own protective gear? Do we insure them? Are they supposed to have their own insurance? This will all get sorted and is an evolving discussion. (Phillips, pers. comm., July 2015)

While freelancers are currently still offered a very meager amount of protection from news outlets, citizen journalists are usually offered none at all, despite the fact that their images routinely appear in major news reports. The death of Rami al-Sayed, a Syrian digital activist whose work had regularly appeared in English-language newscasts, serves as a prime example. Despite the fact that his videos were crucial to the mainstream, English-language news coverage of the 2011–2012 conflict in Homs, it is unclear whether any of these news organizations offered him insurance or safety training. According to former correspondent and Dart Center director Mark Brayne, western news organizations rarely take responsibility for the safety of unpaid digital activists (pers. comm., February 2013). Al-Sayed died only a day before Colvin, and his death did receive some attention from the professional English-language news media. Yet, the melodramatic narrative of Colvin's death dramatically overshadowed his own, distracting viewers from the interpenetration of amateur and professional labor that had defined the coverage of the Syrian conflict.

This undeniable interpenetration perhaps inspires staff correspondents' noticeable efforts at professionally distinguishing themselves from digital activists and even young freelancers. For example, Holmes laments the dangers that freelancers and citizen journalists—both often inexperienced, in his opinion—collectively face (pers. comm., January 2013). This assertion subtly situates freelancers and citizen journalists in a different category from Holmes himself. ABC producer and cameraman Matthew McGarry even goes so far as to overtly say that there is not much difference between a young, inexperienced freelancer running around in the field and a citizen journalist randomly picking up a camera (pers. comm., January 2013). In both of these cases, staff correspondents carefully draw a line between themselves and the freelancers who will do the same work as any war correspondent, albeit for less money. Staff correspondents also draw a distinction between themselves and citizen journalists, implying that professional experience and the support of major news outlets will lead to a better news product.

It could be argued that such notions are rooted in the news industry's anxiety over the status of the professional journalist in today's news market. As Mark Deuze notes, this anxiety inspires professional journalists to insert themselves into their own stories more often, in an attempt to lay claim once again to the monopoly on the flow of information that traditional journalism used to enjoy (2009). Though staff correspondents are increasingly understood as a dying breed in an era when news organizations outsource more and more labor to underpaid freelancers and unpaid citizen journalists, they still represent the gold standard of traditional Anglophone war reporting—possessing a level of cultural capital that is all the more enhanced by the very potential of their death. Colvin exemplified this logic even before she died, marked as her body was by the material imperative of war. She was famous for wearing an eye patch that covered a wound she had sustained in the field. For the rest of her career, that eye patch suggested both past and future encounters with death—not only the deaths of others, but her own death as well. When Colvin finally met her own death, she became the story.

Colvin in the Story

By the time Colvin arrived in Homs, CNN's Arwa Damon had also been inside the beleaguered city, tweeting and giving the occasional phone or Skype interview from the limited space of the media center. But Damon left the area shortly after Colvin arrived, and shortly before the shelling intensified. Throughout January and February of 2012, the siege of Homs became a primary focus for mainstream, Anglophone news outlets, though the danger of keeping correspondents in that region was astronomical. By the time Colvin arrived in Baba Amr, most other journalists that had made it that far were no longer there.

It is, at first glance, difficult to understand why Colvin wanted to remain in Baba Amr when even her photographer Paul Conroy expressed his reservations (Conroy 2013). In his memoir on that final assignment with Colvin, Conroy says that he and Colvin actually went into Baba Amr twice—once just before the CNN crew left and once after that. Conroy and Colvin had originally left Homs with CNN's crew to avoid a ground invasion, but that invasion had not materialized. Furious, Colvin told Conroy that she wanted to smuggle herself back in, something her freelance photographer Conroy was reluctant to do:

> Marie responded flatly with what sounded like regret. "Well, I'm going in, alone if need be. You can go home if you want." She looked resolute and I knew she meant it. She would never drop a story purely on a hunch. "You know I can't let you go alone," I whispered. And that was it. . . . We had a job to do, and I needed a clear head to focus on the task at hand. (ibid., 180)

This passage from Conroy's memoir reveals Colvin's admirable tenacity and her undeniable passion for telling the story of the civilians who were allegedly under attack. Yet, Conroy does not mention the larger industrial imperatives that might cultivate just this type of passion and tenacity in a conflict reporter. Conroy and Colvin returned to Baba Amr without their editor Sean Ryan's knowledge (ibid., 195), but when Colvin finally notified Ryan of where she was, she made sure to emphasize the fact that she was the only "western" reporter in the area (ibid., 197). And though Ryan did express intense concern at his team's decision to linger in Homs, he did not categorically order Colvin to leave. Ryan reportedly implored Colvin to think about leaving soon, but he also let her know that Channel Four News wanted to do a Skype interview with her (ibid., 199).

A *Vanity Fair* article that ran months after Colvin's death quoted Colvin as telling her editor via email: "No other Brits here. Have heard that Spencer and Chulov of the Torygraph and Guardian trying to make it here, but so far we have leap-frogged ahead of them. Heavy shelling this morning" (cited in Brenner 2012). This quote provides rare insight into Colvin's decision to enter Homs when everyone else was leaving. Simply put, Colvin wanted to beat her competitors. The title of a February 19 report that Colvin filed for the *Sunday Times* suggests that her editors felt the same: "'WE LIVE IN FEAR OF A MASSACRE'; The only British newspaper journalists inside the besieged Syrian enclave of Baba Amr report on the terrible cost of the uprising against President Assad" (Colvin 2012). Alongside the drive to tell the world about Assad's attack on his own people, Colvin and her editors were also fiercely competing with other Anglophone news organizations to construct a melodramatic narrative of the war in Syria. Colvin's presence in the conflict zone was crucial to that narrative.

Once Colvin was killed, her own newspaper immediately began publishing archived stories that she had written, along with straight news reports and editorial eulogies memorializing her bravery and her hard work for the *Sunday Times*. Compellingly, some of these pieces—especially those written by her editors—also discussed the difficulty of controlling Colvin's actions in the field, as well as outlining the alleged safety precautions that the *Times* had taken when Colvin returned to Homs. A *Sunday Times* eulogy by editor John Witherow called Colvin "a force of nature," asserting that "the flip side of her dedication to war reporting . . . was an absolute refusal to be ruled by such petty matters as deadlines" ("MARIE COLVIN 1956–2012" 2012). Witherow remarked that Colvin's phone would often go dead, leaving the paper's foreign desk "in a frenzy trying to find her" (ibid.). Later, she would file a brilliant story, and "as usual, she was forgiven" (ibid.). In this sense, Witherow revealed a great deal of admiration for Colvin's talent, while also illuminating the diffuse professional system that offloaded responsibility onto Colvin herself, ultimately rewarding her as long as she wrote a good story.

Another of Colvin's editors, Jon Swain, also talked about Colvin in this fashion. In his piece memorializing Colvin's career, he wrote that Colvin herself "decided she had to go to Syria," because she "felt the truth needed to be told" (Swain and Woods, "Marie Colvin: The Last Assignment" 2012). Describing Colvin's correspondence with her editors, Swain shared a number of Colvin's emails to Ryan, emphasizing Colvin's own decision-making process. He even mentioned that Conroy had sent a separate email to Ryan, voicing his concerns that they were in a far too dangerous situation (ibid.). Still, Swain portrayed Ryan as someone who was merely listening to Colvin's logic and then recommending that she and Conroy "should get out of Baba Amr at the first opportunity" (ibid.). After representing Ryan in this way, Swain wrote of Colvin: "Instead, Marie had a message to get out first, a message for the world about the truth of Baba Amr. In links to the BBC, Channel 4 News and to CNN, the U.S. news network, she described the misery she was witnessing" (ibid.). With this statement, Swain made it sound as though Colvin participated in the television interviews completely of her own accord, instead of with the encouragement of her editors at the *Sunday Times*.

This is rather different than Conroy's own account, where Ryan was the one who first informed Colvin of Channel 4's interview request (Conroy 2013, 199). Though Conroy writes that Ryan quickly followed up with the remark that they should not do the interview if it would be too dangerous, this account still situates Ryan as ambivalently performing the professional doublespeak that simultaneously invokes the safety of the correspondent while also offloading the responsibility for this safety onto the correspondent herself. To his credit, Ryan did begin emailing Colvin in earnest after she completed that particular interview, asking her to respond and discuss the safety of remaining in Homs after that point (ibid., 205). But Conroy's account illuminates the much more complicated dance that unfolds between correspondents like Colvin and the editors located back at headquarters. As Colvin herself told Ryan in their correspondence, she was the only western correspondent currently in Homs, and that was a valuable position to hold; thus, both Colvin and her editors were firmly enmeshed within the professional logic that mandated her precarious presence in the conflict zone.

Following this, the rest of the *Sunday Times* coverage of Colvin's death focused on other issues, instead of exploring the ambivalence that continued to underscore safety culture as the first decade of the twenty-first century drew to a close. These articles examined the atrocities exacted on the Sunni Muslims of Syria, the international stakes in the Syrian civil war, and Colvin's admirable skill as a reporter. Though Colvin very quickly became the *Times*'s big story, there was little mention in this coverage of the economic imperatives that had driven her to smuggle herself back into Homs. Instead, the newspaper focused on deifying her for her bravery, asserting that her death had served a crucial purpose:

> Her powerful report last weekend for this newspaper, and the broadcasts that she did hours before her death, succeeded in exposing the brutality of the Syrian army. She would have been the first to say that the death of a journalist is no more nor less significant than that of the victims around her. But it is fact that her death, simply by being a witness to atrocities, helps focus world attention. ("SYRIA MUST CALL" 2012)

This article portrayed Colvin's death as the ultimate act of verification, "focus[ing] world attention" on the deaths that digital activists had already been discussing. Conroy had also thought about this when he and Colvin were preparing to do the video interviews on Colvin's last night in Homs:

> The so-called "unverified" videos, posted by activists on YouTube, about the brutality of President Assad's assault on the neighborhood, may have slipped past the world largely unnoticed, but things were about to change: the bloodshed was about to be verified by the western eyes of a highly trained, deeply revered and globally respected foreign correspondent. Verified, that is, in a very big way. (2013, 205)

Conroy's statement pointed to the ethnocentrism subtly entangled within Anglophone news industry's drive toward verification. Not only would the YouTube videos streaming out of Syria be verified by a "highly trained" and "globally respected" professional; they would also be verified by this professional's "western eyes." The *Sunday Times* article drew upon this powerful sentiment as well, linking Colvin's death to the professional labor of eye-witnessing—and verifying—the bloodshed that was framed according to a political perspective that aligned with U.S. and British interests. Colvin's persona as a brave individual, tirelessly and incorrigibly braving the perils of an active conflict zone, was made to serve as the nexus between the political, economic, and professional imperatives driving the Anglophone war reporting industry.

Commentators within the broader English-language news industry followed suit, representing Colvin as a "maverick," as someone whose personal passion had always fueled her journeys to dangerous sites. For example, the U.K.'s *Press Gazette* called Colvin "a fearless seeker of truth" ("Marie Colvin" 2012), while also quoting *Sunday Times* owner, Rupert Murdoch, as proclaiming: "She put her life in danger on many occasions because she was driven by a determination that the misdeeds of tyrants and the suffering of the victims did not go unreported" (cited in Pugh 2012). Colvin's own editor wrote a eulogy that appeared in the *Columbia Journalism Review*, calling Colvin "an unflinching witness," one who "spent her life chronicling the horrors of war and oppression" (Swain 2012). Later, the same article quoted Swain as saying that Colvin had always "wanted to experience for herself the destructive forces that surface wherever blood and death run rife" (ibid.).

Interestingly, the discourse on Colvin's death did not tend to represent her in the same sexualized terms associated with Lara Logan. There are a few possible reasons for this. By the time of her death, Colvin was 56 years old, 15 years Logan's senior. She also was not conventionally "beautiful," at least not by the stringent standards of television news. This was partly because she wore an eyepatch, after losing sight in her left eye when she came under attack covering the conflict in Sri Lanka. Yet, even though she was rarely overtly sexualized in news industry discourse, Colvin could not escape the familiar, ambivalent portrayal of her persona as paradoxically "self-sufficient" and "female." For instance, the *Vanity Fair* article that lauded Colvin's "courageous dispatches" also proclaimed that "her nails were a perfect scarlet, and her double strand of pearls was a gift from Yasser Arafat" (Brenner 2012). Colvin's own newspaper published an article about her, which was entitled "Cashmere and Pearls beneath the Combats," juxtaposing Colvin's ostensible affinity for traditionally feminine accessories with her undeniable "know-how" in the war zone (Shulman 2012). Like Logan, Colvin was a discursive contradiction. But after her death, industry commentators especially veered toward emphasizing her bravery and professional experience, more so than accentuating her status as a "female." Marked so visibly by the material realities of war—because of her eyepatch, and eventually because of her violent death in Homs—Colvin seemed the very definition of *extreme*. This extremity tended to overpower (though certainly not erase) the inevitable references to her femininity.

Because she had paid the ultimate price in the field, news industry commentators portrayed Colvin as the quintessential hero of melodrama, rather than as the victim. This rhetorical maneuver obfuscated the ways in which the logic of self-governance continued to inform the safety culture of conflict reporting at the beginning of the twenty-first century, where news organizations continued to offload the responsibility for safety onto the correspondents themselves. The very high likelihood of the correspondent's death was in turn woven into a grand narrative of willing sacrifice, where the correspondent might give her life in order to tell the world about the atrocities of war. Following this logic, Colvin's eulogies repeatedly invoked the death of the Syrian baby that she mentioned in her interviews with CNN, the BBC, and Channel 4, along with numerous other nameless children whose plights in Syria might justify the presence of professional journalists in that dangerous space ("Fallen Heroes" 2012; "More than Numbers" 2012). Colvin's television interviews served as a reference point for the industrial discussion of Colvin's death, as well as for the coverage coming from Colvin's own newspaper. In one sense, these print articles referenced Colvin's television interviews in order to point again to her fearless dedication to sharing the truth with the world, a "truth" that especially centered on the figure of a baby boy whose death Colvin witnessed on YouTube. In another sense, the industrial discourse on Colvin also referenced her final interviews with the television networks as a way of harnessing some of the power of televisual "liveness"—a strategy that CNN, the BBC, and Channel 4 News all deployed in their coverage of Colvin's death.

Each of the television interviews with Colvin drew heavily upon the strategy of "liveness" to "verify" the citizen footage that had been streaming out of Syria for weeks. "Liveness" has been defined as the televisual construction of temporal and spatial immediacy, a construction that bolsters certain socially accepted notions of time and space (White 2004). CNN's *Anderson Cooper 360* drew upon this televisual tactic, opening on February 21, 2012 with the celebrity anchor's own assertions about the dark intentions of the Syrian regime. Yet, Colvin's voice endowed the YouTube images flickering across the screen with a sense of intimacy, immediacy, and authenticity that networks like CNN had sorely been missing. Despite the news industry's long tradition of depending upon the authority of the eyewitness, this intimacy and authenticity did not necessarily hinge upon Colvin's literal positioning in time or space. In fact, Conroy's memoir seems to suggest that Colvin was not technically located in the space where the image of the dying baby had purportedly been recorded, nor had she witnessed that death in person. Conroy asserted that throughout their time in Baba Amr, Colvin had barely been able to venture outside the media center (Conroy 2013). Because of this, Conroy's account implies that the image that Colvin and CNN kept invoking was one that she, like any audience member, had encountered on a laptop screen. Colvin's physical presence in the hospital where the baby died was not the important factor, in other words; instead, it was Colvin's status as a professional journalist that legitimized the amateur video, her vital voice that did the dangerous labor of verifying the "truth" of what was happening in Syria.

Through this strategy, CNN carefully drew upon Colvin's words in order to accentuate the credibility of the YouTube video on which the network had been heavily depending since the early days of the uprising, credibility that had repeatedly been called into question by Assad's officials as well as by industry pundits. Throughout the Syrian uprising, politicians and journalists alike argued over the basic "who, what, when, and where" of the YouTube images flooding the internet. Assad himself repeatedly suggested their falseness, even disputing the graphic images of another dead boy, the 13-year-old who had apparently been tortured to death at the hands of Assad's own forces. In a December 2011 interview with ABC's Barbara Walters, Assad claimed that the boy was alive and that the images were fake. Colvin's words, spoken from the very neighborhood in which the atrocities were alleged to be unfolding, seemed to powerfully contest the words of Syrian officials, and this was precisely because she was a veteran conflict correspondent. The very fact of her precarious professional labor—labor she had lived to tell about for years—secured Colvin's authority to pronounce what was "true" and "false," and what did and did not count as a legitimate political frame.

Colvin's words became even more powerful, however, the day after she died. On February 22, 2012, Cooper announced the death of the witness with whom he had spoken only the day before ("Cooper Remembers" 2012). Replaying Colvin's account of the siege of Homs, CNN now also displayed the banner: "Marie Colvin's Final Talk with Anderson Cooper." This banner, layered over the "live" testimony from the previous night, operated in a few important ways. First, it situated Colvin's very sudden and confusing

Figure 10. CNN remembers its final interview with Marie Colvin.

death within a manageable melodramatic narrative. Though there was a lack of clarity in the hours following Colvin's death over why she had died and where her body could be located, the CNN newscast pretended that history could safely be written, even at this early point. With this goal in mind, CNN focused heavily on the apparently ahistorical evil of the Assad regime, glossing over any tough questions about the international politics that may have contributed to the war in Syria. In turn, CNN glossed over any tough questions that could have been asked about what safety precautions Colvin and her editors had taken to prevent this tragedy from occurring.

Second, this banner claimed ownership of Colvin's last recorded words. Cooper reflected upon his own final words to Colvin ("stay safe"), noting the eerie irony of such a farewell. The repeated reference to the "eeriness" of Colvin's recently recorded voice in fact served to distract viewers from the "past tense" quality of her authority; by casting her as a "specter," speaking from beyond the grave, CNN again deployed the strategy of "liveness," this time attempting to put Colvin to work even when she was dead. Though her physical body was no longer functional, Colvin's voice could continue to communicate the alleged situation in Homs, validating the political frames upon which CNN had been depending. Thus, CNN's "live" report from a dead person was highly lucrative, something that the network disavowed by deploying the rhetoric of individualism. Cooper remarked that Colvin's bravery stemmed from her personal drive to inhabit such dangerous spaces, in order to bear witness to the "truth" of what was happening in Syria. There was no significant mention of the fact that Colvin's decision to do an interview with CNN and other networks might have been the very thing that alerted Syrian officials to the media center's position. Instead, the catastrophe of Colvin's death and of the siege of Homs more generally was made legible through the "ongoing articulations of liveness and historicity," where "normatively distinct temporal and spatial categories of language and experience—proximity and distance, past and present—are brought together in relationships of mutual implication" (White 2004, 78).

But CNN did not solely "own" Colvin's final testimony, since she had also been interviewed on the BBC and Channel 4 News. Both of these networks similarly drew upon the televisual strategy of "liveness" in their February 22 coverage of Colvin's death, replaying the final testimony that she had given to each of them and mentioning that she had spoken on their newscasts only 24 hours before. The BBC and Channel 4 both generated competing discourses of ownership and authority that hinged on the immediacy and intimacy of Colvin's recorded words. The fact that Colvin was now dead did not diffuse this immediacy, nor did it destabilize the authority being invoked in these reports. Instead, Colvin's death endowed her recorded testimony with even more authority because of the fact that she had died in the midst of the dangerous attack she had already been trying to verify.

Like CNN, the BBC coverage invoked the Anglophone news industry's long reliance on "civilian footage" at the beginning of its report ("BBC: Voice of Marie Colvin" 2012). The network's Peter Dobbie opened the report by noting that "since the conflict in Syria began in March of last year, it has been difficult to obtain eyewitness accounts of what's going on there. Much of the evidence—videos, uploaded by civilian journalists, onto the Internet" (ibid.). Dobbie went on to say that more recently, some "international journalists" had been able to get into Syria, subtly suggesting that only the professional international journalists could properly obtain "eyewitness accounts" (ibid.). Thus, the BBC coverage of Colvin's death operated very similarly to the CNN coverage, positing journalists like Colvin as the authority figures who could verify the amateur footage upon which news outlets had long relied in order to cover the Syrian conflict in the first place.

Dobbie then introduced a report by BBC correspondent Fergal Keane, which opened with what was allegedly video of the precise bombing that had killed Colvin—and emblazoned across the top of this footage was the banner, "amateur video." Yet, this video was followed by Colvin's professional headshot, with Keane's voiceover asserting that she was the only British journalist who had been present in Baba Amr at the time of the bombing. The report then reminded viewers that Colvin had been interviewed by the BBC "only yesterday," cutting to her audio interview, which ran over footage attributed to Paul Conroy, courtesy of the *Sunday Times*. In this fashion, the BBC report interwove the amateur footage with Colvin's "live" testimony and Conroy's professional video images, braiding the three together to suggest that the activist accounts of the conflict in Syria could finally be trusted. At the same time, this strategy also attempted to professionally narrativize the war in Syria, implying that this was now a professional and not an amateur news story, despite the fact that amateur footage was still being used.

As in the CNN interview, the BBC report included Colvin's testimony about the death of the Syrian baby, encouraging viewers to sympathize with the Syrian opposition. Though the horrors that Colvin chronicled in Baba Amr were indeed grim, such a rhetorical maneuver was rather simplistic when viewing the conflict on a larger scale. This report did not discuss the international proxy war that was unfolding in Syria at the time, nor did it mention the fragmented nature of the Syrian opposition. Instead, the video portrayed the opposition through Colvin's immersed perspective, representing the people of this movement as innocent victims of a categorically evil villain who operated outside of any historical context. The invocation of the Syrian baby served only to solidify this representation. Meanwhile, Colvin herself was also aligned with western political sentiments in this report when Keane shared a sound bite from the British prime minister paying tribute to Colvin in the House of Commons. Rather than serving as an objective eyewitness, then, in death, Colvin was linked to a very distinct political perspective.

Channel 4 News also politicized Colvin's death in its February 22 coverage of the tragedy, though in this case, Colvin was invoked in order to cast a subtle critique on the British government ("Tributes Paid to Marie Colvin" 2012). In Jon Snow's report on the bombing that killed Colvin, he mentioned that British politicians were speaking out about Colvin's death, and he included that same footage of the British prime minister in the House of Commons (ibid.). Yet, Snow then said: "Political power today marked [Colvin's] death, but had nothing new to say of Syria" (ibid.). With this brief statement, Snow and his Channel 4 editors raised the question of whether western governments would ever intervene in Syria, a question that was common in 2012 and that remains common at the time of this writing. By raising this question, Channel 4 participated in representing the Syrian opposition as a unified population in need of salvation, while also portraying Assad's government as a villainous entity whose evil had no historical context.

Similarly to the BBC and CNN reports, the Channel 4 coverage of Colvin's death also represented Colvin herself as a "one-off," as "the bravest of our age" (Snow, cited in ibid.). As in the other videos, this strategy served to distract from questions of whether or not Colvin's death had been preventable. Yet, at the end of Channel 4's report, Snow interviewed ITN reporter Jonathan Miller, asking him to expound upon the risks that conflict correspondents face in the field. In this discussion, Miller asserted that war reporting "is a profession of enormous risk," and that Colvin was quite aware of "what those risks were" (ibid.). Miller then went on to suggest that Colvin's bravery had hinged upon her awareness of the dangers she faced, interweaving the news industry's continual invocation of Colvin's bravery with a reference to her individual responsibility. Since Miller himself was a conflict correspondent, his statements pointed to the ways in which war reporters internalize the neoliberal logic of self-sufficiency.

While at first glance, this exchange between Snow and Miller may have looked like a conscientious exploration of safety issues in the profession of war reporting, the discussion actually obscured the thornier questions that needed to be asked. Why had Colvin felt so compelled to put herself in this level of danger, for example, when other veteran correspondents like Channel 4's Lindsey Hilsum had refused to do so (Hilsum, cited in ibid.). On top of this, why had her editors told her to leave Baba Amr while at the same time alerting her to the fact that Channel 4 wanted to do an interview with her from that dangerous space? These are questions that needed to be asked after Colvin's death, and sadly, they have not yet been answered today.

Conclusion

In 2013, the *British Journalism Review* published an article about a meeting that had been held in London during October of 2012 (Horsley and Harrison 2013). This meeting included "60 editors and journalists from more than 40 major news organizations around the world," (ibid.). The meeting addressed the growing violence against journalists around the world, in an effort at brainstorming new ways of combating this problem. According to the authors of the article, the meeting focused on the nascent United Nations Action Plan on the Safety of Journalists and Impunity, a plan that eventually led UN officials to claim that "the plan will make a real difference only if the professional news media, journalists' associations and the power of civil society are fully mobilized to hold backsliding governments to account" (ibid.).

Strikingly, there was no mention in the article of news editors and executives brainstorming new ways of holding *themselves* accountable. Other than a very brief and uncritical reference to the competitiveness of the news business, the article did not address the myriad ways in which the professional culture and the political economy of the war reporting industry contributes to the tragedies that correspondents face in the field. Instead, the problem was largely represented as a political issue, one that lay solely in the hands of state or militant actors. Colvin's own death was certainly represented in this way, with the article proclaiming: "When world-famous journalists are killed . . . a clear warning is delivered to all concerned. That chilling effect is multiplied greatly when those responsible for the killing of journalists—often comprising both hitmen and masterminds—are allowed to go unpunished" (ibid.).

Though Colvin's death was undeniably chilling, both for the Anglophone news industry as well as for the world, the incident illuminates some issues that Chapter Five examines carefully. First, the incident highlights the disturbing interconnections between death and the business of conflict reporting, showing how death itself has historically been tied to the news industry's political economy. Conflict correspondents have long been expected to get as close as possible to the dead or dying, risking their own deaths in the process. Yet, these correspondents now share the conflict zone with a number of other people who also encounter the dead and dying, often placing graphic images of this carnage on easily accessible websites like YouTube. These images are highly lucrative for the professional news outlets that use them without compensating the people who capture them. News organizations increasingly rely on unpaid citizen labor, in turn leading professional correspondents to take more risks in an increasingly competitive environment.

Chapter Five also points to another problem: the ways in which western, English-language news organizations write the deaths of conflict correspondents into their melodramatic narratives. This strategy draws upon the incidents faced by reporters in the war zone in order to frame some deaths as more politically and ethically important than others. In Colvin's case, networks like CNN drew upon Colvin's "live" testimony to bolster their rather simplistic representations of the Syrian opposition, aligning Colvin with the civilians in Homs because she had suffered the same fate that many of them had also suffered. Yet, this narrative belied the diversity and complexity of the various groups who comprised the opposition movement, even as early as 2012. And as the conflict in Syria progressed in the years following 2012, it became more and more obvious that this particular war was the product of numerous interlocking factors, factors that had not been adequately explained in the war's early coverage.

Especially in cases like Colvin's, mainstream, English-language news organizations continue to deploy their hero and villain narratives. They also struggle to explain what could be viewed as serious failures of the system: the exploitation, competitiveness, and neglect that all contribute to the very public deaths of their own employees. News organizations need to go further in taking professional responsibility for these tragedies, working to be more proactive in preventing them and investigating ways to improve their practices after the fact. But at the present moment, news organizations avoid such discussions, at least on a level where the public can participate. Instead, news outlets continue to feed the public stock images of correspondents as free individuals, maverick renegades who willingly make the most exacting sacrifices to bring truth and democracy to the world. A renewed attention to the context of conflict, as well as a renewed interest in the histories that drive the wars of the twenty-first century, could help shift the focus from "seeing dead people" to understanding why wars happen in the first place.

Ultimately, the correspondents' precariously embodied labor, "slogging in the mud," as Colvin herself put it (Colvin, cited in Ricchiardi 2012), in order to help the audience "see, smell, and feel" the war zone (Amos, cited in Mawad 2012)—is still grandly narrativized, especially after death. In the discourse on conflict correspondence, there is a subtle connection between the encounter with the deaths of others, and the potential to meet one's own death in the process of seeking those encounters. While the correspondent seeks the dead or dying bodies of others in order to get the story and, thus, to contribute to the construction of the political frame, that correspondent perpetually attempts to evade his or her own death as well. This slippage informs the precarious labor of conflict correspondence. The correspondent's multiple significations cannot be separated from the fact of his or her sensory existence, the laboring body that strives to survive but may encounter a shell at any time.

Conclusion

In some ways, the decade after the September 11 attacks on the World Trade Center seems very recent. The people who remember 9/11 often talk about that event as though it happened "just yesterday." The conflicts that followed the attacks sometimes seem like an inevitable part of the present, part of the world that we inhabit *now*. But this general feeling of temporal simultaneity owes a great deal to the rhetoric that followed 9/11, to the melodramatic narrative that politically simplified the "war on terror" and separated 9/11 from the messy history in which it was entangled. It is crucial for scholars to engage in the tricky but essential work of historicizing every moment, of understanding each event within the broader context that history has to offer. Even a decade that ended only a few years ago has much to tell us, when viewed through a critical historical lens. Applying this lens to the labor of war reporting as it unfolded just after 9/11, we can see the complexity of that labor: how it was shaped by earlier practices and how it veered into new territory. We can also gain a clearer understanding of the ambivalent interplay between war correspondents and the media texts that inform our knowledge of the world's conflicts.

With these issues in mind, this book advances a set of interrelated arguments. First, the book contests that in the first decade of the twenty-first century, conflict reporters grappled with three challenges: industrial, technological, and political. These challenges had connections with the obstacles that conflict correspondents faced in the past, but they intensified in the years between 2002–2012. The first of these challenges was the shifting economic landscape of the Anglophone news industry. At the end of the twentieth century, when corporate buyouts led to the conglomeration of major media industries, U.S. news outlets were compelled to close a number of their foreign bureaus around the world (Barkin 2003; Paterson and Sreberny 2004; Williams 2011). Public and private news outlets in Britain and Canada also faced an array of budget cuts and layoffs over the first years of the twenty-first century. The infrastructure of English-language foreign bureaus around the world had already been dismantled by the time of the September 11 attacks on the World Trade Center, when news organizations suddenly felt that their audiences were displaying a renewed interest in foreign reporting. The lack of infrastructure, on top of the slashing of news budgets and resulting newsroom layoffs, contributed to a much more competitive market in which news outlets relied more heavily on underpaid freelance labor and on the unpaid labor of digital citizen journalists. These dire economic conditions encouraged freelancers and staff correspondents alike to compete more viciously and to place themselves at greater and greater risk.

The second challenge that conflict correspondents faced was related to the changing uses of technology. Intensifying technological practices—practices embedded within the broader sociocultural history of Anglophone war reporting—contributed to shifting expectations for correspondents in the war zone. With the proliferation of lighter and more mobile media technologies as the new century unfolded, correspondents felt the pressure to place themselves closer and closer to the violence. As the "war on terror" progressed and digital practices became even more sophisticated, news organizations also began to deal with the growing "trackability" of their correspondents in the field. For example, regimes like that of Bashar al-Assad in Syria could use satellite GPS technology to locate correspondents operating illegally within the country, a capability that some in the news industry associated with the 2012 death of Marie Colvin (Conroy 2013). Alongside this challenge, correspondents increasingly had to compete with digital activists who used portable media technologies of their own, propagating competing views of what was happening in the world. In this tightly networked technological environment, the conflict correspondent's voice had become one of many.

The third challenge that conflict correspondents faced in the early twenty-first century was political in nature. As the twentieth century drew to a close, the Anglophone war reporting industry began to feel that journalists were increasingly being targeted, just for doing their work. And with the advent of the "war on terror," this feeling only grew. Many of my interviewees asserted that the early twenty-first century was a uniquely dangerous time for war correspondents from the Anglophone world, because they were no longer seen as neutral observers. Instead, journalists were associated with the U.S. government and its allies, or with specific rebel groups that were disliked by other dangerous factions. Journalists were seen as being expendable, since militant groups could simply broadcast their own messages online, rather than relying on professional reporters. Conflict correspondents were also seen as an easy way to make money, since they could be kidnapped and held for ransom.

It is important to remember that Anglophone war correspondents were politically targeted long before the twenty-first century, and they were associated with particular military interests almost as soon as war reporting became a legitimate profession. This is because war correspondents were historically a part of the dominant social establishment and, sometimes, they had even served in the military before becoming journalists (Knightley 2004). Military censorship blurred the lines between journalists and their own governments long before the "war on terror." All the way back in the World Wars, reporters had to travel with the troops, wear military gear, and sign agreements on what they could and could not report (ibid.).

Yet, despite these connections between twenty-first-century war reporting and the political obstacles faced in earlier years, there does appear to be a record number of war reporters dying in the field. The war reporting industry has also seen the rise of journalistic kidnappings, specifically in Syria. This has led news organizations to limit their reporters' visits to Syria and leading editors to refuse work from freelancers who travel there. Thus, while the injuries and deaths of conflict correspondents were in many ways par for the course in earlier years, there has been a marked change in the English-language news industry's attitudes toward safety.

This is related to the second argument I make in this book: the twenty-first century saw the explosion of a paradoxical performance of safety and risk. While editors continued to push correspondents to "get the story," even in the most dangerous of environments, they simultaneously took steps to help correspondents survive the story—and these steps didn't always work. News outlets hired security advisors to guide them in the war zone, they pushed for the use of safety equipment, and they encouraged their staff reporters to engage in safety training that still tended to offload the responsibility for the correspondents' safety onto the correspondents themselves. Many of the staff correspondents I interviewed participated in the highly performative "hazardous environment" courses that simulate warlike conditions. Yet, correspondents such as Bob Woodruff also asserted these courses to be "relatively worthless" (pers. comm., September 2013). Such courses were even less helpful to the freelancers, fixers, and local journalists who could not afford to pay for them on their own. Because of the aforementioned economic landscape, correspondents in the years between 2002–2012 were subjected to a hierarchy of safety preparation, where freelancers and local fixers usually had to pay for their own safety training and medical insurance. The safety of citizen journalists rarely even occurred to news organizations (Brayne, pers. comm., February 2013).

A big part of the problem was the diffuse and heterogeneous nature of news outlets and the news industry more generally. With so many moving parts, it was difficult for war correspondents, their editors, and their organizations to formalize better policies or to hold each other accountable. It didn't help that the mainstream, English-language war reporting industry was obsessed with the notion of individualism, during these years and long before. This leads me to the third and final argument I advance in this book. In the years following 9/11, the Anglophone news industry continued its decades-old tradition of representing its war reporters as self-sufficient individuals—even when they fell prey to the perils of the war zone. Especially in the news coverage of these mishaps, conflict correspondents were portrayed as the neoliberal subjects of late capitalism. In other words, they were cast as "free" individuals (Anker 2014), who were fully responsible for their own safety.

This narrative strategy informed the coverage of Daniel Pearl's 2002 kidnapping in Pakistan. It also surfaced in the coverage of Bob Woodruff's 2006 injury, Maziar Bahari's 2009 imprisonment and exile, Lara Logan's 2011 sexual assault, and Marie Colvin's death in 2012. The only time this strategy was not used in one of the circumstances discussed in this book was in the case of the Iranian reporter Nazila Fathi. This is because Anglophone news organizations barely considered her exile to be worthy of narrativizing at all, until she told her own story. Fathi's experience exemplifies the fact that news organizations' obsession with the plights of certain journalists only obscured the plights of others—most often, the plights of those who were not white westerners.

The narrative strategies I identify in this book are melodramatic strategies. They write certain conflict correspondents into broader stories that assert the villainy of some people, while championing more culturally and politically "recognizable" groups of people (Butler 2004, 2009). Anker argues that melodrama is linked to neoliberalism because it celebrates the notion of the "hero's" freedom (2014). The concept of freedom is a key element of neoliberalism, though Anker states that this notion of individual freedom is actually just a mask for the entitlement that U.S. citizens are taught to feel (ibid.). On an international level, this American "entitlement" takes the form of the unchecked power that the United States has enjoyed for decades (ibid.). This unchecked power has long demarcated who is "good" and who is "bad," who can be recognized as fully "human" and who cannot.

According to Butler, "recognizability" is a decisively ethical question (2004). Drawing from Emanuel Levinas's explication of what is at stake in recognizing the "face of the other," Butler argues that when we cannot see some people as human—when we only see them as enemies, or as collateral damage—we participate in the sociopolitical process of precarity (ibid.). This process determines which groups of people will receive the resources they need, in order to survive and flourish in the world. For Butler, the media play a central role in delimiting who can be recognized as human. She refers to the power of the news camera to meld with the logic of precarity, capturing certain things on screen and leaving other things out (ibid.). Additionally, Butler suggests that the news media are (perhaps inadvertently) helping to construct the philosophical frames that dehumanize the "other." Because of this, she calls on critical scholars to "frame the frame."

This book engages in the ethical practice of "framing the frame," focusing specifically on the war correspondents' ambivalent role in perpetuating these larger philosophical approaches to understanding the world. By studying the labor of war reporting after 9/11, I illuminate the complexity of the work that ultimately results in the news coverage we see on our screens. I also show that war correspondents do not have direct control over the framing processes of which Butler speaks. They cannot be simplistically conflated with their news outlets; nor can a news outlet be simplistically conflated with the government of its home nation. In fact, it is this reductive conflation that sometimes leads to correspondents being targeted in the field. War reporters are not simply "mouthpieces." They are nodes in larger networks of human and nonhuman actors—networks that still perpetuate the logic of precarity, albeit in a diffuse and systemic way. It is also of great ethical importance to remember that war reporters are human subjects and material bodies. They can be emotionally and physically broken by the work that they do, and they take extraordinary risks in the process of covering the world's conflicts. With this book, I have tried to shed light on some of the perils that conflict correspondents face.

Yet, this book is by no means exhaustive. There are still a number of areas that need further exploration. One crucial area of exploration is the issue of psychological injury, a looming problem in war reporting that still needs more study. The material, physical risk is fundamental to my definition of conflict correspondence. But war reporters also perpetually grapple with what former correspondent and current psychoanalyst Mark Brayne has described as the psychic imprint of that labor (pers. comm., February 2013). As Brayne told me, the risk of PTSD is one that haunts the work of war reporting, especially because of the profession's "macho culture" (ibid.). Brayne explained that conflict correspondents are trained to avoid dealing with the emotional fallout from the things they encounter (ibid.). To appear emotional is to appear as though one cannot step back from the events being covered, that one cannot effectively transcend and navigate the site of conflict. According to Brayne, this attitude dominates professional news culture in the Anglophone world, leaving conflict reporters especially vulnerable to the emotions they are not always allowed to process in a healthy way.

Emotional injury potentially affects all war reporters in one manner or another. For example, Marie Colvin suffered very directly from PTSD, receiving medical treatment for it on numerous occasions (Witherow 2012). Lara Logan also reportedly suffered from the disorder after her sexual assault in Egypt (Huff 2012). Even those correspondents who are not diagnosed with PTSD might still suffer from the emotional ramifications of their precarious labor. CNN's Michael Holmes told me of the difficulties he faced on returning to the United States after working in Iraq, for instance, asserting that as he drove down the freeway, he could not easily shake the sense that certain cars might be carrying a bomb (pers. comm., January 2013).

Holmes was not the only interviewee who was emotionally impacted by his experiences. When I was interviewing Ray Homer in Beirut, at one point he began to cry as he discussed the death of an ABC news fixer in Iraq. "I'm sorry," he told me. "I was just thinking about some things" (pers. comm., June 2015). And Sulome Anderson, daughter of the Associated Press's Terry Anderson who was kidnapped in Beirut during the Lebanese Civil War, said: "After what happened to my dad. . . . I mean, everyone I grew up with, all my parents' friends were war correspondents. And they are fucking crazy. This job takes a toll on you. Especially for the people who do hardcore, 'bang-bang' war journalism" (pers. comm., June 2015).

Anderson's testimony points to the fact that the emotional damage incurred through the practice of war reporting is not a new issue. And while organizations like the Dart Center for Journalism and Trauma have pushed news organizations to think more proactively about their correspondents' emotional health, Brayne told me that this kind of industrial change happens very slowly:

> Because this is expensive, and it's awkward. And also a lot of news organizations [have] said, "We only use freelancers, we don't need to take responsibility because they're responsible for themselves. We don't want to get in the

way of our journalists making decisions for themselves." Well, you do have to, actually, because you have a duty of care. (pers. comm., February 2013)

In some respects, news outlets are beginning to embrace this "duty of care," slow though such transformation may be. For instance, in February 2015 an international group of news organizations—including CNN, CBS, ABC, and the BBC—signed a set of guidelines for ensuring the safety of freelancers ("Freelance Journalist Safety Principles" 2015). The guidelines first included a list of precautions that journalists should take, echoing the individualizing rhetoric that has long defined industrial policies on war reporting. But the list of principles also included a set of guidelines for the news organizations more specifically, targeting news editors. Among these guidelines was the call for editors to "show the same concern for the welfare of local journalists and freelancers that they do for staffers" and to "factor in the additional costs of training, insurance and safety equipment in war zones" when determining freelancers' compensation (ibid.). Another meeting on September 30 and October 1 of 2015 resulted in what the Dart Center said were "unprecedented initiatives to share security information; provide subsidized safety training to freelancers; conduct a census of freelancers that could reduce their insurance costs and better inform journalism students of grants and other resources available to freelancers" ("Sotloff Foundation" 2015). These endeavors arguably mark news outlets' productive efforts at thinking more self-reflexively about the safety of freelancers in the field.

Of course, it is too early to determine how helpful these measures will truly be. John Owen, chairman of the Frontline Club, is optimistic, pronouncing that since the late 1990s and especially after 9/11, news organizations have become more collaborative when dealing with safety issues (pers. comm., February 2015). In our interview, Owen cited the aforementioned safety principles as only one example of this collaboration (ibid.). Yet, as the executive director of the Committee to Protect Journalists Joel Simon told me, there are no official mechanisms in place to hold the signatory organizations accountable, should they fail to keep their word and adhere to the principles on the treatment of freelancers:

> There's accountability within news organizations. There's accountability created by the fact that there is some attention on lapses, and there's the sort of shame factor that could function sometimes. But there's no mechanism across the industry to ensure accountability. (pers. comm., April 2015)

Without accountability, it is difficult to ascertain how much the war reporting industry will actually change. On top of that question, it is tough to determine how uniformly these new guidelines will be applied, especially considering the heterogeneity of the English-language news industry. Simon hinted at this issue, arguing that there are key differences between a major international television network versus a smaller online publication (ibid.). These differences might inform the application of the more recent safety guidelines.

There is still very little formal policy on how news organizations should treat their locally based employees, though some of my interviewees say that even this is changing. It is increasingly difficult to speak about "western" news reporting without erasing the critical fact that even those news outlets based in the United States and privileging a U.S. audience still rely heavily on the labor of employees who live and work in diverse geopolitical contexts. Without the drivers, translators, stringers, and "fixers" who live and work in Iraq, for example, news organizations like CNN would never have been able to continue their coverage of the conflict that long outlasted the 2003 invasion of Baghdad. In fact, Iraqi stringers and fixers often acted as "surrogates" for the noticeably more white, westernized reporters who were increasingly being targeted if they stepped outside their Baghdad compounds. Western editors and bureau chiefs sent these Iraqi journalists into dangerous environments, and western networks paid them for this labor. In this sense, when scholars critically invoke the "western" news media, it should be remembered that local journalists and fixers are a crucial part of these institutions.

As conflict itself changes, so does the labor of war reporting. In this book, I define *conflict* as something that describes war and also the political and digital dissent that many traditional war reporters have increasingly covered. The past few years have seen an explosion of uprisings at diverse geopolitical sites, uprisings that sometimes become heavily militarized. Though the twentieth century also saw plenty of uprisings, in this new century the prevalence of digital activism has drawn global attention to protests like those in Egypt and civil wars like that in Syria. Thus, traditional war reporters have turned their gaze to online spaces of dissent that are linked with material sites; the war correspondents of the twenty-first century now operate simultaneously on the ground and on the web, creating online personas and sifting through Twitter feeds, even as they dodge teargas and bullets.

Despite my own broad definition of *conflict*, there are broader definitions still. In the digital era, there is more and more of a focus on the notion of *cyberwarfare*, a type of conflict where the involved parties direct their attacks at information infrastructures. Such attacks can result in data theft, malfunctioning technology, or infrastructural chaos. It remains to be seen whether journalists who report strictly on cyberwarfare will also be called *conflict correspondents*. For my purposes, the *conflict correspondent* is at least partially defined by a highly embodied type of labor that places these news employees at locations that can directly impact their physical well-being. Yet, there are embodied consequences to cyberwarfare, too, and the journalists who report on this phenomenon can also find themselves being targeted along decisively material lines. Thus, this type of journalism also needs further scholarly scrutiny.

On top of this issue, the prevalence of drone warfare raises questions about the meaning of *conflict* in the contemporary moment. When warfare becomes so profoundly one-sided that U.S. pilots can operate war weapons from overseas, dropping missiles on innocent civilians more often than on purported "terrorists," it is difficult to avoid using the word *genocide* rather than *conflict*. In these cases, the attacks can happen so quickly and secretively that traditional war reporters may not be able to get to the scene, leaving the important act of bearing witness to the people who have themselves been attacked. The proliferation of what Lisa Parks refers to as "drone media" (Parks 2017) proves that this "amateur"—but incisively bold and necessary—form of conflict reporting is a very real part of the journalistic landscape at the present moment. These citizen journalists and digital activists certainly put themselves in harm's way to share their experiences with a transnational public. They undoubtedly experience the same, if not more, of the physical and emotional dangers that professional reporters experience.

It may be that we no longer live in a world where these figures can easily be separated from more traditional conflict correspondents. In this convoluted media environment, hard distinctions between "professional" and "amateur" reporting can sometimes appear rather trite, especially when major news organizations rely upon citizen footage more often than they would like to admit. It seems likely that scholars and industry pundits will increasingly talk about those reporters who work with news brands and those who do not, further tightening the hierarchies of safety that define the contemporary news landscape, while also broadening the definition of what it means to cover conflict. In light of these changes, we need more critical theories of the labor of conflict correspondence, more ways of understanding the precarious but still vital work that so often blurs the line between the stories and their storytellers.

Appendix
Research Methods

This book draws upon a mixed set of methods in order to address the many layers that have defined the labor of conflict correspondence in the years following 9/11. First, the book relies heavily on qualitative, semistructured interviews with conflict reporters and the news executives who work with them. Second, the book is informed by my visits to four cities that serve as "hubs" for war reporters. Third, the book benefits from a critical discourse analysis of news industry trade articles and newspaper reports that were relevant to each of my historical case studies. Finally, this project deploys a textual analysis of television news footage in which conflict correspondents were featured as part of the news story. I used each of these methods in an effort at answering the following research questions:

1. How (if at all) has the labor of war reporting changed since the September 11, 2001, attacks on the World Trade Center? How has it stayed the same?
2. What role has digital technology played in this work?
3. How has the question of journalistic safety figured in the discourse and practices of Anglophone news outlets in the first years of the twenty-first century?
4. What are the ethical problems that industry practitioners and media scholars need to address when considering the Anglophone war reporting industry?

In the following sections, I explain the book's research methods in more detail.

Qualitative Interviews

From June 2012 to January 2016, I conducted 85 qualitative, semistructured interviews with war reporters who worked for Anglophone news organizations. I also interviewed 27 news editors and producers who worked with war correspondents in some capacity. These interviews ranged from 20 minutes to 2 hours in length, though they were usually about 45 minutes long. Some of the interviews were conducted via Skype, from my home in Pasadena, California, and later from my office in Madison, Wisconsin. A number of the interviews were also held in person, in the cities where I conducted my site visits. I interviewed people born and raised in the United States, Canada, and Britain; I also spoke to people from places as diverse as Palestine, Pakistan, Lebanon, Egypt, Syria, Turkey, Qatar, Iraq, Iran, and Jordan. I interviewed both freelancers and staff correspondents, as well as television reporters and print journalists, in hopes of getting the broadest possible view of what conflict reporting entails in the digital age. At the end of this appendix, I have included a more detailed list of the journalists and news editors who gave an interview for this research.

Following the suggestion of qualitative researchers Bruce Lawrence Berg and Howard Lune (2011), I intentionally kept the interview template open-ended, allowing each conversation to flow organically from one topic to another. This gave me access to the interviewees' unique anecdotes and memories, which often revealed far more about their past work than did the more direct value judgments they would make about the state of the war reporting industry. In some cases, I relied on these interviews for basic information about the "nuts and bolts" of the labor of war reporting, or for specific details about the events that unfolded in my case studies. Yet, rather than merely relying on these testimonies as factual accounts of what war reporting entails, I also followed John Caldwell's example (2008) in conceptualizing the interviewees' statements as professional performances that could reveal a great deal about the larger economic, political, and technological cultures in which these news employees work. Despite the relative open-endedness of my approach, I did make sure to investigate two important topics with each interviewee: 1) what role has digital technology played in your work, and 2) what measures have been taken to ensure your safety in the field? The answers to these questions served as the backbone of this research project, which explores the precarious labor of war reporting in the context of new safety protocols and in the age of digital convergence.

Site Visits

On top of the qualitative interviews I conducted, I also made a series of short site visits to four cities that serve as hubs for war correspondents, between April of 2013 and July of 2015. I first visited the city of Doha in the tiny Gulf nation of Qatar, from April 1–12, 2013. There, I toured the Al Jazeera English headquarters and conducted a number of in-person interviews with Al-Jazeera English employees. This visit helped me to better understand the unique perspectives of the Al Jazeera employees who work to provide an alternative view of conflict to English-language audiences. I learned that many Al-Jazeera employees previously worked at British, Canadian, or U.S. news outlets, blending those more western viewpoints with viewpoints originating in the

Arab world. This visit taught me that the western or Anglophone news perspective is not as coherent and monolithic as critical media scholars have sometimes argued. From May 27 to June 21, 2015, I visited the Lebanese city of Beirut, which has been a war reporting hub since the civil war of 1975–1990. Not only did I conduct a number of my interviews in Beirut; I was also able to observe some of Beirut's corps of foreign correspondents working in a city that is only a short drive from the Syrian conflict zone. In turn, I got the opportunity to visit the resistance landmark at Mleeta, where much of the conflict between Hezbollah and Israeli forces unfolded during the civil war, and later during the war of 2006. This experience, alongside my forays through the battered streets that had once comprised Beirut's Green Line, helped me to think more historically about the conflict zone, as well as thinking more historically about the long-standing practice of war reporting.

I next visited the Turkish city of Istanbul from July 1–12, 2015. A number of conflict correspondents have chosen to live in Istanbul in more recent years, making this a good place for in-person interviews with a newer generation of war reporters. Though much of the conflict in Turkey occurs miles away, at the Turkish-Syrian border, many war reporters make Istanbul their home because of its proximity to key nations in the Middle East and North Africa and because of its thriving local culture. Freelance journalists also tend to suggest that Istanbul is cheaper than Beirut, making it a more pragmatic choice for them. In Istanbul, I benefited especially from the perspectives of the freelance journalists who navigate the slipperiness of the Anglophone news industry in order to make a living.

Finally, I visited the Egyptian city of Cairo from July 12–24, 2015. There, I spent the majority of my time at the Associated Press's Middle Eastern bureau, observing the labor practices of both the foreign correspondents and the local Egyptian employees. On a daily basis, I was able to "listen in" on the morning conference calls between the Cairo-based editors and the upper management based in New York, London, and Washington, D.C. I was also allowed to observe a bureauwide meeting addressing the growing safety issues that AP employees were experiencing in Egypt during the summer of 2015. These experiences helped me to gain a clearer picture of the complex relationships that form between local and foreign correspondents, as well as between journalists in the field and their editors who live far away from the site of conflict.

Critical Discourse Analysis

Alongside the qualitative interviews and site visits, this book also draws upon a critical discourse analysis of three different types of print publication: 1) news industry trade journals, which are written for journalists and editors to read, 2) newspaper and newsmagazine articles, which are geared toward the general public, and 3) a selection of war reporters' memoirs that were relevant to my case studies. In terms of the memoirs, I relied on these texts first for basic information about the events in question. I also analyzed these texts for examples of war correspondents' participation in constructing the discourse that underscores the Anglophone conflict reporting industry. For example, in Chapter 5, I drew upon the photographer Paul Conroy's account of his last days working with Marie Colvin. His book gave me insight into the basic facts of her death, while also illuminating the ways in which war reporters contribute to the industrial discourse that my research interrogates.

For each of my case studies, I also searched the English-language industry trade articles that were written during the time period in question. Alongside this method, I also analyzed certain news organizations' coverage of the incidents that their own correspondents may have faced in the field. Thus, the discourse analysis was also an archival analysis of a particular historical moment, starting with Pearl's kidnapping in 2002 and ending with Colvin's death in 2012. For example, Chapter One is heavily informed by the discourse found in the English-language trade publications from January 2002 through May 2002 (when CBS aired the footage of Daniel Pearl's execution). This chapter also relies upon an analysis of the *Wall Street Journal* coverage of Pearl's kidnapping that ran from January to May 2002, since Pearl was an employee for the *Journal*.

In this case study, as well as in the other four, I coded the industry trade articles and the newspaper coverage for themes that were relevant to my project—themes such as "safety/security," "digital technology," and "political economy." Following Ruth Wodak's argument that "on the one hand, the situational, institutional and social settings shape and affect discourses, and on the other, discourses influence discursive as well as nondiscursive social and political processes and actions," (2001, 66) I ultimately searched these print publications for instances in which news industry discourse was either *reflecting* or *constructing* journalistic norms. At the end of this appendix, I provide a list of the industry trade publications and the newspapers/ newsmagazines I analyzed in this research.

Textual Analysis of Video Footage

For the fourth and final method used in this research, I conducted a textual analysis of select television news reports. These reports were each chosen because they portrayed a conflict correspondent as part of the news story itself. Rather than approaching these videos through the lens of critical discourse analysis, I explored the videos' filmic *structure*, while also "examining the political or ideological values that shape[d] or underpin[ned]" these televisual news reports (Gillespie and Toynbee 2006, 1–2). In other words, I investigated the different elements of the video at the level of both form and content, in an effort at better understanding the ways in which war reporters are circulated in the public imaginary as semiotic signs, loaded with sociopolitical meaning.

I also watched over 100 television news reports that were relevant to each of my historical case studies, ranging from the 2002 coverage of Daniel Pearl's kidnapping to the 2012 death of Marie Colvin in Syria. The vast majority of these reports were viewed at the Vanderbilt Television News Archive, which houses a large collection of U.S. news footage. It is far more difficult to access British or Canadian television news footage, especially when the researcher is based in the United States. Thus, I watched a smaller selection of videos from the BBC and Channel Four News that were available to me online. Finally, I watched a small selection of videos posted on Al Jazeera English's website, in order to get a different perspective on events such as the 2011 Egyptian uprising. At the end of this appendix, I have included a list of the television news networks whose reports I viewed for this research.

List of Interviewees

CORRESPONDENTS:

1. Anonymous retired NBC correspondent, interviewed June 2012
2. Anonymous retired NBC field producer, interviewed June 2012
3. Anonymous CBS correspondent, interviewed December 2012
4. Anonymous CNN camerawoman, interviewed December 2012
5. Lama Hasan, ABC correspondent, interviewed January 2013
6. Zeina Khodr, Al Jazeera English correspondent, interviewed January 2013
7. Alexander Marquardt, ABC correspondent, interviewed January 2013
8. Matt McGarry, ABC field producer, interviewed January 2013
9. Rachel Anderson, freelancer correspondent, interviewed January 2013
10. Don Duncan, former freelance correspondent, interviewed January 2013
11. Michael Holmes, CNN correspondent and anchor, interviewed January 2013
12. Fred Scott, freelance cameraman, interviewed February 2013
13. Sebastian Junger, freelance filmmaker and correspondent, interviewed February 2013
14. John Wendle, freelance correspondent, interviewed February 2013
15. Paul Wood, BBC correspondent, interviewed February 2013
16. Rosie Garthwaite, freelance correspondent, interviewed February 2013
17. Ben Gittleson, freelance correspondent, interviewed February 2013
18. Oliver Holmes, Reuters correspondent, interviewed February 2013
19. Bill Gentile, freelance multimedia correspondent, interviewed February 2013
20. Angus Hines, ABC field producer, interviewed February 2013
21. Aaron Ross, freelance correspondent, interviewed February 2013
22. Hala Gorani, CNN correspondent and anchor, interviewed February 2013
23. Abigail Hauslohner, *Washington Post* correspondent, interviewed February 2013
24. Kevin Sites, freelance multimedia correspondent, interviewed February 2013 and 2014

25. David Degner, freelance photojournalist, interviewed February 2013
26. Shawn Baldwin, freelance photojournalist, interviewed February 2013
27. Ben Solomon, *New York Times* videographer, interviewed February 2013
28. Christina Paschyn, former freelance correspondent, interviewed April 2013
29. Hashem Ahelbarra, former Abu Dhabi TV correspondent, current Al Jazeera English correspondent, interviewed April 2013
30. Yasmine Ryan, former Al Jazeera English web correspondent, interviewed April 2013
31. Sherine Tadros, former Al Jazeera English correspondent, current Sky News correspondent interviewed April 2013
32. Anonymous Al Jazeera English field producer, interviewed April 2013
33. Salman Siddiqui, former AFP stringer and freelance fixer, April 2013
34. Hoda Abdel-Hamid, former ABC field producer, Al Jazeera English correspondent, interviewed April 2013
35. Andrew Mills, former *Toronto Star* reporter and freelancer, interviewed April 2013
36. Janet Key, former *New York Times* correspondent, interviewed April 2013
37. Alastair Leithead, BBC correspondent, interviewed May 2013
38. Jonathan Miller, ITN correspondent, interviewed May 2013
39. Jonathan Rugman, ITN correspondent, interviewed May 2013
40. Susan Ormiston, CBC correspondent, interviewed May 2013
41. Caroline Wyatt, BBC correspondent, interviewed May 2013
42. Leena Saidi, former freelance correspondent and fixer, interviewed May 2013
43. Lindsey Hilsum, ITN correspondent, interviewed May 2013 and April 2015
44. Judith Matloff, former freelance correspondent, interviewed June 2013
45. Kate Adie, BBC correspondent, interviewed June 2013
46. Anonymous freelance correspondent and fixer, interviewed July 2013
47. Anonymous freelance correspondent and fixer, interviewed July 2013
48. Holly Pickett, freelance correspondent, interviewed July 2013
49. Bob Woodruff, ABC correspondent and former anchor, interviewed September 2013 and February 2014
50. Lourdes Garcia-Navarro, NPR correspondent, interviewed July 2014
51. Abeer Ayyoub, news fixer, interviewed September 2014
52. Erin Banco, freelance correspondent, interviewed December 2014
53. Anonymous freelancer and stringer for wire service, interviewed February 2015
54. Taghreed El-Khodary, former stringer for the *New York Times*, interviewed April 2015
55. Anna Lekas Miller, freelance correspondent, interviewed May 2015

56. Liz Sly, *Washington Post* Beirut bureau chief, interviewed June 2015
57. Patrick Baz, photo editor for AFP Beirut bureau, interviewed June 2015
58. Roy Samaha, former video journalist for Beirut production house, interviewed June 2015
59. Mohamad al-Sayed, news fixer, interviewed June 2015
60. Rana Moussaoui, AFP Beirut correspondent, interviewed June 2015
61. Samya Kullab, Lebanon *Daily Star* correspondent, interviewed June 2015
62. Habib Battah, freelance correspondent, interviewed June 2015
63. Jeff Neumann, freelance correspondent, interviewed June 2015
64. Abd Nova, former news fixer, interviewed June 2015
65. Dalia Khamissy, former AP photo editor, current freelance photographer, interviewed June 2015
66. Jessica Dheere, former freelance correspondent, interviewed June 2015
67. Moe Ali Nayel, news fixer, interviewed June 2015
68. Josh Wood, freelance correspondent, interviewed June 2015
69. Ammar Abd Rabbo, freelance photojournalist, interviewed June 2015
70. Luna Safwan, former news fixer and correspondent at NOW Lebanon, interviewed June 2015
71. Sulome Anderson, freelance correspondent, interviewed June 2015
72. Kareem Shaheen, stringer for the *Guardian*, interviewed June 2015
73. Suzan Haidamous, news assistant for the *Washington Post*, interviewed June 2015
74. Nour Malas, *Wall Street Journal* correspondent, interviewed June 2015
75. Rami Aysha, freelance correspondent, interviewed June 2015
76. Nabih Bulos, news assistant for the *Los Angeles Times*, interviewed June 2015
77. Hwaida Saad, news assistant for the *New York Times*, interviewed June 2015
78. Anonymous Turkish correspondent for U.S. newspaper, interviewed July 2015
79. Yusuf Sayman, freelance photojournalist, interviewed July 2015
80. Anonymous news fixer and freelance photographer, interviewed July 2015
81. Nada Bakri, former *New York Times* correspondent, interviewed July 2015
82. Mostafa Sheshtawy, former news fixer, interviewed July 2015
83. Nazila Fathi, former contract correspondent for the *New York Times*, interviewed July 2015
84. Samad, news fixer, interviewed August 2015
85. Nadine Marroushi, freelance correspondent, interviewed January 2016

NEWS EDITORS AND EXECUTIVES:

1. Mark Brayne, former BBC correspondent and DART Center executive, interviewed February 2013

2. Noreen Jameel, former chief crew producer for Al Jazeera, interviewed February 2013

3. Tamara Bralo, former CNN editor, Al Jazeera English safety consultant, interviewed April 2013

4. Jason Samuels, former ABC web producer, interviewed February 2015

5. Alexis Gelber, former *Newsweek* editor, interviewed February 2015

6. Owen Ullmann, *USA Today* managing editor of world news, interviewed February 2015

7. Philip Bennett, former *Washington Post* managing editor, interviewed February 2015

8. John Geddes, former *New York Times* managing editor, interviewed February 2015

9. Marquita Pool-Eckert, former CBS correspondent and executive producer, interviewed February 2015

10. David Hoffman, former *Washington Post* foreign editor, interviewed February 2015

11. John Owen, former head of CBC Television News, interviewed February 2015

12. Scott Anderson, former CNN web producer, interviewed February 2015

13. Charlie Beckett, former program editor for ITN, interviewed February 2015

14. Paul Ingrassia, former Reuters managing editor, interviewed February 2015

15. David Nayman, former CBC executive producer, interviewed March 2015

16. Kathleen Carroll, former Associated Press executive editor, interviewed March 2015

17. William Schmidt, former *New York Times* deputy managing editor, interviewed March 2015

18. Paul Knox, former *Globe and Mail* foreign editor, interviewed March 2015

19. Jamie Wilson, *Guardian* foreign desk editor, interviewed March 2015

20. Joel Simon, Committee to Protect Journalists executive director, interviewed April 2015

21. Roger Matar, CEO of Newsgate production house, interviewed June 2015

22. Jonathan Giesen, CEO of Transterra Media, interviewed June 2015

23. Ray Homer, former ABC Baghdad bureau chief and current Transterra Media content officer, interviewed June 2015

24. Ian Phillips, Associated Press Middle East bureau director, interviewed July 2015

25. Bill Spindle, former *Wall Street Journal* Middle East bureau chief, interviewed July 2015

26. Christopher Dickey, former *Newsweek* editor, interviewed December 2015

27. Susan Chira, former *New York Times* foreign news editor, interviewed November 28, 2016

LIST OF NEWS INDUSTRY TRADE JOURNALS

1. *American Journalism Review*
2. *Columbia Journalism Review*
3. *Broadcasting & Cable*
4. *Editor & Publisher*
5. *MEDIA Magazine*
6. *Ryerson Review of Journalism*
7. *British Journalism Review*
8. *Press Gazette*

LIST OF NEWSPAPERS/NEWSMAGAZINES

1. *The Wall Street Journal*
2. *Newsweek*
3. *The New York Times*
4. *The Toronto Star*
5. *The Globe and Mail*
6. *The Sunday Times of London*

LIST OF TELEVISION NEWS NETWORKS

1. NBC
2. ABC
3. CBS
4. CNN
5. Fox
6. BBC
7. Channel 4 News
8. Al Jazeera English

Notes

Chapter 1. The "Blood Messenger"

President Bush's admonition at the beginning of this chapter appeared in an official statement on Pearl's death, which CNN covered at the time. "President Bush on Pearl: Americans 'Deeply Saddened.'" 2002. CNN. February 21. http://www.cnn.com/2002/US/02/21/pearl.bush.reaction/index.html (accessed April 27, 2017).

1. This phrase comes from the *New York Times* correspondent David Rohde's memoir on his own 2008 kidnapping. In that book, Rohde's captors say they will use him to "send a 'blood message' to President Barack Obama." David Rohde and Kristen Mulvihill, 2010, *A Rope and a Prayer: The Story of a Kidnapping.* New York: Viking. Kindle edition.

Chapter 4. The "Intimate Threat"

1. Stelter, "CBS Reporter Recounts a 'Merciless' Assault," 2011.

2. In a Fox News report with Shepard Smith on January 26, 2011, Jonathan Hunt remarks that Mubarak "may have ruled as an autocrat, Shep, but he has in a sense been 'our' autocrat" (Vanderbilt Television News Archive, record number 1004335). On January 27, 2011, ABC's Martha Raddatz lamented that Egypt's "spirit of protest" had spread to Yemen, "a place that harbors terrorists." Raddatz added that while we might celebrate uprisings in some places, protests in other places should "make Americans nervous" (Vanderbilt Television News Archive, record number 986149). CNN's *AC360* anxiously addressed the role of the Muslim Brotherhood in the Egyptian demonstration as early as January 28, 2011 (Vanderbilt Television News Archive, record number 986170), and then the next day opened the show with the declaration that "Israel's neighbor, America's ally" was "under crisis" (Vanderbilt Television News Archive, record number 986855). On the same day, NBC's Richard Engel worriedly

claimed that the protests had suddenly become more "Islamic," with more and more people chanting Allah's name. *NBC Nightly News*, January 28, 2011 (Vanderbilt Television News Archive, record number 988820). And on February 1, 2011, Logan herself was reporting from a neighboring protest in Alexandria; oddly, she said that this "violent" protest, driven by the "extremist" Muslim Brotherhood was, "even here," being driven by the people's own voices (Vanderbilt Television News Archive, record number 986766).

3. For examples of the reference to "spreading," see the *CBS Evening News*, January 25, 2011 (Vanderbilt Television News Archive, record number 986091); the *NBC Nightly News*, January 25, 2011 (Vanderbilt Television News Archive, record number 988433); the *ABC World News Tonight*, January 27, 2011 (Vanderbilt Television News Archive, record number 986149); and "Protests and the Role of Social Media," BBC, January 28, 2011, http://www.bbc.co.uk/news/technology-12304750 (accessed June 3, 2013).

Chapter 5. The "Living Dead"

1. Colvin, "The Shot Hit Me," 2012a.

Bibliography

"About Us." 2016. AKE Security. http://akegroup.com/about-us/.

Ackermann, Kristina. 2011. "Tackable Gives Order to Citizen Journalism." *Editor & Publisher* 144 (April). http://www.editorandpublisher.com/feature/tackable-gives-order-to-citizen-journalism/.

Allan, Stuart. 2009. "Histories of Citizen Journalism." In *Citizen Journalism: Global Perspectives*, eds. Stuart Allan and Einar Thorsen. New York: Peter Lang. 17–32.

Allan, Stuart, and Barbie Zelizer, eds. 2004. *Reporting War: Journalism in Wartime.* London: Routledge.

Amar, Paul. 2011. "Turning the Gendered Politics of the Security State Inside Out?" *International Feminist Journal of Politics* 13 (3): 299–328. doi:10.1080/14616742.2011.587364.

"American Pie 01.11.01." 2001. *Press Gazette* (October 31). http://www.pressgazette.co.uk/node/27628.

Anker, Elisabeth. 2014. *Orgies of Feeling: Melodrama and the Politics of Freedom.* Durham: Duke UP.

Appadurai, Arjun. 1988. "Putting Hierarchy in Its Place." *Cultural Anthropology* 3, no. 1 (1988): 36–49.

———. 2010. "Disjuncture and Difference in the Global Cultural Economy. In *International Communication, a Reader*, ed. Daya Thussu. New York: Routledge. 383–392.

Armoudian, Maria. 2017. *Reporting from the Danger Zone: Frontline Journalists, Their Jobs, and an Increasingly Perilous Future.* New York: Routledge.

Arnot, Bob. 2003. "Embedded/Unembedded I." *Columbia Journalism Review* 42 (May/June): 42–43.

Azeez, Wale. 2003. "ITN Presses Hoon for Inquiry into Missing Duo." *Press Gazette* (May 14). http://www.pressgazette.co.uk/itn-presses-hoon-for-inquiry-into-missing-duo/.

Bach, Trevor. 2014. "When Reporters Are Kidnapped." *Columbia Journalism Review* (August 20). http://www.cjr.org/behind_the_news/journos_and_kidnapping.php.

Bahari, Maziar. 2001a. "Moving Forward; Iranian President Mohammad Khatami Prepares to Tackle the Anti-Reform Establishment. Will the United States Come Up with a Suitable Response?" *Newsweek Web Exclusive*, June 20. http://global.factiva.com/redir/default.aspx?P=sa&an=nwbe0000020011211dx6k000i7&cat=a&ep=ASE.

———. 2001b. *Football, Iranian Style*. Documentary, 50:00.

———. 2003. *And Along Came a Spider*. Documentary, 1:58:00.

———. 2009a. "Mohammad Khatami: 'The Country Can Be Run Better'; Iran's Ex-President on Why Change Is on the Way." *Newsweek*, June 1. http://global.factiva.com/redir/default.aspx?P=sa&an=NSWK000020090527e5610000f&cat=a&ep=ASE.

———. 2009b. "Iran Turns against Its President." *Newsweek*, June 15. http://global.factiva.com/redir/default.aspx?P=sa&an=NSWK000020090608e56f0003a&cat=a&ep=ASE.

———. 2010. "Maziar Bahari: My Sentence in an Iranian Court." *Newsweek*, May 9. http://www.newsweek.com/maziar-bahari-my-sentence-iranian-court-72691.

———. 2012. *Then They Came for Me: A Story of Injustice and Survival in Iran's Most Notorious Prison*. London: Oneworld Publications.

Bahari, Maziar, and Carla Power. 2001. "Freedom for Film; Iranian Cinema, Long Popular Abroad, Is Finally Having Its Day at Home." *Newsweek International*, May 28. http://global.factiva.com/redir/default.aspx?P=sa&an=newi000020010712dx5s000fx&cat=a&ep=ASE.

Baker, Peter. 2003. "Inside View." *American Journalism Review* 25 (May): 36–39. http://ajrarchive.org/article.asp?id=2993.

Baker, Russ. 2001. "The Journal on the Run." *Columbia Journalism Review* 40 (Nov/Dec): 16–17.

Barkin, Steve Michael. 2003. *American Television News: The Media Marketplace and the Public Interest*. Armonk: M. E. Sharpe.

Barrett, Liz Cox. 2008. "On Last Week's Lara Logan 'News.'" *Columbia Journalism Review* (July 2). http://www.cjr.org/behind_the_news/lara_logan.php.

———. 2011. "Lara Logan, Foreign Correspondents, and Sexual Abuse." *Columbia Journalism Review* (February 17). http://www.cjr.org/the_kicker/lara_logan_foreign_corresponde.php.

Baxter, Kylie, and Shahram Akbarzadeh. 2012. *US Foreign Policy in the Middle East: The Roots of Anti-Americanism*. London: Routledge.

"BBC: Voice of Marie Colvin." 2012. *BBC's The Hub*, YouTube video. https://www.youtube.com/watch?v=7PxSiDYVHhU.

Berg, Bruce L., and Howard Lune. 2011. *Qualitative Research Methods for the Social Sciences*. 8th ed. Boston: Pearson.

Blyth, Jeffrey. 2002. "Execution of Daniel Pearl Causes Worldwide Disgust." *Press Gazette* (February 27). http://www.pressgazette.co.uk/node/21289.

Borzou, Daragahi. 2003. "In Iraq, Everyone Is Media-Savvy." *Columbia Journalism Review* 42 (May/June): 40.

Bossone, Andrew. 2014. "The Thankless Work of a 'Fixer.'" *Columbia Journalism Review* 52 (May/ June): 24–25. http://www.cjr.org/reports/the_thankless_work_of _a_fixer.php?page=all#sthash.oUHvsYW5.dpuf.

Bourrie, Mark. 2012. *Fighting Words: Canada's Best War Reporting*. Toronto: Dundern Press.

Brenner, Marie. 2012. "Marie Colvin's Private War." *Vanity Fair*, August. www.vanity fair.com/politics/2012/08/marie-colvin-private-war.

Brodbeck, Sam. 2011. "CPJ investigation reveals extent of sexual assaults on journalists." *Press Gazette* (June 8). http://www.pressgazette.co.uk/wire/7914.

Brown, Kimberly. 2009. "Do Foreign Correspondents Matter?" *Media Magazine* (Winter): 30.

Buford, William. 1978. Introduction. In Gellhorn, *Travels with Myself and Another*. New York: Eland. Kindle Version.

Bunder, Leslie. 2001. "Cyberview 280901." *Press Gazette* (September 26). http://www .pressgazette.co.uk/node/27705.

Butler, Judith. 2004. *Precarious Life: The Powers of Mourning and Violence*. London: Verso.

———. 2009. *Frames of War: When Is Life Grievable?* New York: Verso.

Caldwell, John. 2008. *Production Culture: Industrial Reflexivity and Critical Practice in Film and Television*. Durham: Duke UP.

Campion-Smith, Bruce. 2009. "Jailed Detainee's Wife Prays 'Complete Nightmare' Ends; Hopes Canadians at UN Will Press Case to Free Husband Held in Iran." *Toronto Star*, September 23. http://search.proquest.com.ezproxy.library.wisc.edu/ docview/439608121?accountid=465.

Carey, James. 2002. "American Journalism On, Before, and After September 11." In *Journalism after 9/11*, eds. Barbie Zelizer and Stuart Allan. New York: Routledge. 85–103.

Carruthers, Susan. 2011. *The Media at War*. Basingstoke, U.K.: Palgrave Macmillan.

"CBS News' Lara Logan Assaulted during Egypt Protests." 2011. *CBS News*, February 16. http://www.cbsnews.com/news/cbs-news-lara-logan-assaulted-during-egypt -protests/.

Chakrabarty, Dipesh. 2000. *Provincializing Europe: Postcolonial Thought and Historical Difference*. Princeton: Princeton University Press.

Chambers, Deborah, Linda Steiner, and Carole Fleming. 2004. *Women and Journalism*. London: Routledge.

Cohn, Martin Regg. 2009. "From Tehran to Toronto for the Times." *Toronto Star*, November 17. http://search.proquest.com.ezproxy.library.wisc.edu/docview/439 627751?accountid=465.

Colvin, Jill. 2009. "Ottawa Urges Canadian's Release." *Globe and Mail*, June 23. http:// search.proquest.com.ezproxy.library.wisc.edu/docview/382629327?accountid=465.

Colvin, Marie. 2012a. "The Shot Hit Me: Blood Poured from my Eye—I Felt a Profound Sadness I was Going to Die," in *On the Front Line: The Collected Journalism of Marie Colvin*. London: Harper Press, 199–200.

———. 2012b. "'WE LIVE IN FEAR OF A MASSACRE.'" *Sunday Times*, February 19. http://global.factiva.com/redir/default.aspx?p=sa&an=ST0000002012021ge82 j00080&cat=a&ep=ASE.

Conroy, Paul. 2013. *Under the Wire: Marie Colvin's Final Assignment*. New York: Weinstein Books. Kindle Edition.

"Cooper Remembers Final Colvin CNN Report." 2012. CNN. http://www.cnn.com/videos/bestoftv/2012/02/22/jk-cooper-colvin-last-report-mpg.cnn.

Cottle, Simon. 2016. "Keeping Safe(r) in Unruly, Uncivil Places: Journalist Voices in a Changing Communication Environment." In *Reporting Dangerously: Journalist Killings, Intimidation, and Security*, eds. Simon Cottle, Richard Sambrook, and Nick Mosdell. London: Palgrave. 145–170.

Cottle, Simon, Richard Sambrook, and Nick Mosdell, eds. 2016. *Reporting Dangerously: Journalist Killings, Intimidation, and Security*. London: Palgrave.

"Could Death of Syrian Boy Make Him Arab Spring Martyr?" 2011. *BBC News*, June 1. http://www.bbc.com/news/world-middle-east-13620407.

Couldry, Nick, and Anna McCarthy, eds. 2004. *MediaSpace: Place, Scale and Culture in a Media Age*. London: Routledge.

Cushion, Stephen, and Justin Lewis. 2010. *The Rise of 24-Hour News Television*. New York: Peter Lang.

Deacon, David. 2008. *British News Media and the Spanish Civil War*. Edinburgh: Edinburgh UP.

Delano, Anthony. 2009. "Trust: Journalistic License." *British Journalism Review* 20 (December): 9–11. doi:10.1177/0956474809020004020 3.

Derian, James Der. 2009. *Virtuous War: Mapping the Military-Industrial-Media-Entertainment-Network*. New York: Routledge.

Deuze, Mark. 2009. "Technology and the Individual Journalist: Agency beyond Imitation and Change." In *The Changing Faces of Journalism*, ed. Barbie Zelizer. New York: Routledge. 82–98.

Dew, Gwen. 1943. *Prisoner of the Japs*. New York: Alfred A. Knopf.

Dickey, Christopher, Maziar Bahari, Mark Hosenball, Owen Matthews, and Stryker Mcguire. 2003. "Scaring the Ayatollahs; Is Washington Now Aiming for 'Regime Change' in Iran?" *Newsweek*, June 9. http://global.factiva.com/redir/default.aspx?P=sa&an=nswk000020030605dz6900009&cat=a&ep=ASE.

Dickey, Christopher, Maziar Bahari, Reem Haddad, Dan Ephron, Tara Pepper, and Roy Gutman. 2002. "The Iran Connection; Washington Believes Tehran Is Developing Weapons of Mass Destruction—and Worries They Could Wind Up in the Hands of Lebanon's Hizbullah." *Newsweek*, February 18. http://global.factiva.com/redir/default.aspx?P=sa&an=nswk000020020211dy2i0000b&cat=a&ep=ASE.

DiMaggio, Anthony. 2010. *When Media Goes to War: Hegemonic Discourse, Public Opinion, and the Limits of Dissent*. New York: NYU Press.

Dimiero, Ben. 2011. "Jim Hoft Blames Lara Logan for Her Sexual Assault." *Media Matters for America* (February 16). http://mediamatters.org/blog/2011/02/16/jim-hoft-blames-lara-logan-for-her-sexual-assau/176520.

Dobkin, Bethami. 1992. *Tales of Terror: Television News and the Construction of the Terrorist Threat.* Westport, Conn.: Praeger.

"Don't Forget This Detainee." 2009. *Globe and Mail,* September 16. http://search .proquest.com.ezproxy.library.wisc.edu/docview/382613731?accountid=465.

Doyle, Molly. 2009. "Guerillas in Our Midst." *Ryerson Review of Journalism* (April 16). http://rrj.ca/guerillas-in-our-midst/.

"Editorial: Fallen Heroes." 2012. *Broadcasting & Cable* (May 14). http://www.broadcasting cable.com/article/484496-Editorial_Fallen_Heroes.php.

"Editorial Freedom to Choose." 2002. *Boston Phoenix* (June). http://www.boston phoenix.com/boston/news_features/editorial/documents/02299081.htm.

"Editorial: In the Line of Duty." 2013. *Broadcasting & Cable* (January 14). http:// www.broadcastingcable.com/article/491320-Editorial_In_the_Line_of_Duty.php.

"Editorial: More than Numbers." 2012. *Broadcasting & Cable* (March 5). http://www .broadcastingcable.com/article/481333-Editorial_More_Than_Numbers.php.

Eggerton, John. 2009. "Obama Points to New Media in Bringing Struggle in Iran to World." *Broadcasting & Cable* (June 23). http://www.broadcastingcable.com/ news/washington/obama-points-new-media-bringing-struggle-iran-world/56215.

"Egyptian Women Protesters Sexually Assaulted in Tahrir Square." 2012. *The Guardian,* June 8. https://www.theguardian.com/world/2012/jun/09/egyptian-women -protesters-sexually-assaulted.

Farhi, Paul. 2001. "Double Whammy." *American Journalism Review* 23 (November): 54–55. http://ajrarchive.org/article_printable.asp?id=2379.

Fathi, Nazila. 2001a. "Iran Won't Join U.S. Campaign, Leader Says." *New York Times,* September 27. http://global.factiva.com/redir/default.aspx?P=sa&an=nytf00002001 0927dx9r00032&cat=a&ep=ASE.

———. 2001b. "Iranian Soccer Fans Celebrate; This Time, No Protest Breaks Out." *New York Times,* November 1. http://global.factiva.com/redir/default.aspx?P=sa &an=nytf000020011101dxb10001j&cat=a&ep=ASE.

———. 2001c. "Iranians Welcome Winter with a Ritual from Ancient Persia." *New York Times.* December 23. http://www.nytimes.com/2001/12/23/world/iranians -welcome-winter-with-a-ritual-from-ancient-persia.html.

———. 2002. "Bush's 'Evil' Label Rejected by Angry Iranian Leaders." *New York Times,* February 1. http://global.factiva.com/redir/default.aspx?P=sa&an=nytf00002002020 dy210002d&cat=a&ep=ASE.

———. 2003. "U.N. Nuclear Inspection Chief Is Examining Iranian Facilities." *New York Times,* February 22. http://global.factiva.com/redir/default.aspx?P=sa&an= nytf000020030222dz2m0002a&cat=a&ep=ASE.

———. 2004. "Beckham's Kid Sister." *New York Times,* February 8. http://global.factiva .com/redir/default.aspx?P=sa&an=NYTF000020040208e02800015&cat=a&ep =ASE.

———. 2005. "Iranian Women Defy Authority to Protest Sex Discrimination." *New York Times,* June 13. http://global.factiva.com/redir/default.aspx?P=sa&an=NYT F000020050613e16d0002j&cat=a&ep=ASE.

——. 2009. "Iran's Top Leader Dashes Hopes for a Compromise." *New York Times*, June 20. http://global.factiva.com/redir/default.aspx?p=sa&an=NYTF00002009 0620e56k0000k&cat=a&ep=ASE.

——. 2010. "The Exile's Eye." *New York Times*, January 17. http://global.factiva.com/ redir/default.aspx?p=sa&an=NYTF000020100117e61h0006q&cat=a&ep=ASE.

——. 2014. *The Lonely War: One Woman's Account of the Struggle for Modern Iran.* New York: Basic Books.

Fitzgerald, Mark. 2002. "No Brilliant Disguise." *Editor & Publisher* (April 1).

Fleeson, Lucinda. 2003. "Bureau of Missing Bureaus." *American Journalism Review* 25 (Oct/Nov): 32–39. http://ajrarchive.org/article.asp?id=3409.

Freedman, Des, and Daya Kishan Thussu, eds. 2012. *Media and Terrorism: Global Perspectives.* London: SAGE.

Freedman, Robert O. 2012. "Russia and the Arab Spring: A Preliminary Appraisal." In *The Arab Spring: Change and Resistance in the Middle East*, eds. Mark L. Hass and David W. Lesch. Boulder: Westview Press. 195–218.

"Freelance Journalist Safety Principles." 2015. Dart Center for Journalism and Trauma. February 12. http://dartcenter.org/content/global-safety-principles-and-practices.

Friedman, Paul. 2003. "TV: A Missed Opportunity." *Columbia Journalism Review* 42 (May/June): 29–31.

Gaber, Ivor. 2009. "Them and Us: Is There a Difference?" *British Journalism Review* 20 (March): 41–46. doi:10.1177/0956474809104202.

Garrels, Anne. 2006. "INTO THE ABYSS: Reporting Iraq, 2003–2006: An Oral History." *Columbia Journalism Review* 45 (Nov/Dec): 53.

Gazze, Mary. 2009. "Getting the Most out of Facebook." *Media Magazine* (Summer): 24–27.

Geiss, Robin. 2010. "How Does International Humanitarian Law Protect Journalists in Armed-Conflict Situations?" *International Committee of the Red Cross* (July 27). https://www.icrc.org/eng/resources/documents/interview/protection-journalists -interview-270710.htm.

Gray, Ken. 2012. "The Sad Triumph of the Tweet." *Media Magazine* (Winter): 13–14.

Greenslade, Roy. 2002. "So Who Needs Newspapers?" *British Journalism Review* 13: 41–49. doi:10.1177/095647480201300107.

Grego, Melissa. 2011a. "EXECS ON EGYPT: ABC Says Budget Cuts Have Had 'No Impact.'" *Broadcasting & Cable* (February). http://stg.broadcastingcable.com/news/ programming/execs-egypt-abc-says-budget-cuts-have-had-no-impact/37430.

——. 2011b. "EXECS ON EGYPT: NBC Brass Says 'We Are Lowering Our Profile' in Egypt." *Broadcasting & Cable* (February). http://stg.broadcastingcable.com/news/ programming/execs-egypt-nbc-brass-says-we-are-lowering-our-profile-egypt/ 37429.

Greppi, Michele. 2007. "News Emmy Sights and Sounds." *Television Week*, October 1.

Grewal, Inderpal, and Caren Kaplan, eds. 1994. *Scattered Hegemonies: Postmodernity and Transnational Feminist Practices.* Minneapolis: University of Minnesota Press.

Griffin, Michael. 2004. "Picturing America's 'War on Terrorism' in Afghanistan and Iraq: Photographic Motifs as News Frames." *Journalism* 5: 381–402. doi:10.1177/1464884904044201.

Grindstaff, Davin Allen, and Kevin Michael DeLuca. 2007. "The Corpus of Daniel Pearl." *Critical Studies in Media Communication* 21: 305–324. doi:0.1080/0739318042000245345.

Guthrie, Marisa. 2008. "TCA: McManus, Couric Stand Behind Logan." *Broadcasting & Cable* (July). http://www.broadcastingcable.com/news/programming/tca -mcmanus-couric-stand-behind-logan/28907.

——. 2009. "A Vested Interest in Covering Wars." *Broadcasting & Cable* (December). https://www.broadcastingcable.com/news/fifth-estate/vested-interest-covering -wars/124948.

Hagerty, Bill. 2009. "The Web Could Spell Catastrophe." *British Journalism Review* 20: 35–43. doi:10.1177/0956474809348262.

Hall, Stuart. 1996. "Cultural Identity and Cinematic Representation." *Black British Cultural Studies: A Reader* (1996): 210–222.

Hallin, Daniel. 1989. *The Uncensored War: The Media and Vietnam.* Berkeley: UC Press.

Hamilton, John Maxwell. 2011. *Journalism's Roving Eye: A History of American Foreign Reporting.* Baton Rouge: LSU Press.

Harcup, Tony. 2013. *Alternative Journalism, Alternative Voices.* New York: Routledge.

Harms, Gregory. 2010. *Straight Power Concepts in the Middle East: US Foreign Policy, Israel and World History.* London: Pluto Press.

Hayhoe, Anita. 2002. "Fuck Corporate Media. We Want the Truth." *Ryerson Review of Journalism* (June 16). http://rrj.ca/fuck-corporate-media-we-want-the-truth/.

Healy, Tory. 2002. "Hack of All Trades, Master of None." *Ryerson Review of Journalism* (June 16). http://rrj.ca/hack-of-all-trades-master-of-none/.

Hewlett, Steve. 2009. "For TV News, News Isn't All Bad." *British Journalism Review* 20 (September): 41–46. doi: 10.1177/0956474809106670.

Higgins, John M. 2005. "Battle Tested." *Broadcasting & Cable* (May). http://www .broadcastingcable.com/news/news-articles/battle-tested/107084.

Hinton, Les. 2009. "They're Stealing Our Lifeblood." *British Journalism Review* 20 (September): 13–18. doi:10.1177/0956474809348258.

Holt, Jennifer, and Alisa Perren, eds. 2011. *Media Industries: History, Theory, and Method.* West Sussex: Wiley-Blackwell.

Horsley, William, and Jackie Harrison. 2013. "Censorship by Bullet." *British Journalism Review* 24 (March): 39–46. doi: 10.1177/0956474813481932.

Huff, Richard. 2012. "Lara Logan: Life Is Not about Dwelling on the Bad." *NY Daily News,* July 3. http://www.nydailynews.com/entertainment/tv-movies/lara-logan -life-not-dwelling-bad-article-1.1009501.

Hume, Mark. 2009. "Jailed Journalist's Wife Begs PM for Help." *Globe and Mail,* September 15. http://search.proquest.com.ezproxy.library.wisc.edu/docview/382606497 ?accountid=465.

"Iran Elections: Journalists Expelled and Jailed in Press Crackdown." 2009. *Press Gazette* (June 22). http://www.pressgazette.co.uk/node/43827.

"Iranian Authorities Block BBC Election Coverage." 2009. *Press Gazette* (June 15). http://www.pressgazette.co.uk/node/43789.

"Iran vs. the Media." 2009. *Toronto Star*, July 28. http://search.proquest.com.ezproxy .library.wisc.edu/docview/439597904?accountid=465.

Jacobs, Matthew F. 2011. *Imagining the Middle East: The Building of an American Foreign Policy, 1918–1967*. Chapel Hill: University of North Carolina Press.

Jessell, Harry A. 2003. "Let's Televise the War." *Broadcasting & Cable* (March). http:// www.broadcastingcable.com/news/news-articles/lets-televise-war/74356.

"Journal Staffer's Abductors Deliver a Second Message." 2002. *Wall Street Journal*, January 31. http://global.factiva.com/redir/default.aspx?P=sa&an=j0000000200 20131dy1v0000s&cat=a&ep=ASE.

Katz, Harry L., and Vincent Virga. 2012. *Civil War Sketch Book: Drawings from the Battlefront*. New York: W. W. Norton and Company.

Keath, Lee, and Robert H. Reid. 2006. "Fewer Reporters Embedded in Iraq." *Washington Post* (October 15). http://www.washingtonpost.com/wp-dyn/content/article/ 2006/10/15/AR2006101500386.html.

Kellner, Douglas. 1992. *The Persian Gulf TV War*. Boulder: Westview Press.

———. 2003. *From 9/11 to Terror War: The Dangers of the Bush Legacy*. Lanham: Rowman and Littlefield.

Kennedy, Liam. 2008. "Securing Vision: Photography and US Foreign Policy." *Media, Culture, and Society 30* (3): 279–294. doi: 10.1177/0163443708088788.

Kerschbaumer, Ken. 2003a. "The Rules of War." *Broadcasting & Cable* (March). http:// www.broadcastingcable.com/news/news-articles/rules-war/98187.

———. 2003b. "News Ops Marshal Digital Gear for War." *Broadcasting & Cable* (March). http://www.broadcastingcable.com/news/news-articles/news-ops-marshal -digital-gear-war/98274.

———. 2003c. "Rather's Wary of Embedding." *Broadcasting & Cable* (March). http:// www.broadcastingcable.com/news/news-articles/rathers-wary-embedding/98408.

Kind-Kovács, Friederike, and Jessis Labov. 2013. *Samizdat, Tamizdat, and Beyond: Transnational Media during and after Socialism*. New York: Berghahn Books.

Kinder, John. 2015. *Paying with Their Bodies: American War and the Problem of the Disabled Veteran*. Chicago: U Chicago P.

Knightley, Phillip. 2003. "History, or Bunkum?" *British Journalism Review* 14 (June): 7–14. doi: 10.1177/09564748030142002.

———. 2004. *The First Casualty: The War Correspondent as Hero and Myth-Maker from the Crimea to Iraq*. Baltimore: JHU Press.

Korte, Barbara. 2009. *Represented Reporters: Images of War Correspondents in Memoirs and Fiction*. Bielefeld: Transcript Verlag.

Kumar, Deepa. 2012. *Islamophobia and the Politics of Empire*. Chicago: Haymarket Books.

Lalami, Laila. 2011. "The Attack on Lara Logan: War of the Words." *Nation*, February 16. http://www.thenation.com/article/attack-lara-logan-war-words/.

"Lara Logan Pregnant with Joe Burkett's Baby, Couple Will Wed." 2011. *Huffington Post*, May 25. http://www.huffingtonpost.com/2008/07/08/lara-logan-pregnant-with_n_111392.html.

Learmonth, Michael. 2006. "CBS Beefs Up News Team." *Daily Variety*, February 3.

Lefebvre, Henri. 1992. *The Production of Space*, trans. Donald Nicholson-Smith. Oxford: Blackwell.

Lewis, Justin. 2012. "Terrorism and News Narratives." In *Media and Terrorism: Global Perspectives*, eds. Des Freedman and Daya Kishan Thussu. London: SAGE. 257–270.

Lewis, Justin, Rod Brookes, Nick Mosdell, Terry Threadgold. 2006. *Shoot First and Ask Questions Later: Media Coverage of the 2003 Iraq War*. New York: Peter Lang.

Loyn, David. 2007. "Local Heroes: Risk-taking in Iraq." *British Journalism Review* 18 (June): 21–25. doi: 10.1177/0956474807080928.

Machin, David, and Sarah Niblok. 2006. *News Production: Theory and Practice*. New York: Routledge.

Mander, Mary S. 2010. *Pen and Sword: American War Correspondents, 1898–1975*. Urbana-Champaign: University of Illinois Press.

Manthorpe, Jonathan. 1999. "The Rush to Parochialism." *Media Magazine* (Spring). http://caj.ca/wp-content/uploads/2010/mediamag/spring99/media99_9.html.

Marash, Dave. 2011. "Fade to Black." *Columbia Journalism Review* 50 (September): 24–28. http://www.cjr.org/feature/fade_to_black.php?page=all.

Marie, Gillespie, and Toynbee Jason, eds. 2006. *Analysing Media Texts*. Volume 4. Berkshire: McGraw-Hill Education (U.K).

"Marie Colvin: 'Full of Passion, Full of Belief.'" 2012. *Press Gazette* (March 13). http://www.pressgazette.co.uk/marie-colvin-full-of-passion-full-of-belief/.

Massey, Doreen. 1994. *Space, Place and Gender*. Cambridge: Polity Press.

Matheson, Donald, and Stuart Allan. 2009. *Digital War Reporting*. Cambridge: Polity Press.

Matloff, Judith. 2011. "Safety Tips for Female Correspondents." *Columbia Journalism Review* (February 22). http://www.cjr.org/campaign_desk/safety_tips_for_female_corresp.php.

Mawad, Dalal. 2012. "Syria: Too Much Information?" *Columbia Journalism Review* (February 24). http://www.cjr.org/behind_the_news/syria_too_much_information.php.

"Maziar Bahari Canadian Scapegoat in Iran." 2009. *Globe and Mail*, July 8. http://search.proquest.com.ezproxy.library.wisc.edu/docview/382627072?accountid=465.

McAlister, Melani. 2005. *Epic Encounters: Culture, Media, and U.S. Interests in the Middle East since 1945*. Berkeley: University of California Press.

McChesney, Robert. 2002. "September 11 and the Structural Limitations of US Journalism." In *Journalism after 9/11*, eds. Barbie Zelizer and Stuart Allan. London: Routledge. 104–112.

McClellan, Steve. 2001. "TV Mobilizes for 'Global War.'" *Broadcasting & Cable* (September 24). https://www.highbeam.com/doc/1G1-78800917.html.

McClintock, Pamela. 2003. "Youth Movement under Way." *Daily Variety*, October 30. https://www.highbeam.com/doc/1G1-110457501.html.

McKie, David. 2002. "The Objectivity of Method." *Media Magazine* (Fall/Winter).

———. 2009. "What Are Journalists For?" *Media Magazine* (Summer): 4.

McLaughlin, Greg. 2002. *The War Correspondent.* London: Pluto Press.

McLean, Jesse. 2009. "Iran Frees Jailed Canadian; After Nearly Four Months in Custody, Journalist Gets Bail, Magazine Reports." *Toronto Star*, October 18. http://search.proquest.com.ezproxy.library.wisc.edu/docview/439622871?accountid=465.

McLeary, Paul. 2006. "The Stringers." *Columbia Journalism Review* 44 (March/April): 20–22.

McNally, Paul. 2009. "Social Media Breaks Through Iran News Blackout Attempt." *Press Gazette* (June 17). http://www.pressgazette.co.uk/node/43808.

McNamara, Martin. 2001. "National Dailies up by One Million." *Press Gazette* (September 19). http://www.pressgazette.co.uk/node/21007.

Meadows, Susannah. 2006. "Lara Logan; MEDIA: How a Former Swimsuit Model Became CBS's Chief Foreign Correspondent." *Newsweek*, December 25. https://www.highbeam.com/doc/1G1-156414788.html.

Miller, Toby. 2007. *Cultural Citizenship: Cosmopolitanism, Consumerism, and Television in a Neoliberal Age.* Philadelphia: Temple University Press.

Mirkinson, Jack. 2011. "Nir Rosen to Anderson Cooper on Lara Logan Assault Tweets: 'I Was a Jerk.'" *Huffington Post*, February 17. http://www.huffingtonpost.com/2011/02/17/nir-rosen-anderson-cooper-lara-logan_n_824411.html.

Moallem, Minoo. 2005. *Between Warrior Brother and Veiled Sister: Islamic Fundamentalism and the Politics of Patriarchy in Iran.* Berkeley: University of California Press.

Moffat, Sarah. 2009. "Photojournalism: an Eminent History." *Media Magazine* (Summer): 34.

Mohanty, Chandra Talpade. 2003. *Feminism without Borders: Decolonizing Theory, Practicing Solidarity.* Durham: Duke UP.

Morabito, Andrea. 2011a. "EXECS ON EGYPT: CBS's McManus: Challenges of Covering Egypt 'Apparent on Video.'" *Broadcasting & Cable* (February). http://stg.broadcastingcable.com/news/programming/execs-egypt-cbss-mcmanus-challenges-covering-egypt-apparent-video/37426.

———. 2011b. "EXECS ON EGYPT: CNN's Maddox: It's Up to Our Journos if They Want to Stay in Egypt." *Broadcasting & Cable* (February). http://stg.broadcastingcable.com/news/programming/execs-egypt-cnns-maddox-its-our-journos-if-they-want-stay-egypt/37427.

———. 2012. "The Trouble with Syria." *Broadcasting & Cable* (February 27). http://www.broadcastingcable.com/article/481015-The_Trouble_With_Syria.php.

Morgan, Jean. 2001a. "Rivals Launch Backlash against 'Foolhardy' Ridley." *Press Gazette* (October 10). http://www.pressgazette.co.uk/node/21092.

———. 2001b. "Shock as 80 Wapping Jobs Come under Threat." *Press Gazette* (October 17). http://www.pressgazette.co.uk/node/21034.

Mosco, Vincent. 2005. *The Digital Sublime: Myth, Power, and Cyberspace*. Cambridge: MIT Press.

Mostafa, Karim. 2001. "Wsj.com Stood Tall in Shards of Sept. 11." *Editor & Publisher* 134 (November): 20A.

Naficy, Hamid. 1993. *The Making of Exile Cultures: Iranian Television in Los Angeles*. Minneapolis: U Minnesota P.

———, ed. 2013 [1999]. *Home, Exile, Homeland: Film, Media, and the Politics of Place*. New York: Routledge.

Narayan, Kirin. 2003."How Native Is a 'Native' Anthropologist. In *Feminist Postcolonial Theory: A Reader*, eds. Reina Lewis and Sara Mills. New York: Routledge. 285–305.

"New Media Hits Profits at Guardian." 2001. *Press Gazette* (September 5). http://www.pressgazette.co.uk/new-media-hits-profits-at-guardian/.

Nicholas, Sian. 2005. "*War Report* (BBC 1944–5) and the Birth of the BBC War Correspondent." In *War and the Media: Reportage and Propaganda, 1900–2003*, eds. Mark Connelly and David Welch. London: I. B. Taurus. 139–161.

Offman, Craig. 2003. "Fager May Turn Back the Clock." *Variety*, February 2. https://variety.com/2003/tv/news/fager-may-turn-back-the-clock-1117879848/.

"178 Journalists Killed in Iraq since 1992/Motive Confirmed." Committee to Protect Journalists. https://cpj.org/killed/mideast/iraq/.

"Pakistani Group Says It Seized Daniel Pearl, Journal Correspondent." 2002. *Wall Street Journal*, January 28. http://global.factiva.com/redir/default.aspx?P=sa&an=j000000020020128dy1s0001k&cat=a&ep=ASE.

Palmer, Lindsay. 2012. "'iReporting' an Uprising: CNN and Citizen Journalism in Network Culture." *Television & New Media* (June). doi:10.1177/1527476412446487.

———. 2016. "'Being the Bridge': News Fixers' Perspectives on Cultural Difference in Reporting the 'War on Terror.'" *Journalism*. Advance online copy. doi:10.1177/1464884916657515.

Palser, Barb. 2002. "Is It Journalism?" *American Journalism Review* 24 (June): 62. http://ajrarchive.org/article.asp?id=2540.

———. 2009a. "Shining Through the Gloom." *American Journalism Review* 31 (February/March): 48. http://ajrarchive.org/article.asp?id=4701.

———. 2009b. "Amateur Content's Star Turn." *American Journalism Review* 31 (August/September): 42. http://ajrarchive.org/article.asp?id=4821.

Parks, Lisa. Forthcoming. "Drone Media: Grounded Dimensions of the US Drone War in Pakistan." In *Public, Space, and Mediated Communication: Exploring Context Collapse*, eds. Carolyn Marvin and Sun-ha Hong. New York: Routledge.

Paterson, Chris. 2010. "The Hidden Role of Television News Agencies: 'Going Live' on 24-Hour News Channels." In *The Rise of 24-Hour News Television: Global Perspectives*, eds. Stephen Cushion and Justin Lewis. New York: Peter Lang. 99–112.

———. 2014. *War Reporters under Threat: The United States and Media Freedom.* London: Pluto Press.

Paterson, Chris, and Annabelle Sreberny, eds. 2004. *International News in the 21st Century.* Hants: University of Luton Press.

Perigoe, Ross, and Mahmoud Eid. 2014. *Mission Invisible: Race, Religion, and News at the Dawn of the 9/11 Era.* Vancouver: UBC Press.

Perlmutter, David, and John Maxwell Hamilton. 2007. *From Pigeons to News Portals: Foreign Reporting and the Challenge of New Technology.* Baton Rouge: LSU Press.

Petrick, Stephen. 2002. "Camera Ready." *Ryerson Review of Journalism* (March 16). http://rrj.ca/camera-ready/.

Pintak, Lawrence. 2011. "Breathing Room: Toward a New Arab Media." *Columbia Journalism Review* 50 (May/June): 22–28. http://www.cjr.org/cover_story/breathing_room.php.

Podger, Pamela J. 2009. "The Limits of Control." *American Journalism Review* 31 (August/September): 32–37. http://ajrarchive.org/article.asp?id=4816.

Poniewozik, James. 2011. "Lara Logan Speaks Out about Her Assault." *Time*, April 28. http://entertainment.time.com/2011/04/28/lara-logan-speaks-out-about-her-assault/.

Pugh, Andrew. 2012. "Colvin: Sometimes War Reporters 'Pay the Ultimate Price.'" *Press Gazette* (February 22). http://www.pressgazette.co.uk/node/48803.

Regier, Terry, and Muhammad Ali Khalidi. 2009. "The Arab Street: Tracking a Political Metaphor." *The Middle East Journal* 63 (1): 11–29. https://muse.jhu.edu/journals/the_middle_east_journal/v063/63.1.regier.html.

"Regime Detains Canadian Citizen." 2009. *Toronto Star*, June 22. http://search.proquest.com.ezproxy.library.wisc.edu/docview/439573799?accountid=465.

Remy, Ruane. 2012. "The Question of Rape." *Ryerson Review of Journalism* (February 17). http://rrj.ca/the-question-of-rape/.

"Reuters' Bureau Chief on Reporting from Baghdad." 2006. *Press Gazette* (October 1). http://www.pressgazette.co.uk/reuters-bureau-chief-on-reporting-from-baghdad/.

Ricchiardi, Sherry. 2000. "Highway to the Danger Zone." *American Journalism Review* 22 (April): 42–49. http://ajrarchive.org/article.asp?id=746.

———. 2002a. "A Killing Field for Journalists." *American Journalism Review* 24 (January/February): 32–37. http://ajrarchive.org/Article.asp?id=2398.

———. 2002b. "Dangerous Journalism." *American Journalism Review* 24 (April): 28–33. http://ajrarchive.org/article.asp?id=2495.

———. 2003a. "Preparing for War." *American Journalism Review* 25 (March): 29–33. http://ajrarchive.org/article.asp?id=2794.

———. 2003b. "Close to the Action." *American Journalism Review* 25 (May): 28–35. http://ajrarchive.org/article.asp?id=2991.

———. 2006. "Out of Reach." *American Journalism Review* 28 (April/May): 24–31. http://ajrarchive.org/article.asp?id=4078.

———. 2011. "Out of the Shadows." *American Journalism Review* 33 (Oct/Nov): 28–33. http://ajrarchive.org/Article.asp?id=5137.

———. 2012. "Remembering Two Splendid Journalists." *American Journalism Review* (February/March). http://ajrarchive.org/Article.asp?id=5263.

Rid, Thomas. 2007. *War and Media Operations: The US Military and the Press from Vietnam to Iraq.* London: Routledge.

Ridley, Yvonne. 2003. "In the Fog of War." In *War and the Media: Reporting Conflict 24/7.* Thousand Oaks: Sage. 248–252.

Rieder, Rem. 2002. "Being There." *American Journalism Review* 24 (April): 6. http://ajrarchive.org/article.asp?id=2477.

———. 2003. "In the Zone." *American Journalism Review* 25 (May): 6. http://ajrarchive.org/article_printable.asp?id=2966.

Riley, Robin L., Chandra Talpade Mohanty, and Minnie Bruce Pratt, eds. 2008. *Feminism and War: Confronting US Imperialism.* London: Zed Books.

Robins, J. Max. 2006a. "In the Line of Duty." *Broadcasting & Cable* (February). http://www.broadcastingcable.com/news/news-articles/line-duty/78748.

———. 2006b. "Big Bucks for What?" *Broadcasting & Cable* (April). http://www.broadcastingcable.com/news/news-articles/big-bucks-what/79684.

———. 2006c. "Where Go ABC News?" *Broadcasting & Cable* (May). http://www.broadcastingcable.com/news/news-articles/where-go-abc-news/70854.

Robins, Wayne. 2001a. "The Web Fails First Big Test." *Editor & Publisher* 134 (September 17): 4.

———. 2001b. "Coming to Your Senses." *Editor & Publisher* 134 (October 15): 16B.

Rodgers, Gavin. 2013. "Sunday Times Tells Freelances Not to Submit Photographs from Syria." *Press Gazette* (February 5). http://www.pressgazette.co.uk/sunday-times-tells-freelances-not-submit-photographs-syria.

Rodgers, Walter. 2005. *Sleeping with Custer and the 7th Cavalry: An Embedded Reporter in Iraq.* Carbondale: Southern Illinois University Press.

Rogoff, Irit. 2000. *Terra Infirma: Geography's Visual Culture.* London: Routledge.

Romano, Allison. 2003. "Embeds Return, Laden with Stories." *Broadcasting & Cable* (April). https://www.broadcastingcable.com/news/news-articles/embeds-return-laden-stories/98743.

———. 2006a. "A New Era in Network News." *Broadcasting & Cable* (April). http://www.broadcastingcable.com/news/news-articles/new-era-network-news/74217.

———. 2006b. "ABC News Taps Gibson as Solo Anchor." *Broadcasting & Cable* (May). http://www.broadcastingcable.com/news/news-articles/abc-news-taps-gibson-solo-anchor/80143.

Rosaldo, Renato. 1993. *Culture and Truth: The Remaking of Social Analysis.* Boston: Beacon Press.

"RSF Annual Roundup: 110 Journalists Killed in 2015." Reporters without Borders. https://rsf.org/en/news/rsf-annual-round-110-journalists-killed-2015.

Said, Edward W. 2000. *Reflections on Exile and Other Essays*. Cambridge: Harvard University Press.

Samuel-Azran, Tal. 2010. *Al-Jazeera and US War Coverage*. New York: Peter Lang Publishing.

Schlussel, Debbie. 2011. "How Muslims Celebrate Victory: Egypt's 'Peaceful, Moderate, Democratic' Protesters." *Debbie Schlussel* (February 15). http://www.debbie schlussel.com/33031/how-muslims-celebrate-victory-egypts-peaceful-moderate -democratic-protesters/.

Schmidt, Elizabeth. 2013. *Foreign Intervention in Africa: From the Cold War to the War on Terror*. New York: Cambridge University Press.

Schmidt, Natasha. 2014. "The Lessons of Rosewater for All Campaigners." *IranWire*, October 17. http://en.iranwire.com/features/6080/.

Seipp, Catherine. 2002. "Online Uprising." *American Journalism Review* 24 (June): 42–47. http://www.ajrarchive.org/article.asp?id=2555.

Sengupta, Ken. 2012. "Taking Orders from the Insurgents." *British Journalism Review* 23 (September): 55–60. doi:10.1177/0956474812460471.

Shadid, Anthony. 2006. "INTO THE ABYSS: Reporting Iraq, 2003–2006: An Oral History." *Columbia Journalism Review* 45 (Nov/Dec): 50.

Shields, Todd. 2001. "'POST' GAME PLAN STILL IN PLACE." *Editor & Publisher* 134 (October 15): 12.

Shulman, Alexandra. 2012. "Cashmere and Pearls beneath the Combats." *Sunday Times of London*. February 26. http://www.thesundaytimes.co.uk/sto/newsreview/ features/article877584.ece.

Silberstein-Loeb, Jonathan. 2014. *The International Distribution of News: The Associated Press, Press Association, and Reuters 1848–1947*. Cambridge: Cambridge UP.

Silverman, Craig. 2011. "Unknown Quantities: How Social Network Verification Can Show Us What We Don't Know." *Columbia Journalism Review* (September 30). http://www.cjr.org/behind_the_news/unknown_quantities.php?page=all.

Silvio, Ann. 2010. "Lara Logan under Fire." *CBS News* video, September 26. http:// www.cbsnews.com/videos/lara-logan-under-fire/.

Singer, Jane B. 2008. "Ethnography of Newsroom Coverage." In *Making Online News: The Ethnography of New Media Production*, eds. Chris Paterson and David Domingo. New York: Peter Lang.

Smith, Terrence. 2003. "Hard Lessons." *Columbia Journalism Review* 42 (May/June): 26–28.

Smolkin, Rachel. 2006. "Hold That Obit." *American Journalism Review* 28 (August/ September): 18–27. http://ajrarchive.org/article.asp?id=4157.

"Sotloff Foundation, Four U.S. TV Networks Sign onto Safety Principles." 2015. Dart Center for Journalism and Trauma, October 6. http://dartcenter.org/content/sotloff -foundation-and-four-us-television-networks-sign-onto-safety-principles.

Spurr, David. 1993. *The Rhetoric of Empire: Colonial Discourse in Journalism, Travel Writing, and Imperial Administration*. Durham: Duke UP.

Stahl, Roger. 2009. *Militainment, Inc.: War, Media, and Popular Culture.* New York: Routledge.

Starr, Ryan. 2002. "Under the Weather." *Ryerson Review of Journalism* (March 16). http://rrj.ca/under-the-weather/.

Steinberg, Jacques. 2005. "War Zone 'It Girl' Has a Big Future at CBS News." *New York Times*, November 23. http://www.nytimes.com/2005/11/23/arts/television/war-zone-it-girl-has-a-big-future-at-cbs-news.html?_r=0.

Stelter, Brian. 2011. "CBS Reporter Recounts a 'Merciless' Assault." *New York Times*, April 28. http://www.nytimes.com/2011/04/29/business/media/29logan.html.

Strupp, Joe. 2009a. "Top News Outlets Scramble to Get Full Story out of Iran." *Editor & Publisher* (June 15). http://www.editorandpublisher.com/news/top-news-outlets-scramble-to-get-full-story-out-of-iran/.

———. 2009b. "SPECIAL REPORT: The Many Rewards—and Risks—of Social Media for Newspapers." *Editor & Publisher* (August 24). http://www.editorandpublisher.com/news/special-report-the-many-rewards-and-risks-of-social-media-for-newspapers/.

Swain, Jon. 2003. "War Doesn't Belong to the Generals." *British Journalism Review* 14 (March): 23–29. doi: 10.1177/0956474803014001802.

———. 2012. "An Unflinching Witness." *Columbia Journalism Review* (May 8). http://www.cjr.org/on_the_job/an_unflinching_witness.php?page=all.

Swain, Jon, and Richard Woods. 2012. "MARIE COLVIN: THE LAST ASSIGNMENT." *Sunday Times*, February 26. http://search.proquest.com.ezproxy.library.wisc.edu/docview/923427789?accountid=465.

"SYRIA MUST CALL AN IMMEDIATE CEASEFIRE." 2012. *Sunday Times*, February 26. http://search.proquest.com.ezproxy.library.wisc.edu/docview/923428062?accountid=465.

Tang, Colleen. 2010. "Much Ado about Precious Little." *Ryerson Review of Journalism* (June 23). http://rrj.ca/much-ado-about-precious-little-2/.

Thussu, Daya Kishan, and Des Freedman, eds. 2003. *War and the Media: Reporting Conflict 24/7.* London: SAGE.

"To Iraq and Back: Bob Woodruff Reports." 2008. *ABC News* video. YouTube. https://www.youtube.com/watch?v=B31l7v9NCto.

Tomlin, Julie. 2001a. "Broadcasters Count Cost of War Coverage." *Press Gazette* (September 26). http://www.pressgazette.co.uk/node/21029.

———. 2001b. "US 'Short-Changed' on World Coverage." *Press Gazette* (October 24). http://www.pressgazette.co.uk/node/21038.

———. 2001c. "BBC Crew's Trek to Make Kabul Rendezvous." *Press Gazette* (November 14). http://www.pressgazette.co.uk/node/21153.

Torregrosa, Luisita Lopez. 2015. "The Rise of the Female TV War Correspondent as Global Celebrity." *The New York Times*, August 21. http://nytlive.nytimes.com/womenintheworld/2015/08/21/the-rise-of-the-female-tv-war-correspondent-as-global-celebrity/.

"Tributes Paid to Marie Colvin." 2012. Channel 4 News YouTube video, February 23. https://www.youtube.com/watch?v=akrMoU5CFNw.

Trigoboff, Dan. 2002a. "Careful News Crews in Pakistan." *Broadcasting & Cable* (February 3). http://www.broadcastingcable.com/news/news-articles/careful-news -crews-pakistan/91170.

———. 2002b. "Journalists' Survival Schools." *Broadcasting & Cable* (May 5). http:// www.broadcastingcable.com/news/news-articles/journalists-survival-schools/ 92388.

———. 2003. "Networks Get Ready for War." *Broadcasting & Cable* (February 2). http://www.broadcastingcable.com/news/news-articles/networks-get-ready-war/ 97693.

Trinh, Minh-ha T. 1994. "Other than Myself/My Other Self." In *Travellers' Tales: Narratives of Home and Displacement*, eds. Jon Bird, Barry Curtis, Melinda Mash, Tim Putnam, George Robertson, Lisa Tickner. New York: Routledge. 9–26.

Trombly, Maria. 2003. "Reference Guide to the Geneva Conventions." Indianapolis: Society of Professional Journalists. https://www.spj.org/gc-index.asp?#journalists.

"Try, Try Again at 'World News Tonight.'" 2006. *Broadcasting & Cable* (May). http://www .broadcastingcable.com/news/news-articles/try-try-again-world-news-tonight/ 76585.

Tumber, Howard, and Frank Webster. 2006. *Journalists under Fire: Information War and Journalistic Practices*. London: SAGE.

Vane, Sharyn. 2002. "Days of Rage." *American Journalism Review* 24 (July/August): 32–37. http://ajrarchive.org/Article.asp?id=2567.

Varadarajan, Tunku. 2002. "This Is a Phoenix That Stoops instead of Rising." *Wall Street Journal*, June 11. http://global.factiva.com/redir/default.aspx?P=sa&an=joo 0000020020611dy6b00036&cat=a&ep=ASE.

Vaughan, Jenny. 2009. "Taking the 'Free' out of 'Freelance.'" *Ryerson Review of Journalism* (December 9). http://rrj.ca/taking-the-free-out-of-freelance/.

Verma, Sonia. 2009. "Wife Appeals to Iran to Free Jailed Spouse." *Globe and Mail*, October 14. http://search.proquest.com.ezproxy.library.wisc.edu/docview/382615166 ?accountid=465.

Vranckx, Rudi. 2002. "Now Truth Is the First Target." *British Journalism Review* 13 (September): 71–74. doi:10.1177/095647480201300313.

Ward, Olivia. 2009. "Jailed Canadian Touted for Peace Prize; Journalist Charged with Inciting Uprisings in Iran Is a Top Contender for Prestigious Spanish Award." *Toronto Star*, September 9. http://search.proquest.com.ezproxy.library.wisc.edu/ docview/439608621?accountid=465.

Ward, Stephen. 2003. "In Bed with the Military." *Media Magazine* (Spring): 6–7.

White, Mimi. 2004. "The Attractions of Television: Reconsidering Liveness." In *MediaSpace: Place, Scale, and Culture in a Media Age*, eds. Nick Couldry and Anna McCarthy. New York: Routledge. 90.

"Who We Are." 2016. Centurion Risk Assessment Services, Ltd. http://www.centurionsafety.net/about-us/.

Wilford, Hugh. 2011. "America's Great Game: The CIA and the Middle East." In *Challenging US Foreign Policy: America and the World in the Long 20th Century*, eds. Bevan Sewell and Scott Lucas. Houndmills, Basingstoke, U.K.: Palgrave MacMillan. 99–112.

Williams, Kevin. 2011. *International Journalism*. Los Angeles: SAGE.

Williams, Raymond. [1974] 2003. *Television: Technology and Cultural Form*. London: Routledge.

Winslow, George. 2011. "Egyptian Coverage Boosts Streaming Media Sites." *Broadcasting & Cable* (February). http://www.broadcastingcable.com/news/programming/egyptian-coverage-boosts-streaming-media-sites/37431.

Witherow, John. 2012. "MARIE COLVIN 1956–2012." *Sunday Times*, February 26. http://search.proquest.com.ezproxy.library.wisc.edu/docview/923428888?accountid=465.

Wodak, Ruth. 2001. "The Discourse-Historical Approach." In *Methods of Critical Discourse Analysis*, eds. Ruth Wodak and Michael Meyer. London: SAGE. 63–94.

Wolfe, Lauren. 2011. "The Silencing Crime: Sexual Violence and Journalists." Committee to Protect Journalists (June 7). https://cpj.org/reports/2011/06/silencing-crime-sexual-violence-journalists.php.

Woodruff, Lee, and Bob Woodruff. 2007. *In an Instant: A Family's Journey of Love and Healing*. New York: Random House.

Wooten, Jim. 2002. "Three Minutes from Death." *Columbia Journalism Review* 40 (January/February): 36–38.

———. 2006. "The Cameramen." *Columbia Journalism Review* 45 (May/June): 33–37.

Worth, Robert F., and Nazila Fathi. 2009. "Ahmadinejad Stages Huge Campaign Rally in Tehran, but Challenger's Event Is Bigger." *New York Times*, June 9. http://global.factiva.com/redir/default.aspx?P=sa&an=NYTF000020090609e5690002s&cat=a&ep=ASE.

Zayed, Dina. 2011. "Attack on Egyptian Women Protesters Spark Uproar." *Reuters*, December 21. http://www.reuters.com/article/us-egypt-protests-women-idUSTRE7BK1BX20111221.

Zelizer, Barbie. 1999. "CNN, the Gulf War, and Journalistic Practice." In *News: A Reader*, ed. Howard Tumber. Oxford: Oxford University Press. 340–355.

———. 2007. "On 'Having Been There': 'Eyewitnessing' as a Journalistic Key Word." *Critical Studies in Media Communication* 24 (5): 408–428. doi:10.1080/07393180701694614.

———, ed. 2009. *The Changing Faces of Journalism: Tabloidization, Technology, and Truthiness*. New York: Routledge.

———. 2010. *About to Die: How News Images Move the News Public*. Oxford: Oxford UP.

Zelizer, Barbie, and Allan, Stuart. 2002. *Journalism after 9/11*. New York: Routledge.

Index

LINDSAY PALMER is an assistant professor of global media ethics at the University of Wisconsin, Madison.

THE HISTORY OF COMMUNICATION

Speech Rights in America: The First Amendment, Democracy, and the Media
  Laura Stein
Freedom from Advertising: E. W. Scripps's Chicago Experiment   *Duane C. S. Stoltzfus*
Waves of Opposition: The Struggle for Democratic Radio, 1933–58
  Elizabeth Fones-Wolf
Prologue to a Farce: Democracy and Communication in America   *Mark Lloyd*
Outside the Box: Corporate Media, Globalization, and the UPS Strike
  Deepa Kumar
The Scripps Newspapers Go to War, 1914–1918   *Dale Zacher*
Telecommunications and Empire   *Jill Hills*
Everything Was Better in America: Print Culture in the Great Depression
  David Welky
Normative Theories of the Media   *Clifford G. Christians, Theodore L. Glasser,*
  Denis McQuail, Kaarle Nordenstreng, and Robert A. White
Radio's Hidden Voice: The Origins of Public Broadcasting in the United States
  Hugh Richard Slotten
Muting Israeli Democracy: How Media and Cultural Policy Undermine
  Free Expression   *Amit M. Schejter*
Key Concepts in Critical Cultural Studies   *Edited by Linda Steiner*
  and Clifford Christians
Refiguring Mass Communication: A History   *Peter Simonson*
Radio Utopia: Postwar Audio Documentary in the Public Interest   *Matthew C. Ehrlich*
Chronicling Trauma: Journalists and Writers on Violence and Loss   *Doug Underwood*
Saving the World: A Brief History of Communication for Development
  and Social Change   *Emile G. McAnany*
The Rise and Fall of Early American Magazine Culture   *Jared Gardner*
Equal Time: Television and the Civil Rights Movement   *Aniko Bodroghkozy*
Advertising at War: Business, Consumers, and Government in the 1940s
  Inger L. Stole
Media Capital: Architecture and Communications in New York City   *Aurora Wallace*
Chasing Newsroom Diversity: From Jim Crow to Affirmative Action
  Gwyneth Mellinger
C. Francis Jenkins, Pioneer of Film and Television   *Donald G. Godfrey*
Digital Rebellion: The Birth of the Cyber Left   *Todd Wolfson*
Heroes and Scoundrels: The Image of the Journalist in Popular Culture
  Matthew C. Ehrlich and Joe Saltzman
The Real Cyber War: The Political Economy of Internet Freedom   *Shawn M. Powers*
  and Michael Jablonski
The Polish Hearst: *Ameryka-Echo* and the Public Role of the Immigrant Press
  Anna D. Jaroszyńska-Kirchmann
Acid Hype: American News Media and the Psychedelic Experience   *Stephen Siff*
Making the News Popular: Mobilizing U.S. News Audiences   *Anthony M. Nadler*
Indians Illustrated: The Image of Native Americans in the Pictorial Press
  John M. Coward

The University of Illinois Press
is a founding member of the
Association of American University Presses.

Composed in 10.5/13 Adobe Minion Pro
by Lisa Connery
at the University of Illinois Press
Cover designed by Dustin J. Hubbart
Cover illustration: French photographer Remi Ochlik in Cairo,
Egypt, November 23, 2011. (Reuters/Julien de Rosa/Handout)
Manufactured by Sheridan Books, Inc.

University of Illinois Press
1325 South Oak Street
Champaign, IL 61820-6903
www.press.uillinois.edu